**WEBER'S**

# BIG BOOK OF
# BURGERS™

## BY JAMIE PURVIANCE

PHOTOGRAPHY BY TIM TURNER
ILLUSTRATIONS BY LINDA KELEN

# ACKNOWLEDGMENTS

Writing this book felt like throwing a big ole barbecue that lasted about a year. I had the good fortune of planning, cooking, and collaborating with many of my favorite people. Some were with me from start to finish. Some stopped by for just a short visit. But each and every person contributed something wonderful to this burger extravaganza.

The first people on the scene were Mike Kempster and Brooke Jones from Weber. They dreamed a big dream for this book and then gave me everything I needed to make it real. Thank you, Mike and Brooke. It is an honor and pleasure to work with you. Susan Maruyama was right there with us every step of the way, sharing superb ideas and her good graces with everyone involved. Several other people at Weber stepped up with grilling inspiration, grilling equipment, and all-around support. I want to express my appreciation to Kim Lefko, Kevin Kolman, Jeanine Thompson, and Kim Durk. Amy Dorsch and Deanna Budnick also deserve special mentions for their awesome work on the finished look of these pages.

The hardest-working person of all was Marsha Capen. I am awed and inspired by her extraordinary dedication to getting every element just right. As the managing editor, Marsha worked closely with a top-notch design team led by creative director Shum Prats and designer Carrie Tilmann. Marsha also collaborated with the wonderful editor and writer Abby Wilson and the pure genius of their boss, Christina Schroeder. Just one of Christina's brilliant moves was bringing Kerry Trotter onto the writing team. Thank you, Kerry, for your hilarious wit and your unfailing kindness.

I have been working on Weber cookbooks with photographer Tim Turner for more than 15 years. I used to think he was great at his job. Now I think that great doesn't begin to describe his actual level of technical skills, his impressive range of creative solutions, and his impressive artistry with light and lens. I want to send special thanks to Tim's photo assistant, Christy Clow, and the other members of his team, including Joe Bankmann, Matt Gagné, Josh Marrah, David Raine, Meghan Ross, and Donte Tatum. For the gorgeousness of the food and the colorful variety of presentations, we can all thank the delightful food stylist Lynn Gagné and her very talented assistant, Nina Albazi.

Wanting to write a cookbook is one thing, but actually doing it in ways that are ultimately successful requires a publishing house with a deep understanding of the business and an unwavering professionalism about how to get it done right and on time. I am grateful that Jim Childs at Oxmoor House supported this book from start to finish. Thank you, Leah McLaughlin, Felicity Keane, and Pam Hoenig, for caring so deeply about all aspects and for giving your expertise so generously. I also want to acknowledge others at Oxmoor House whose hard work and collaborative attitudes I really appreciate, specifically Tom Mifsud, Steve Sandonato, Susan Hettleman, and Vanessa Tiongson.

When we talk about the food at this yearlong barbecue, I have enormous gratitude and admiration for my culinary team (the "Purviance Alliance"). These people finessed each and every recipe again and again so they taste as great as they possibly can. Many thanks, especially to the following grillers: Lynda Balslev, Brigit Binns, Lena Birnbaum, David Bonom, Angela Brassinga, Linda Carucci, Tara Duggan, Sarah Epstein, Elizabeth Hughes, Allison Kociuruba, Alex Novielli, Rick Rodgers, Cheryl Sternman Rule, Andrew Schloss, and Terri Wuerthner. You guys are the best. I hope you will all come back and enjoy our next barbecue together.

# FOREWORD

I can't imagine a world without hamburgers. Some of my fondest memories are accompanying my dad to our favorite burger drive-ins for meaty treats, along with sides of fries and shakes. Dad and I also liked to explore. When a new burger place opened, we had to give it a try. I guess you could say that I became an accomplished burger critic before even reaching my teenage years.

At home, though, hamburgers just didn't seem to be nearly as tasty and adventuresome—that is, until my dad started grilling them in the backyard. Burgers cooked in a skillet on the range top were okay, but they were a meal, not a celebration. Burgers cooked on the grill were smoky and fun, and flames sizzled the patties, imparting a special flavor.

Then, when I started grilling, I was like most backyard chefs: I started with hamburgers. Burgers were an easy entry point to the world of grilling for friends and family, but what I didn't understand was that *everyone* is a hamburger expert. Grilling hamburgers is like walking out on stage: expectations are high, and preparation, technique, and creativity are closely scrutinized by a semicircle of hungry grill watchers. When I pleased the onlookers with technique—the dimpled patty, the perfectly timed flip, and the addition of cheese at the right moment— I felt like a true backyard hero.

*Weber's Big Book of Burgers*™ stretches the definition of the hamburger as it takes you on a journey of imaginative burger recipes—but we didn't stop there. You'll also find recipes for hot dogs, sausages, brats, sides, toppings, and drinks. Plus, there are plenty of helpful tips to improve your grilling technique, so you're sure to have crowd-pleasing results every time.

### THE BURGER GUY

Here at Weber we devoted a newsletter exclusively to hamburgers several years back, and in it we introduced an illustrated character we named "Burger Guy." The newsletter generated an amazing level of interest, and readers thought that the illustrations successfully captured the casual fun of a burger barbecue. When we decided to create a book celebrating burgers and sausages of all kinds, it was a unanimous decision to bring back Burger Guy. As you flip through the pages, you'll see him shimmying his way through special features, revealing recipe-related fun facts, and causing all sorts of saucy mischief every step of the way.

This book is all about fun and flavor. Use your imagination and let Burger Guy be your guide to a whole new world that is filled with big, beautiful burgers—that's my kind of world!

*Mike Kempster*

# INTRODUCTION

Imagine you are seven years old. It's the first day of second grade, and you're the new kid in class. All morning long you have a sinking feeling that you really don't belong. At lunch, you sit in the cafeteria and watch with skepticism as a few classmates pile potato chips on their cheeseburgers.

To your surprise, they motion for you to do the same, and they wait as you balance your last delicate chip in place and hold the top bun over your little tower. In unison, you and your new classmates crush each tower of chips to smithereens, laugh instinctively, and then bite into the warm cheesy patties that are dripping with meaty juices and flecked with salty chips. The ladies in the kitchen wearing paper hats shake their heads but break into laughter right along with you. I was that seven-year-old kid, and that was when I started to love burgers and the way they made me feel.

Since then, like a lot of us, I've eaten a ridiculous number of burgers. Most estimates are that Americans eat about 50 billion burgers per year. That's three burgers per week for each and every American. For most of my childhood, a burger meant a predictably basic version involving a thin ground beef patty tucked inside a soft enriched bun. Sometimes they had cheese, sometimes they had lettuce and tomato, but back then, we didn't have a lot of burger options. On big birthdays, my parents treated me to dinner at a fancy restaurant where I inevitably ordered some kind of super-deluxe burger, like a double-decker bacon cheeseburger with the house sauce. That was as crazy as burgers got.

In the 1980s and '90s, a funny thing happened ... "alternative burgers" started showing up all over America. The first time I saw chicken burgers at a barbecue, I thought to myself, *this is not quite right. Where's the respect for our beloved hamburger? What's next, a pizza with fish on top?* Well, like pizzas, burgers proved to be very adaptable. It wasn't long before lots of people were raving about burgers made from chicken, turkey, and other surprising ingredients. When I moved to California for college and came across fish burgers, I smirked at the idea at first, especially at the weird toppings like alfalfa sprouts and guacamole. But now that pigs were flying every which way, I let go of preconceived notions and just took a bite. My mind changed quickly when I tasted the lightly smoked and charred edges of a moist fish patty held inside a warm bun glistening with butter. Whoa, it was good. Really good.

All the while, beef burgers were getting bigger and better in America. Celeb chefs rescued us from the redundancy of fast-food burgers and made headlines with outrageously expensive versions starring ingredients like Kobe beef, black truffle shavings, and béarnaise sauce. As restaurants loaded the humble burger with the trappings of exalted steaks, folks like you and me who throw backyard barbecues

showed a new open-mindedness about burgers of all types and styles. We cleared room on the grill for whatever our guests preferred, even ... gasp ... vegetarian burgers. We let people put whatever wacky toppings they wanted on their burgers, and if someone wanted a burger without a bun, we toasted to their individual style.

Which begs the question: what is a burger anyway? At Weber, we are not purists when it comes to a definition. In fact I'm not convinced there really is a strict definition. Even the purists disagree about which types of meat and buns qualify. Early versions of the "Hamburg sandwich" actually used thinly sliced bread, so a burger has been a flexible idea since its beginnings and has always been evolving.

This book covers a full range of interpretations over time—not only for burgers, but also for the great food and drinks that we associate with burgers. You'll find many recipes for hot dogs, sausages, and brats, along with a selection of side dishes, toppings, and drinks. As with burgers, many of these items now reflect our most modern tastes, and yet the early versions from decades ago remain as popular as ever. In other words, our options haven't really changed as much as they have just grown in numbers and creativity. With each new take on a burger, a hot dog, or even a potato salad, we can ask whether or not it's authentic, but for me the more important question is: how does it make you *feel*? I figure that if it makes me smile like I did when I ate "crunch burgers" (for the recipe, see page 25) back in the second grade, that is all I really need to know.

Jamie Purviance

# TABLE OF **CONTENTS**

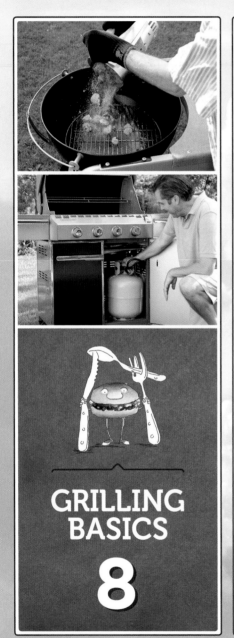

# GRILLING
# BASICS

# STARTING A
# CHARCOAL GRILL

Got a match? You and your charcoal grill, right? All jokes aside, plan on carving out 15 to 20 minutes to get your fire going.

**1. LIFE'S EASIER WITH A CHIMNEY STARTER.** This metal cylinder with a wire rack and handles provides a snug spot for getting a fire going quickly. Simply fill the space under the wire rack with some wadded-up newspaper or paraffin cubes, then fill the cylinder with charcoal briquettes.

**2. LIGHT, CHIMNEY, ACTION.** Once you light the newspaper or paraffin cubes, the briquettes will fire up with little risk of a flameout. You'll see the chimney smoking at first, but don't make a move until the top coals are covered in white ash.

**3. GLOVES ON.** Wearing insulated barbecue mitts or gloves, grab both of the chimney handles and carefully pour the hot coals onto the charcoal grate. That swinging handle is designed to make it safer and easier to aim the coals.

**4. COAL PLAY.** We like the flexibility of a two-zone fire, where all the coals are pushed to one side of the charcoal grate, providing you with both direct and indirect cooking options. An area of indirect heat will also give you a "safety zone"— a place to temporarily move food if it begins to flare up over direct heat.

**5. JUST ABOUT GO TIME.** Put the cooking grate back in place, and cover the grill with the lid. In 10 to 15 minutes, the temperature of the grill should be close to 500°F. This is when you want to brush the grate clean.

**6. MAKE SURE THE TOP AND BOTTOM VENTS ARE OPEN.** While grilling, the vent on the bottom half of the grill should be wide open and clear of ashes, to provide enough air for the fire. Keep the vent on the top open as well, unless you want to lower the temperature a bit by closing the top vent about halfway.

# STARTING A
# GAS GRILL

Skills required: lid lifting and knob turning. The huge advantage of gas grilling is its ease, but there are a few important tips to follow:

**1. FIRST THINGS FIRST.**
Check the propane tank; replace it if it's empty or near empty.

**2. LIFT THE GRILL LID AND LIGHT THE GRILL.**
Follow your Owner's Guide for lighting instructions.

**3. GRILL ON, LID GOES DOWN.**
Close the lid and wait 10 to 15 minutes for the grill to preheat. This creates the oven-like environment needed for efficient cooking and gets the cooking grates good and hot for the perfect sear. It also makes the grates much easier to clean.

# DIRECT AND INDIRECT
# COOKING

It's time for us to be direct—
and indirect—regarding heat.

There are two basic ways of grilling your food:
directly over hot coals or fired-up burners, or
indirectly, off to the side of the heat source. Direct
cooking doles out a hefty blast of heat, which gives
food that satisfying, crunchy sear, while indirect
heat is gentler, transforming the grill into an oven
that cooks your meal more gradually.

Direct heat is best used when grilling thinner, tender
items that don't need a lot of time to cook all the way
through—your basic hot dogs and beef burger patties
would fall under this category.

Indirect heat is the way to go when you want to
cook foods more gently from all directions. It's
great for roasting fresh sausages and toasting
buns, for example.

In many cases, we like to dabble in both types
of heat to achieve a good external crust with the
preferred internal doneness level to match. This
approach leads to more dependable outcomes and
not as many awkward "surprise—it's raw!" moments
at the dinner table. To ensure tasty success, start
your item over direct heat to sear on both sides,
and then move it to the indirect zone to finish up
without getting torched. You'll need to build a simple
two-zone fire for this, where the hot coals are pushed
to one side in a charcoal grill, or where some of the
burners are turned off on a gas grill.

In order for all this direct-indirect stuff to work,
however, you need know that the lid is your friend.
Keeping it closed as much as possible is what
retains the swirling radiant heat you need for
indirect cooking, as well as staving off flare-ups
in direct use. You'll still need to turn your food, but
when the heat can cook the food from the top and
bottom simultaneously, grilling tends to go much
faster, which, of course, means the eating part arrives
more quickly, and that's the whole point of this
delicious exercise, isn't it?

**CHARCOAL: DIRECT COOKING**
With direct heat, the fire
is right below the food.
The heat radiates off the
charcoal and conducts
through the metal cooking
grate to create those dark,
handsome grill marks.

**CHARCOAL:
INDIRECT COOKING**
With indirect heat, the
charcoal is arranged to
one side of the food, or it
is on both sides of the food.

**GAS: DIRECT AND
INDIRECT COOKING**
Using direct heat on a gas
grill is simply a matter of
grilling the food right over lit
burners. To use indirect heat,
light the burners on the far left
and far right of the grill, and
grill the food over the unlit
burner(s) between them. If your
grill has just two burners, light
one of them and grill over the
unlit one for indirect cooking.

# GRILL
# MAINTENANCE

Outdoorsy types tend to be pretty low maintenance—grills included. That said, embracing a couple of simple upkeep rituals can keep your grill going, and going strong, for a very long time.

To achieve the coveted grill marks, keep food from sticking, and eliminate the chances of old burned barnacles on your burger, the cooking grates need to be cleaned before every use. Close the lid and preheat your grill to about 500°F for 10 minutes. Slip your hand into an insulated barbecue mitt or glove and use a long-handled grill brush to do a quick once-over of the grates, dislodging any charred bits left behind from past meals. That quick treatment does the trick.

Keep your grill in tip-top, efficient shape by giving it a more thorough cleaning every month or so. Check the instructions in your Owner's Guide, but start by wiping down the outside of your grill with warm, soapy water. Scrape any accumulated debris from the inside of the lid. Gas grillers should remove the cooking grates, brush the burners, and clean out the bottom of the cook box and drip pan. Charcoal grillers should regularly remove all ash sitting at the bottom of the kettle.

Check your Owner's Guide to get the full report on the ultimate deep clean, upkeep, and maintenance for your grill.

## GRILL SAFETY

Please read your Owner's Guide and familiarize yourself with and follow all "dangers," "warnings," and "cautions." Also follow the grilling procedures and maintenance requirements listed in your Owner's Guide.

If you cannot locate the Owner's Guide for your grill model, please contact the manufacturer prior to use. If you have any questions concerning the "dangers," "warnings," and "cautions" contained in your Weber® gas, charcoal, or electric grill Owner's Guide, or if you do not have an Owner's Guide for your specific grill model, please visit www.weber.com to access your Owner's Guide or for the toll-free number for Weber-Stephen Products LLC Customer Service before using your grill.

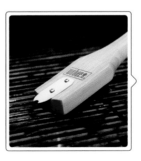

A sturdy grill brush with stainless-steel bristles is essential for cleaning your cooking grate. A notched scraper on the grill head is especially good at loosening hardened bits.

GRILLING BASICS

TOOLS

# TOOLS OF
# THE TRADE

These are our must-have tools for creating perfectly cooked, easily flipped, deftly served masterpieces.

## 5
### PERFORATED GRILL PAN

Use this when cooking foods that are either too small or too delicate for the grates, and say good-bye to saying good-bye to food dropped in the fire.

## 1
### CHIMNEY STARTER

This is the secret to charcoal grilling success. Pile in briquettes; fill the space underneath with paraffin cubes or wadded-up newspaper; strike a match; and a safe, quickly lit fire is at the ready—lighter fluid need not apply. See "Starting a Charcoal Grill" (page 10) for more details.

## 2
### BARBECUE GLOVES

Choose gloves that are insulated and that cover both hand and wrist.

## 3
### TIMER

Ensure that nothing gets overdone or underdone by setting a timer. Simple is best, so select something easy to use that emits a sound you can hear.

## 4
### INSTANT-READ THERMOMETER

Get a quick and accurate read on internal temperatures. Easy to find and relatively inexpensive, this all but guarantees grilling success.

## 6

### BURGER PRESS

Become a patty-forming machine with this. Your burgers will be the same size and thickness, which means they will cook at the same rate.

## 7

### GRILL BRUSH

Keep your cooking grates clean with one of these. Your burgers and sausages won't stick or be speckled with old, burned bits.

## 8

### SPATULA

Long-handled spatulas with offset (bent) necks are what we flip for. These are the easiest for lifting burgers off the grates.

## 9

### GRILL-PROOF GRIDDLE

A griddle brings another kitchen convenience to your grill top for cooking fish and vegetable patties too delicate to put right on an open grate.

## 10

### TONGS

Turn hot dogs, brats, and sausages in seconds without piercing them and losing those precious juices. Look for a pair with low tension, a good grip, and a lock for storage.

# TEN TIPS
## FOR GRILLING GREATNESS

### 1 THOSE WHO PREHEAT WELL, EAT WELL.

Cold grills are no place for burgers and sausages. Without that ample surge of heat to kick off the cooking, food will stick to the grates and you'll miss out on those coveted grill marks. Even if a recipe calls for medium or low heat, the grill should be preheated first. Lift the lid, fire up the coals or burners, close the lid, and let the grill do its intensely hot thing for 10 to 15 minutes—the internal temperature should reach about 500°F.

### 2 CLEANLINESS IS GRILL-LINESS.

Unless you prefer your burgers speckled with burned, crusty old bits of food, a swift sweep of a grill brush over the grates is your second order of business. There's usually "stuff" left behind after grilling, and, if not removed, it will bind itself to your food, and your food to the grates. So, after a good preheat, grab a sturdy, long-handled, stainless steel–bristled grill brush and give your grates a good cleaning.

### 3 GET IT TOGETHER, MAN!

Once your grill is preheated and the cooking grates are brushed clean, gather everything you will need and bring it to your grill. That includes tools, oiled and seasoned food, and any additional sauces or sides you're using. Don't forget a clean platter or plates to use as a landing pad for your grilled burgers, sausages, and sides. Running back and forth to the kitchen could lead to something great getting overcooked or burned.

### 4 PLAY (HEAT) ZONE DEFENSE.

Thinner beef burgers tend to cook pretty quickly over direct heat, as do hot dogs, but sometimes you'll use ingredients that benefit from indirect cooking— think big, raw sausages, or super thick burger patties. In those instances, and many others, a two-zone fire is the way to go. Also, you can brown your items directly above the heat source to get good grill marks, and then slide them onto the indirect, cooler side to finish in gentler, roasting confines.

## 5 THEY JUST NEED SOME SPACE.

Burgers and sausages were designed to feed a crowd, but they don't necessarily want to be part of one. All food cooks a little better on a grill with a little space around it. This allows heat to move freely up and around, as well as giving you some elbow room to wedge tongs or a spatula in between items. Also, leave about a quarter of the grate space clear in case you have to move something quickly to a warmer or cooler spot.

## 6 GIVE A LID-DLE.

Yes, it's more than just a heavy-duty rain shield. The grill's lid is actually an integral part of the cooking. Leaving the lid on while grilling keeps the interior at a consistent temperature, which makes for better and more predictable results. Also, dripping fat plus too much air whooshing in can trigger flare-ups. Not good. Charcoal grillers, remember to keep the lid vents at least halfway open. All fires need at least some air to keep on burning.

## 7 HANDS OFF THE MERCHANDISE.

When you put a cold, raw patty on a hot cooking grate, it sticks. As the meat begins to cook, it attaches itself to the cooking grate for the first couple of minutes. If you try to turn a patty during this time, you are bound to tear it and leave some meat sticking to the grate. However, if you can manage to wait four minutes or so, that's enough time for the meat to develop a caramelized crust that releases naturally from the grate.

## 8 KEEP THE GRILL FIRES BURNING.

Charcoal fires, if left to their own devices, reach their hottest temperatures first and then start to lose heat—that rate is determined by the type and amount of fuel used, and your interference. Refuel your fire every 45 minutes or so to keep the temperature up, and move coals around to get your heat zones in order. Keep the bottom vent free of ash, and the top vent adjusted to your preferred airflow.

## 9 KNOW WHEN TO PULL THE RIP CORD.

This means getting your burgers and sausages off the grill at just the right moment. The surest approach involves a thermometer slipped into the center of the meat, but forget about that old, dial thermometer bouncing around your kitchen drawer. For much more reliable readings, trust a digital instant-read thermometer.

## 10 NOW, WAIT JUST A MINUTE.

As burgers cook, the heat pushes meat juices out to the surface. If you let hot burgers "rest" for just a minute or two off the grill before diving in, the juices have a chance to be reabsorbed into the meat, and that makes a better burger. On decadent days, drop a thin slice of butter on top of each burger while resting and let the lusciousness seep inside.

# BURGERS

# 5 STEPS TO BURGER BRILLIANCE

## 1 MEAT MATTERS

Prepackaged "hamburger" often means you get ground scraps of questionable quality. Once that meat has been compressed in a tray, it will never have the loose, tender texture of a great burger. You are much better off with "ground beef" (by law, it can't include fat scraps), or, if perfection is your goal, buy freshly ground beef from a butcher you trust.

## 2 THOROUGH SEASONING

Burgers taste significantly better with seasonings dispersed throughout the meat, not just on the surface. Use salt and pepper at a minimum. Wet ingredients like minced onion, ketchup, mustard, and Worcestershire sauce improve not only the taste but also the juiciness. Mix in the seasonings as gently possible with your fingertips so you don't compress the texture too much.

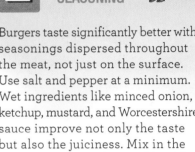

Consider this one of life's great turning points.
Before: burgers were at times dry, tough, tasteless, or the
unfortunate all-of-the-above abomination. After: burgers
are juicy, flavorful, and consistently brilliant. Here's why.

## 3 PORTION CONTROL

Inside the bowl, divide the meat into equal portions so that you don't end up with mismatched sizes. Form each portion into a loose, round ball, then gently flatten it until it's ¾ to 1 inch thick. This is your ideal thickness for giving the surface a nicely charred crust just as the center is reaching a juicy medium doneness.

## 4 DIMPLING

Most burgers tend to puff up in the middle as they cook, making the tops rounded and awkward for piling on toppings. To avoid this trouble, use your thumb or the back of a spoon to press a shallow indentation in the center of each raw patty. As each patty cooks, that well will fill in and flatten out, giving you a nice level surface instead of a big fat meatball.

## 5 HANDLING THE HEAT

The grill has to be hot (400° to 500°F) and clean. You have to be cool and patient. Close the lid as soon as the patties hit the grate. Give them 8 to 10 minutes total to reach a medium doneness, turning them only once—any more and you run the risk of ripping the surface before it has turned into a tasty crust. Oh, and don't ever smash burgers with a spatula! The juices will run out quickly and cause a flare-up.

# TEXAS BURGERS WITH CHEDDAR CHEESE AND BARBECUE SAUCE

SERVES: **4** | PREP TIME: **15 MINUTES, PLUS ABOUT 30 MINUTES FOR THE SAUCE** | GRILLING TIME: **8 TO 10 MINUTES**

**BEEF**

## SAUCE
- 1 tablespoon vegetable oil
- ½ medium yellow onion, finely chopped
- 1 cup ketchup
- ¼ cup water
- 2 tablespoons Worcestershire sauce
- 1 tablespoon packed dark brown sugar
- 1 tablespoon prepared chili powder
- 1 tablespoon cider vinegar
- ½ teaspoon garlic powder

## PATTIES
- 1½ pounds ground chuck (80% lean)
- 1 tablespoon prepared chili powder
- ½ teaspoon garlic powder
- ½ teaspoon kosher salt

- 4 slices cheddar cheese, each about 1 ounce
- 4 hamburger buns, split
- 4 leaves romaine lettuce, shredded
- 16 sweet pickle chips (optional)

**1.** In a heavy, medium saucepan over medium heat, warm the oil. Add the onion and cook until super soft and as dark as possible, 12 to 15 minutes, stirring occasionally. Add the remaining sauce ingredients and bring to a boil over medium-high heat. Regulate the heat so that the sauce simmers gently. Cook until thickened, 15 to 20 minutes, stirring frequently. Let cool to room temperature.

**2.** Mix the patty ingredients, and then gently form four patties of equal size, each about ¾ inch thick. With your thumb or the back of a spoon, make a shallow indentation about 1 inch wide in the center of the patties to prevent them from forming a dome as they cook. Refrigerate the patties until ready to grill.

**3.** Prepare the grill for direct cooking over medium-high heat (400° to 500°F).

**4.** Grill the patties over *direct medium-high heat*, with the lid closed, until cooked to medium doneness (160°F), 8 to 10 minutes, turning once. During the last 30 seconds to 1 minute of grilling time, place a slice of cheese on each patty to melt, and toast the buns, cut side down, over direct heat.

**5.** Build each burger on a bun with lettuce, a patty, barbecue sauce, and pickles, if desired. Serve warm. The extra sauce can be stored in the refrigerator in a covered container for up to 1 week.

For this barbecue sauce, cook the onions until super soft and as dark as possible to extract as much flavor as you can before adding the ketchup and other wet ingredients.

# CRUNCH BURGERS

SERVES: **4 (MAKES 8 SLIDERS)** | PREP TIME: **10 MINUTES** | GRILLING TIME: **ABOUT 6 MINUTES**

## PATTIES

1½ pounds ground chuck (80% lean)
1 tablespoon ketchup
½ teaspoon Worcestershire sauce
½ teaspoon onion powder
½ teaspoon kosher salt
¼ teaspoon freshly ground black pepper

2 slices cheddar cheese, each about 1 ounce, cut into quarters
8 slider buns, split
Ketchup (optional)
16 dill pickle chips
8 handfuls thin potato chips, such as Lay's® Classic

1. Mix the patty ingredients, and then gently form eight patties of equal size, each about ½ inch thick. Refrigerate the patties until ready to grill.

2. Prepare the grill for direct cooking over medium-high heat (400° to 500°F).

3. Grill the patties over *direct medium-high heat*, with the lid closed, until cooked to medium doneness (160°F), about 6 minutes, turning once. During the last 30 seconds to 1 minute of grilling time, place a quarter-slice of cheese on each patty to melt, and toast the buns, cut side down, over direct heat.

4. Place a patty on each bottom bun half and top with ketchup (if using), a patty, pickles, and a stack of chips. Put the bun tops on and then press down. Serve immediately.

Go ahead and have some fun with your cheeseburgers. Making a tower of chips and crushing them into smithereens is bound to bring back the little kid in you.

# VERMONT BURGERS WITH MAPLE-MUSTARD GLAZE

SERVES: **4** | PREP TIME: **20 MINUTES** | GRILLING TIME: **9 TO 11 MINUTES**

## PATTIES

1½ pounds ground chuck
(80% lean)
½ cup finely chopped
yellow onion
2 teaspoons
Worcestershire sauce
1 teaspoon mustard powder
1 teaspoon kosher salt
½ teaspoon freshly ground
black pepper

## GLAZE

3 tablespoons pure maple syrup
2 tablespoons
coarse-grain mustard
1 tablespoon balsamic vinegar
¼ teaspoon freshly ground
black pepper

6 ounces aged cheddar
cheese, cut into four slices,
at room temperature
4 pretzel rolls, split
1½ cups baby arugula
½ small red onion,
cut into thin slices
8 slices cooked thick-cut bacon

1. Mix the patty ingredients, and then gently form four patties of equal size, each about 1 inch thick. With your thumb or the back of a spoon, make a shallow indentation about 1 inch wide in the center of the patties to prevent them from forming a dome as they cook. Refrigerate the patties until ready to grill.

2. Prepare the grill for direct cooking over medium-high heat (400° to 500°F).

3. Combine the glaze ingredients.

4. Grill the patties over *direct medium-high heat*, with the lid closed, until cooked to medium doneness (160°F), 9 to 11 minutes, turning once. Once the burgers have been turned, baste with the glaze frequently. During the last 30 seconds to 1 minute of grilling time, place a slice of cheese on each patty to melt, and toast the rolls, cut side down, over direct heat.

5. Build each burger on a roll with arugula, a patty, onion, and two slices of bacon. Serve warm.

# BACON AND EGG BEEF BURGERS WITH CHEDDAR

SERVES: **4** | PREP TIME: **25 MINUTES** | GRILLING TIME: **9 TO 11 MINUTES**

## PATTIES

1½ pounds ground chuck
(80% lean)
¼ cup finely chopped
yellow onion
2 tablespoons ketchup
2 teaspoons
Worcestershire sauce
1 teaspoon kosher salt
¼ teaspoon freshly ground
black pepper

8 slices bacon
4 slices cheddar cheese,
each about 1 ounce
4 kaiser rolls, split
4 large eggs
Kosher salt
Freshly ground black pepper
8 slices ripe tomato

1. Mix the patty ingredients, and then gently form four patties of equal size, each about 1 inch thick. With your thumb or the back of a spoon, make a shallow indentation about 1 inch wide in the center of the patties to prevent them from forming a dome as they cook. Refrigerate the patties until ready to grill.

2. In a skillet over medium heat, fry the bacon until crisp, 10 to 12 minutes, turning occasionally. Transfer the bacon to paper towels to drain. Pour off and discard all but 2 tablespoons of the bacon fat from the skillet.

3. Prepare the grill for direct cooking over medium-high heat (400° to 500°F).

4. Grill the patties over *direct medium-high heat*, with the lid closed, until cooked to medium doneness (160°F), 9 to 11 minutes, turning once. During the last 30 seconds to 1 minute of grilling time, place a slice of cheese on each patty to melt, and toast the rolls, cut side down, over direct heat.

5. Return the skillet over medium heat and warm the bacon fat. Crack the eggs into the skillet and cook until the yolks are still slightly runny, about 3 minutes, turning once. Season with salt and pepper.

6. Build each burger on a roll with two tomato slices, a patty, two slices of bacon, and an egg. Serve warm.

This one is for all the breakfast lovers. Who says you can't have bacon and eggs for dinner? After you fry the bacon, leave a little fat in the pan and heat it just until it barely sizzles before you add the eggs. If your eggs are really fresh, the yolks will sit up proudly in the center and the whites will not spread far and wide in the pan. For really tender eggs, cover the pan while frying. The moisture trapped by the lid will gently steam the tops of the eggs.

# TEX-MEX BEEF BURGERS

SERVES: **4** | PREP TIME: **25 MINUTES** | GRILLING TIME: **9 TO 11 MINUTES**

## PATTIES

1½ pounds ground chuck (80% lean)
 1 teaspoon granulated onion
½ teaspoon ground cumin
½ teaspoon granulated garlic
½ teaspoon prepared chili powder

  Kosher salt
  Freshly ground black pepper

## SALSA

 3 ripe plum tomatoes, cored, seeded, and
   cut into ¼-inch dice
¼ cup roughly chopped fresh cilantro leaves
 3 tablespoons finely diced red onion
 2 tablespoons seeded and minced jalapeño
   chile peppers
1½ tablespoons fresh lime juice

 8 slices sourdough bread, each about ½ inch thick
   Extra-virgin olive oil
 4 whole green chile peppers (from a can), chopped
 4 slices sharp cheddar cheese, each about 1 ounce
½ cup sour cream

**1.** Mix the patty ingredients, including ½ teaspoon salt and ¼ teaspoon pepper, and then gently form four patties of equal size, each about 1 inch thick. With your thumb or the back of a spoon, make a shallow indentation about 1 inch wide in the center of the patties to prevent them from forming a dome as they cook. Refrigerate the patties until ready to grill.

**2.** Prepare the grill for direct cooking over medium-high heat (400° to 500°F).

**3.** Meanwhile, combine the salsa ingredients, including ½ teaspoon salt and ¼ teaspoon pepper.

**4.** Lightly season the patties on both sides with salt and pepper, and brush one side of each bread slice with oil. Grill the patties over *direct medium-high heat*, with the lid closed, for 5 minutes. Turn the patties over and top with an equal amount of chopped chiles and a slice of cheese. Continue grilling until the patties are cooked to medium doneness (160°F), 4 to 6 minutes more. During the last 30 seconds to 1 minute of grilling time, toast the bread, oiled side down, over direct heat (do not turn).

**5.** Stir the salsa. Build each burger on a bread slice with a patty, 1 tablespoon salsa, 1 tablespoon sour cream, and the remaining bread slice. Serve warm with the remaining salsa and sour cream on the side.

**FUN FACT**

The word "Tex-Mex" first entered the English language around 1875, in reference to the Texas-Mexican Railway. Since then, the term has turned much tastier, generally referring to the now mainstream Mexican–influenced cuisine, such as fajitas, chilis, nachos, tacos, and burritos.

# FOUR-ALARM JALAPEÑO CHEESEBURGERS

SERVES: **4**  |  PREP TIME: **15 MINUTES**  |  GRILLING TIME: **8 TO 10 MINUTES**

**SAUCE**
- ¾ cup mayonnaise
- 2 canned chipotle chile peppers in adobo sauce, minced
- 2 teaspoons fresh lime juice

**PATTIES**
- 1½ pounds ground chuck (80% lean)
- 3 tablespoons ketchup
- 2 teaspoons Worcestershire sauce
- 1 teaspoon garlic powder
- ¾ teaspoon ancho chile powder
- ¾ teaspoon kosher salt

- 4 slices pepper jack cheese, each about 1 ounce
- 4 hamburger buns, split
- 1 ripe beefsteak tomato, about 10 ounces, cut crosswise into 4 slices
- 4 pickled jalapeño chile peppers (from a jar), each cut lengthwise into quarters

1. Whisk the sauce ingredients.

2. Mix the patty ingredients, and then gently form four patties of equal size, each about ¾ inch thick. With your thumb or the back of a spoon, make a shallow indentation about 1 inch wide in the center of the patties to prevent them from forming a dome as they cook. Refrigerate the patties until ready to grill.

3. Prepare the grill for direct cooking over medium-high heat (400° to 500°F).

4. Grill the patties over *direct medium-high heat*, with the lid closed, until cooked to medium doneness (160°F), 8 to 10 minutes, turning once. During the last 30 seconds to 1 minute of grilling time, place a slice of cheese on each patty to melt, and toast the buns, cut side down, over direct heat.

5. Build each burger on a bun with sauce, a patty, a tomato slice, and four jalapeño quarters. Serve warm.

---

### WHERE DID THE WORD "HAMBURGER" COME FROM?

Etymologists will contend that the Hamburg steak, the hamburger's plated knife-and-fork predecessor, is also the hamburger's etymological derivative. Named after the port city of Hamburg, Germany, the Hamburg steak (simply a seasoned chopped beefsteak patty) made its way to America alongside its emigrant creators in the seventeenth century. America's industrialization and the advent of lunch wagons then provoked the Hamburg steak's historic leap from plate to sandwich, making standing lunches—sans plates or utensils—both possible and plausible. Filling, cheap, and convenient, the "hamburger steak sandwich" was born, and the rest, as they say, is history.

# ROUTE 66 BURGERS

SERVES: **4** | PREP TIME: **15 MINUTES** | GRILLING TIME: **8 TO 10 MINUTES**

## SAUCE
- ⅓ cup mayonnaise
- 2 tablespoons ketchup
- 1 tablespoon sweet pickle relish
- 1 tablespoon finely chopped shallot

## PATTIES
- 1½ pounds ground chuck (80% lean)
- ¾ teaspoon garlic powder
- ¾ teaspoon kosher salt
- ¼ teaspoon freshly ground black pepper

- 4 slices American cheese
- 4 hamburger buns, split
- 4 leaves Boston lettuce
- 1 ripe beefsteak tomato, about 6 ounces, cut crosswise into 4 slices

1. Combine the sauce ingredients.

2. Mix the patty ingredients, and then gently form four patties of equal size, each about ¾ inch thick. With your thumb or the back of a spoon, make a shallow indentation about 1 inch wide in the center of the patties to prevent them from forming a dome as they cook. Refrigerate the patties until ready to grill.

3. Prepare the grill for direct cooking over medium-high heat (400° to 500°F).

4. Grill the patties over *direct medium-high heat*, with the lid closed, until cooked to medium doneness (160°F), 8 to 10 minutes, turning once. During the last 30 seconds to 1 minute of grilling time, place a slice of cheese on each patty to melt, and toast the buns, cut side down, over direct heat.

5. Build each burger on a bun with sauce, a lettuce leaf, a tomato slice, and a patty. Serve warm.

Like the great ole highway that stretched from Chicago to Los Angeles, these burgers represent a classic Americana style. If you ever drove Route 66 and ate in the mom-and-pop restaurants along the way, you might have had burgers just like these.

# BEEF FAJITA BURGERS WITH GUACAMOLE

SERVES: **4** | PREP TIME: **25 MINUTES** | GRILLING TIME: **8 TO 10 MINUTES**

1 tablespoon extra-virgin olive oil
½ red bell pepper, cut into thin strips
½ yellow bell pepper, cut into thin strips

## GUACAMOLE
1 Hass avocado
1 tablespoon fresh lime juice
1 plum tomato, seeded and finely chopped
1 tablespoon finely chopped fresh cilantro leaves
1 tablespoon minced shallot
½ teaspoon kosher salt, or to taste

## PATTIES
1½ pounds ground chuck (80% lean)
1 tablespoon prepared chili powder
1 teaspoon ground cumin
½ teaspoon kosher salt

4 slices pepper jack cheese, each about 1 ounce
4 sesame seed buns, split

1. In a large skillet over medium heat, warm the oil. Add the bell peppers and cook until softened, about 10 minutes, stirring frequently. Remove from the heat.

2. Mash the guacamole ingredients. Cover with plastic wrap, pressing the wrap directly onto the surface of the guacamole to prevent it from browning. Refrigerate until ready to serve.

3. Mix the patty ingredients, and then gently form four patties of equal size, each about ¾ inch thick. With your thumb or the back of a spoon, make a shallow indentation about 1 inch wide in the center of the patties to prevent them from forming a dome as they cook. Refrigerate the patties until ready to grill.

4. Prepare the grill for direct cooking over medium-high heat (400° to 500°F).

5. Grill the patties over *direct medium-high heat*, with the lid closed, until cooked to medium doneness (160°F), 8 to 10 minutes, turning once. During the last 30 seconds to 1 minute of grilling time, place a slice of cheese on each patty to melt, and toast the buns, cut side down, over direct heat.

6. Build each burger on a bun with a patty, peppers, and guacamole. Serve warm.

# CHEDDAR-STUFFED BURGERS WITH CHOPPED ONION

SERVES: **4** | PREP TIME: **20 MINUTES** | GRILLING TIME: **9 TO 11 MINUTES**

## PATTIES

1½  pounds ground chuck
(80% lean)
½  cup finely chopped
yellow onion
1  teaspoon kosher salt
¾  teaspoon granulated garlic
½  teaspoon freshly ground
black pepper

4  slices cheddar cheese,
stacked and quartered to make
4 blocks, each about 1¼ inches
square and ½ inch thick
4  hamburger buns, split
Ketchup *or* Sweet and
Spicy Tomato Chutney
(for recipe, see page 235)

Use whatever type of cheddar cheese you like with your burgers. The "sharpness" of the cheese is an indication of its pungency. Sharp cheddar is an aged cheese, usually for 6 to 9 months, so it has a stronger taste than mild cheddar. Extra-sharp cheddar is often aged for 1½ to 2 years. Regardless of its sharpness, a good cheddar should have a nutty taste and a firm but creamy texture. Its color is naturally off-white, but a lot of American producers color it orange with annatto seeds or other ingredients.

1. Mix the patty ingredients, and then gently form eight patties of equal size, each about ⅓ inch thick. Place four patties on a work surface and center a cheese block on top of each. Center the remaining four patties over the top and press down until each double patty is about 1 inch thick. Pinch the edges together tightly to seal the cheese inside. Refrigerate the patties until ready to grill.

2. Prepare the grill for direct cooking over medium-high heat (400° to 500°F).

3. Grill the patties over *direct medium-high heat*, with the lid closed, until cooked to medium doneness (160°F), 9 to 11 minutes, turning once (don't worry if a little cheese leaks out). During the last 30 seconds to 1 minute of grilling time, toast the buns, cut side down, over direct heat.

4. Build each burger on a bun with a patty and ketchup or chutney. Serve warm.

# CHEESEBURGERS WITH GRILLED APPLE

SERVES: **4**  |  PREP TIME: **15 MINUTES**  |  GRILLING TIME: **9 TO 11 MINUTES**

## PATTIES

- 1½ pounds ground chuck (80% lean)
- 1 teaspoon kosher salt
- ¼ teaspoon ground nutmeg
- ¼ teaspoon freshly ground black pepper

- 1 large, ripe apple, cored and cut crosswise into four ½-inch slices
- 1½ teaspoons extra-virgin olive oil
- 4 ounces Tilsit or Havarti cheese, cut into 8 pieces
- 4 round pretzel rolls or hamburger buns, split
  Spicy brown mustard
- 4 leaves lettuce

1. Mix the patty ingredients, and then gently form four patties of equal size, each about 1 inch thick. With your thumb or the back of a spoon, make a shallow indentation about 1 inch wide in the center of the patties to prevent them from forming a dome as they cook. Refrigerate the patties until ready to grill.

2. Prepare the grill for direct cooking over medium-high heat (400° to 500°F).

3. Brush the apple slices on both sides with the oil.

4. Grill the patties over *direct medium-high heat*, with the lid closed, until cooked to medium doneness (160°F), 9 to 11 minutes, turning once. At the same time, grill the apple slices over *direct medium-high heat* until tender and nicely marked, 3 to 4 minutes, turning once. During the last 30 seconds to 1 minute of grilling time, place two pieces of cheese on each patty to melt, and toast the rolls, cut side down, over direct heat.

5. Build each burger on a roll with mustard, a lettuce leaf, a patty, and a grilled apple slice. Serve warm.

# WEBER'S EXTREME BURGERS

SERVES: **4** | PREP TIME: **25 MINUTES** | GRILLING TIME: **6 TO 8 MINUTES**

4 slices thick-cut bacon

## MAYO
⅓ cup mayonnaise
1 teaspoon minced garlic

Kosher salt
Freshly ground black pepper

## GUACAMOLE
2 ripe Hass avocados
1 tablespoon fresh lime juice
2 teaspoons minced garlic

2 pounds ground chuck (80% lean)
1 tablespoon Worcestershire sauce
½ teaspoon smoked paprika
½ teaspoon onion powder
8 thin slices cheddar cheese
4 hamburger buns, split
4 leaves Boston lettuce
1 ripe beefsteak tomato, cut crosswise
into 4 slices about ⅓ inch thick

1. In a skillet over medium heat, fry the bacon until crisp, 10 to 12 minutes, turning occasionally. Drain on paper towels.

2. Whisk the mayo ingredients, including ¼ teaspoon salt and ⅛ teaspoon pepper.

3. Mash the guacamole ingredients, including ½ teaspoon salt and ¼ teaspoon pepper.

4. Mix the ground chuck with the Worcestershire sauce, 1 teaspoon salt, ½ teaspoon pepper, the smoked paprika, and onion powder, and then gently form eight patties of equal size, each about ½ inch thick and a little wider than the buns. Refrigerate the patties until ready to grill.

5. Prepare the grill for direct cooking over medium-high heat (400° to 500°F).

6. Grill the patties over *direct medium-high heat*, with the lid closed, until cooked to medium doneness (160°F), 6 to 8 minutes, turning once. During the last 30 seconds to 1 minute of grilling time, place a slice of cheese on each patty to melt, and toast the buns, cut side down, over direct heat.

7. Build each burger on a bun with garlic mayo, a lettuce leaf, a tomato slice, two patties, as much guacamole as you like, a slice of bacon (torn in half), and more garlic mayo. Serve immediately.

Behold an extreme example of what's good, renowned, and entirely decadent about burgers. This cheesy double-decker of grilled beef gets a dollop of garlic mayonnaise smeared on the bun, all of which would make a spectacular sandwich if we stopped right there, but we don't take the word "extreme" lightly. So bring on the layers of lettuce and tomato. Bring on the glorious guacamole. And as long as we're going over the top, bring on the bacon, too.

# BUILDING A
# BETTER BURGER

The burger is about as foolproof a meal as we know: open bun, insert patty, close bun, eat. Not much to it, right? Nor should there be, but some small adjustments can yield delicious results.

 **1** CHOOSE FIRM BUNS

Grocery store brands can be too soft and may fall apart as the juices run. A good bun should be slightly dense but still pillowy. Sound contradictory? The potato bun and the kaiser roll pull off this duality well.

 **2** MAKE IT TOASTY

Tossing your split buns on the grill for 30 seconds to 1 minute creates a dry surface that will absorb juices without total bun disintegration. That slight crunch does a lot for texture, too.

### 3 ▸ SPREAD LIGHTLY

A light slathering of condiments inside your bun reinforces that toasty barrier while adding flavor and just the right amount of moisture. Limit yourself to one condiment per half so you can appreciate the taste of each.

### 4 ▸ TOP SMART

While a sky-high burger with the works may suit your cravings, it rarely suits the size of the human mouth. Stick to what is fresh, good quality, and complementary. The idea is that the toppings should play ball, not stage a bench-clearing brawl between the buns.

### 5 ▸ ORDER MATTERS

Place the drier toppings, such as lettuce and raw onion, closest to the bun, with juicier toppings, like tomato slices, closest to the patty. The bun stays dry, the toppings stay put, and no clean shirts will be harmed while you build your perfect burger.

# BRONCO BURGERS WITH SMOKED MOZZARELLA AND BARBECUE SAUCE

SERVES: **4** | PREP TIME: **15 MINUTES** | GRILLING TIME: **8 TO 10 MINUTES**

## PATTIES

1½ pounds ground chuck (80% lean)
 1 teaspoon ground cumin
 1 teaspoon prepared chili powder
 1 teaspoon onion powder
 1 teaspoon kosher salt
 ½ teaspoon freshly ground black pepper

 4 slices smoked mozzarella cheese
 4 hamburger buns, split
 ¾ cup Cherry Cola Barbecue Sauce (for recipe, see page 237) *or* store-bought barbecue sauce
 4 thin slices sweet onion
16 dill pickle chips

1. Mix the patty ingredients, and then gently form four patties of equal size, each about ¾ inch thick. With your thumb or the back of a spoon, make a shallow indentation about 1 inch wide in the center of the patties to prevent them from forming a dome as they cook. Refrigerate the patties until ready to grill.

2. Prepare the grill for direct cooking over medium-high heat (400° to 500°F).

3. Grill the patties over *direct medium-high heat*, with the lid closed, until cooked to medium doneness (160°F), 8 to 10 minutes, turning once. During the last 30 seconds to 1 minute of grilling time, place a slice of cheese on each patty to melt, and toast the buns, cut side down, over direct heat.

4. Build each burger on a bun with barbecue sauce, an onion slice, a patty, and pickles. Serve warm.

*Serving suggestion: Smoky Barbecued Baked Beans (for recipe, see page 226).*

**FUN FACT**

Pickle perfection is all about the snap. The best dill pickles, according to professional pickle purveyors, pack an audible crunch from 10 paces away, whereas pickles that can be heard from only one pace are known as "denture dills."

# SUN-DRIED TOMATO BEEF BURGERS WITH SMOKED MOZZARELLA

SERVES: **4** | PREP TIME: **20 MINUTES** | GRILLING TIME: **6 TO 8 MINUTES**

## PATTIES

- 1 pound ground chuck (80% lean)
- 2 tablespoons minced shallot
- 2 tablespoons freshly grated Parmigiano-Reggiano® cheese
- 2 tablespoons minced oil-packed sun-dried tomatoes
- 1 tablespoon panko bread crumbs
- 1 tablespoon minced fresh Italian parsley leaves
- 1 teaspoon dried oregano

  Kosher salt
  Freshly ground black pepper
- 4 slices olive bread, each about ½ inch thick
  Extra-virgin olive oil
- 3 ounces smoked mozzarella cheese, thinly sliced
- ⅓ cup baby arugula

1. Mix the patty ingredients, including ¾ teaspoon salt and ¼ teaspoon pepper, and then gently form four patties of equal size, each about ½ inch thick. Refrigerate the patties until ready to grill.

2. Prepare the grill for direct cooking over medium heat (350° to 450°F).

3. Brush the bread slices on both sides with oil and lightly season the bread and the patties with salt and pepper. Grill the patties over *direct medium heat*, with the lid closed, for 3 to 4 minutes. Turn the patties over and distribute the cheese evenly on top of the patties. Continue grilling until cooked to medium doneness (160°F), 3 to 4 minutes more. During the last minute of grilling time, toast the bread over direct heat until slightly golden, turning once.

4. Top each bread slice with a patty and arugula. Serve warm.

# DOUBLE-TRUFFLED CHEESEBURGERS

SERVES: **4** | PREP TIME: **15 MINUTES** | GRILLING TIME: **9 TO 11 MINUTES**

## PATTIES

1½ pounds ground chuck
(80% lean)
1½ tablespoons minced shallot
4 teaspoons white or
black truffle oil
1 tablespoon Dijon mustard
1 tablespoon minced fresh
Italian parsley leaves
½ teaspoon Worcestershire sauce

Kosher salt
Freshly ground black pepper
2½ ounces truffle cheese, cut into
8 slices, at room temperature
2 focaccia squares, each about
4½ inches in diameter, split
4–8 cornichons, thinly sliced

1. Mix the patty ingredients, including ½ teaspoon salt and ¼ teaspoon pepper, and then gently form four patties of equal size, each about 1 inch thick. With your thumb or the back of a spoon, make a shallow indentation about 1 inch wide in the center of the patties to prevent them from forming a dome as they cook. Refrigerate the patties until ready to grill.

2. Prepare the grill for direct cooking over medium-high heat (400° to 500°F).

3. Lightly season the patties on both sides with salt and pepper, and then grill over *direct medium-high heat*, with the lid closed, until cooked to medium doneness (160°F), 9 to 11 minutes, turning once. During the last 30 seconds to 1 minute of grilling time, place two slices of cheese on each patty to melt, and toast the focaccia, cut side down, over direct heat.

4. Top each focaccia square with a patty and cornichons. Serve warm.

The first dose of truffle comes from a soft, melting cheese that is speckled with tiny bits of the mushroom-y tuber. The second dose comes from oil that is infused with truffle aroma and worked into the meat.

# REUBEN BURGERS

SERVES: **4** | PREP TIME: **20 MINUTES** | GRILLING TIME: **13 TO 15 MINUTES**

## PATTIES

- 1 pound ground chuck (80% lean)
- 4 ounces pancetta or lean bacon, finely chopped
- 2 teaspoons whole-grain mustard
- 1 teaspoon granulated onion
- ½ teaspoon granulated garlic

  Kosher salt
  Freshly ground black pepper

## DRESSING

- ½ cup mayonnaise
- 2 tablespoons sour cream
- 1½ tablespoons ketchup
- 2 teaspoons prepared horseradish
- 1 teaspoon Worcestershire sauce
- 1 teaspoon minced fresh dill
- 1 garlic clove, minced or pushed through a press
- ¼ teaspoon white wine vinegar

- 8 slices rye bread
- 2 tablespoons unsalted butter, melted
- 8 slices Swiss cheese, each about 1 ounce
- 1 cup sauerkraut, drained

**1.** Mix the patty ingredients, including ½ teaspoon salt and ¼ teaspoon pepper, and then gently form four patties of equal size, each about 1 inch thick. With your thumb or the back of a spoon, make a shallow indentation about 1 inch wide in the center of the patties to prevent them from forming a dome as they cook. Refrigerate the patties until ready to grill.

**2.** Prepare the grill for direct cooking over medium-high heat (400° to 500°F).

**3.** Combine the dressing ingredients, including ⅛ teaspoon salt.

**4.** Lightly season the patties on both sides with salt and pepper, and then grill over *direct medium-high heat*, with the lid closed, until cooked to medium doneness (160°F), 9 to 11 minutes, turning once.

**5.** Brush one side of each bread slice with the melted butter, and place them on a work surface, buttered side down. Spread the unbuttered side of the bread with the dressing. Build each burger with a bread slice (dressing side up), one slice of cheese, a patty, another slice of cheese, sauerkraut, and a second bread slice (dressing side down). Place the burgers over *direct medium-high heat*, close the lid, and cook until the cheese is melted and the bread is toasted, about 4 minutes, carefully turning once. Serve warm.

Pancetta is easier to chop if it is very cold, so chill it in the freezer for 15 minutes just before chopping.

# BAGUETTE BEEF BURGERS WITH BRIE

SERVES: **4** | PREP TIME: **15 MINUTES** | GRILLING TIME: **8 TO 10 MINUTES**

BEEF

## PATTIES

1½ pounds ground chuck
(80% lean)

1½ tablespoons minced fresh
Italian parsley leaves

2 garlic cloves, minced or
pushed through a press

1 teaspoon dried thyme

Kosher salt
Freshly ground black pepper

4 ounces Brie cheese,
rind removed, chilled,
and cut into four chunks

4 slices French baguette,
each about ½ inch thick,
cut on a sharp diagonal

2 teaspoons unsalted
butter, softened

4 teaspoons whole-grain mustard

1 small head frisée,
pale inner heart only

1. Mix the patty ingredients, including ½ teaspoon salt and ¼ teaspoon pepper, and then divide into four equal-sized balls (don't compact the meat too much). With your forefinger, make a dimple in the center of each ball of meat and insert a piece of cheese. Close the meat over the cheese. Gently press the meat into oblong patties of equal size (to match the size of the bread slices), each about ¾ inch thick. Refrigerate the patties until ready to grill.

2. Prepare the grill for direct cooking over medium-high heat (400° to 500°F).

3. Lightly season the patties on both sides with salt and pepper, and then grill over *direct medium-high heat*, with the lid closed, until cooked to medium doneness (160°F), 8 to 10 minutes, turning once. During the last minute of grilling time, toast the baguette slices over direct heat, turning once.

4. Spread the butter on the baguette slices and top each with mustard, a patty, and frisée. Serve warm.

# FONTINA-STUFFED BURGERS WITH PROSCIUTTO

SERVES: **4** | PREP TIME: **15 MINUTES** | GRILLING TIME: **10 TO 12 MINUTES**

## PATTIES

1½  pounds ground chuck
    (80% lean)
1  tablespoon minced fresh
    sage leaves
½  teaspoon kosher salt
¼  teaspoon freshly ground
    black pepper

2  ounces fontina cheese,
    cut into 4 pieces
⅓  cup mayonnaise
½  teaspoon finely grated
    lemon zest
4  hamburger buns, split
4  ounces thinly sliced prosciutto
2  cups baby arugula

The keys to keeping the
cheese inside a burger are:
(1) using just a little of it and
(2) creating a tight seal all
the way around each patty.

**1.** Mix the patty ingredients, and then gently form eight patties of equal size, each about ½ inch thick. Center one piece of cheese on top of four patties. Center the remaining four patties over the top and press down until each double patty is about 1 inch thick. Pinch the edges together tightly to seal the cheese inside. Refrigerate the patties until ready to grill.

**2.** Mix the mayonnaise and lemon zest. Cover and refrigerate until ready to use.

**3.** Prepare the grill for direct cooking over medium heat (350° to 450°F).

**4.** Grill the patties over *direct medium heat*, with the lid closed, until cooked to medium doneness (160°F), 10 to 12 minutes, turning once.

**5.** Build each burger on a bun with lemon mayonnaise, a patty, prosciutto, arugula, and more lemon mayonnaise. Serve immediately.

# BEEF BURGERS WITH CAMEMBERT AND RED ONION JAM

SERVES: **4** | PREP TIME: **15 MINUTES, PLUS ABOUT 30 MINUTES FOR THE JAM** | GRILLING TIME: **9 TO 11 MINUTES**

## JAM

  2 tablespoons extra-virgin olive oil
  2 large red onions, 1½ pounds total, slivered
  3 tablespoons granulated sugar
  ¾ cup cabernet sauvignon
  2 tablespoons balsamic vinegar

    Kosher salt
2½ tablespoons unsalted butter, softened
  8 slices rye bread
1½ pounds ground chuck (80% lean)
    Freshly ground black pepper
  4 ounces Camembert cheese, cut into 8 slices

1. In a large, heavy skillet over medium heat, warm the oil. Add the onions and sugar and sauté until the onions are very soft, about 15 minutes, stirring occasionally. Pour in the cabernet and vinegar and cook until almost evaporated, 13 to 14 minutes, stirring occasionally. Season with ½ teaspoon salt. Keep warm until ready to serve.

2. Butter both sides of each bread slice.

3. Mix the ground chuck, 1 teaspoon salt, and ½ teaspoon pepper, and then gently form four patties of equal size, each about 1 inch thick. With your thumb or the back of a spoon, make a shallow indentation about 1 inch wide in the center of the patties to prevent them from forming a dome as they cook. Refrigerate the patties until ready to grill.

4. Prepare the grill for direct cooking over medium-high heat (400° to 500°F).

5. Grill the patties over *direct medium-high heat*, with the lid closed, until cooked to medium doneness (160°F), 9 to 11 minutes, turning once. During the last minute of grilling time, place two slices of cheese on each patty to melt, and toast the bread over direct heat, turning once.

6. Build each burger on a bread slice with a patty, red onion jam, a generous grinding of pepper, and the remaining bread slice. Serve warm.

This great sweet-and-sour jam requires cooking the red onions with a bit of sugar until very, very tender and then infusing them with red wine and vinegar. Use any leftover jam for a topping on steaks, leg of lamb, or pork chops.

# PARMESAN BURGERS WITH BALSAMIC KETCHUP

SERVES: **4** | PREP TIME: **20 MINUTES** | GRILLING TIME: **11 TO 14 MINUTES**

## PATTIES

1½  pounds ground chuck
    (80% lean)
2   tablespoons balsamic vinegar
2   teaspoons minced fresh
    rosemary leaves
3   small garlic cloves, minced

    Kosher salt
    Freshly ground black pepper

## KETCHUP

¼   cup ketchup
2   tablespoons balsamic vinegar
1   tablespoon Dijon mustard
1½  teaspoons mayonnaise

1   ounce Parmigiano-Reggiano®
    cheese, at room temperature,
    shaved into pieces with a
    vegetable peeler, divided
4   slices rustic Italian bread,
    each about ⅓ inch thick
    Extra-virgin olive oil

1. Mix the patty ingredients, including ½ teaspoon salt and ¼ teaspoon pepper, and then gently form four patties of equal size, each about 1 inch thick. With your thumb or the back of a spoon, make a shallow indentation about 1 inch wide in the center of the patties to prevent them from forming a dome as they cook. Refrigerate the patties until ready to grill.

2. Prepare the grill for direct and indirect cooking over medium-high heat (400° to 500°F).

3. Whisk the ketchup ingredients.

4. Lightly season the patties on both sides with salt and pepper, and then grill over *direct medium-high heat*, with the lid closed, until cooked to medium doneness (160°F), 9 to 11 minutes, turning once. Remove from the grill, immediately top the patties with half of the cheese, and let rest for 2 to 3 minutes.

5. Brush the bread on both sides with oil, and then grill over *indirect medium-high heat* for 30 seconds. Turn the bread over and top with the remaining cheese. Cook until the cheese softens, 1 to 2 minutes. Serve each cheese-topped patty atop a cheese-topped piece of bread with the balsamic ketchup on the side.

# CROQUE-MONSIEUR BEEF BURGERS

SERVES: **4** | PREP TIME: **15 MINUTES** | GRILLING TIME: **8 TO 10 MINUTES** | SPECIAL EQUIPMENT: **GRILL-PROOF GRIDDLE**

## PATTIES

- 1½ pounds ground chuck (80% lean)
- 2 tablespoons Dijon mustard
- 1 tablespoon Worcestershire sauce
- ¾ teaspoon kosher salt

- 3 tablespoons unsalted butter, softened
- 8 slices sourdough or French bread
- 6 ounces Gruyère cheese, grated
- ¼ teaspoon ground nutmeg
- 8 thin slices deli ham
  Dijon mustard
  Cornichons (optional)

**1.** Mix the patty ingredients, and then gently form four patties of equal size, each about ¾ inch thick. With your thumb or the back of a spoon, make a shallow indentation about 1 inch wide in the center of the patties to prevent them from forming a dome as they cook. Refrigerate the patties until ready to grill.

**2.** Prepare the grill for direct cooking over medium-high heat (400° to 500°F) and preheat a grill-proof griddle.

**3.** Butter both sides of each bread slice. Mix the cheese with the nutmeg.

**4.** Grill the patties on the cooking grates over *direct medium-high heat*, with the lid closed, until cooked to medium doneness (160°F), 8 to 10 minutes, turning once. After you turn the patties, place two ham slices on each patty to warm. At the same time, cook the bread on the griddle for 2 minutes, turn, top equally with the cheese, and cook for 2 minutes more.

**5.** Place one slice of bread on each serving plate, cheese side up, and then add a patty. Top with another slice of bread, cheese side down. Serve immediately with mustard and cornichons, if desired.

**FUN FACT**

The *croque-monsieur* is a classic French ham-and-Gruyère-cheese sandwich that's traditionally spread with béchamel sauce and then grilled to a crisp (in fact, it literally translates to "crunch, mister"). Seeking even more French decadence? Slap a sunny-side-up fried egg on top, and you've made it a *croque-madame*.

# WILD MUSHROOM CHEESEBURGERS

SERVES: **4** | PREP TIME: **25 MINUTES** | GRILLING TIME: **9 TO 11 MINUTES**

2 tablespoons extra-virgin olive oil

8 ounces assorted mushrooms, such as shiitake, oyster, and chanterelle, cleaned and cut into slices

½ cup thinly sliced shallots

3 garlic cloves, thinly sliced

1 teaspoon minced fresh thyme leaves *or* ½ teaspoon dried thyme

½ cup Madeira wine
  Kosher salt
  Freshly ground black pepper

1½ pounds ground chuck (80% lean)

2 tablespoons low-sodium soy sauce

4 thick slices Gruyère cheese

4 French rolls, split

¼ cup mayonnaise

1. In a large skillet over medium-high heat, warm the oil. Add the mushrooms, shallots, garlic, and thyme, and sauté until lightly browned, 10 to 11 minutes, stirring occasionally. Pour in the wine and cook until it has evaporated, about 2 minutes, stirring often. Remove the mushroom mixture from the heat and season with ¼ teaspoon salt and ¼ teaspoon pepper.

2. Mix the ground chuck, soy sauce, ½ teaspoon salt, and ¼ teaspoon pepper, and then gently form four patties of equal size, each about 1 inch thick. With your thumb or the back of a spoon, make a shallow indentation about 1 inch wide in the center of the patties to prevent them from forming a dome as they cook. Refrigerate the patties until ready to grill.

3. Prepare the grill for direct cooking over medium-high heat (400° to 500°F).

4. Grill the patties over *direct medium-high heat*, with the lid closed, until cooked to medium doneness (160°F), 9 to 11 minutes, turning once. During the last 30 seconds to 1 minute of grilling time, place a slice of cheese on each patty to melt, and toast the rolls, cut side down, over direct heat.

5. Build each burger on a roll with mayonnaise, a patty, and the mushroom mixture. Serve warm.

The stems of wild chanterelles (far left) are a little tougher than the caps but still edible; however, the stems of cultivated shiitakes (left) are almost always too tough, so cut them off before sautéing the caps in a hot skillet.

# WEBER'S IDEAL CHEESEBURGERS

SERVES: **4**  |  PREP TIME: **15 MINUTES**  |  GRILLING TIME: **9 TO 11 MINUTES**

## PATTIES

1½   pounds ground chuck (80% lean), preferably
    ground to order by your butcher
2   tablespoons minced white or yellow onion
1½   teaspoons Dijon mustard
½   teaspoon Worcestershire sauce
½   teaspoon dried oregano

    Ketchup
    Kosher salt
    Freshly ground black pepper
2   tablespoons unsalted butter, softened
4   hamburger buns, split
4   slices aged cheddar cheese, each about 2 ounces
4   leaves butter lettuce
16   dill pickle chips

1. Mix the patty ingredients, including 1 tablespoon ketchup, ½ teaspoon salt, and ¼ teaspoon pepper, and then gently form four patties of equal size, each about 1 inch thick. With your thumb or the back of a spoon, make a shallow indentation about 1 inch wide in the center of the patties to prevent them from forming a dome as they cook. Refrigerate the patties until ready to grill.

2. Prepare the grill for direct cooking over medium-high heat (400° to 500°F).

3. Lightly season the patties on both sides with salt and pepper. Butter the cut side of the buns. Grill the patties over *direct medium-high heat*, with the lid closed, until cooked to medium doneness (160°F), 9 to 11 minutes, turning once. During the last 30 seconds to 1 minute of grilling time, place a slice of cheese on each patty to melt, and toast the buns, cut side down, over direct heat.

4. Build each burger on a bun with a lettuce leaf, a patty, pickles, and ketchup, if desired. Serve immediately.

*Serving suggestion: Classic Buttermilk Onion Rings (for recipe, see page 228).*

*(for recipe, see page 228).*

---

### THE GLORY OF MUSTARD

In life, we consider it prudent to live by the golden rule. That is, put mustard on everything.

From smooth and vibrant to spicy and granular, mustard and mankind have moved lockstep through history. Ancient Romans used ground mustard seed in sauces; Greeks treated scorpion bites (yikes) with the stuff; and healers of all eras relied on mustard ointments for medicinal cure-alls.

The *mères* and *pères* of the modern marvel we love come from thirteenth-century Dijon, France, where ingenious folk whipped up a spread of the ground seed, wine, vinegar, and spices—the predecessor of the spicy, nuanced Dijon-style we know today.

The word "mustard" has a number of possible origins, but one comes from its rightful home of old Dijon. The town's coat of arms bore the phrase *Moult Me Tard* ("I ardently desire"), which became associated with its delicious export and was eventually whittled down to *moutarde*, or, anglicized, "mustard."

BEEF

# WHO INVENTED THE
# HAMBURGER?

**Was it "Hamburger Charlie" Nagreen with the bread-enveloped meatballs in Seymour, Wisconsin? Or could it have been the Menches brothers with the burger sandwiches in Hamburg, New York? Like a century-long game of hamburger Clue, the hunt for the true inventor of "America's National Sandwich" has turned up no shortage of likely suspects.**

The late nineteenth and early twentieth centuries, however, did provoke a plethora of alleged originators—all with fiercely contested credentials. Let us present you with just a few claims to hamburger fame.

Fletcher "Old Dave" Davis said that he did it first in the 1880s at a lunch counter in Athens, Texas, where he served fried ground beef patties between two slices of homemade bread. From there, his hamburger invention got its first widespread national exposure at the 1904 World's Fair in St. Louis, Missouri. Oh, and for what it's worth, in 2006 the Texas State Legislature went ahead and designated Athens as the "Original Home of the Hamburger."

Around the same time that Old Dave allegedly invented the hamburger, 15-year-old Charlie Nagreen started selling a similar product at the 1885 Outagamie County

Fair in Seymour, Wisconsin: meatballs that were smashed between bread slices. The town of Seymour still stands staunchly by the claim, even erecting a 12-foot statue of "Hamburger Charlie" proudly presenting his famous burger for all to affirm.

And then there were the Menches brothers of Akron, Ohio. While little Charlie the entrepreneur was busy slinging meatballs in the Midwest, Frank and Charles Menches were pioneering ground beef patties in the East. Legend has it that during a stop at the Erie County Fair in Hamburg, New York, the two traveling concessionaires ran out of their standard sausage sandwich, so they started serving beef patties between two pieces of bread. They declared it "the hamburger," supposedly naming it after the town in which they sold their first.

Other folklore attributes the hamburger's invention—specifically, the first-known hamburger on a bun—to Oscar Weber Bilby of Tulsa, in 1891. While there is little documentation to prove this, the mystery further multiplied when Oklahoma's governor proclaimed April 12, 1995, as "The *Real* Birthplace of the Hamburger in Tulsa Day."

Lastly (but that doesn't mean *anything*), came Louis' Lunch in New Haven, Connecticut. Founder Louis Lassen purportedly sold the United States' first hamburger in 1900 from his small lunch wagon: a vertically broiled ground beef patty on white bread. These guys even got the Library of Congress on board with their allegation, affirming their claim and calling Louis' Lunch a "Connecticut Legacy."

What began as a bun-less, immigrant-inspired Hamburg steak is now an indisputably juicy, towering symbol of American prosperity. Perhaps the real question is: who *wouldn't* want to lay claim to its invention? Whether the true creator was one of the five aforementioned, or perhaps even another undocumented (gasp!) innovator, we may never know. Unsolved mysteries aside, the hamburger and its many purveyors have established a satisfying global icon, here for the long haul.

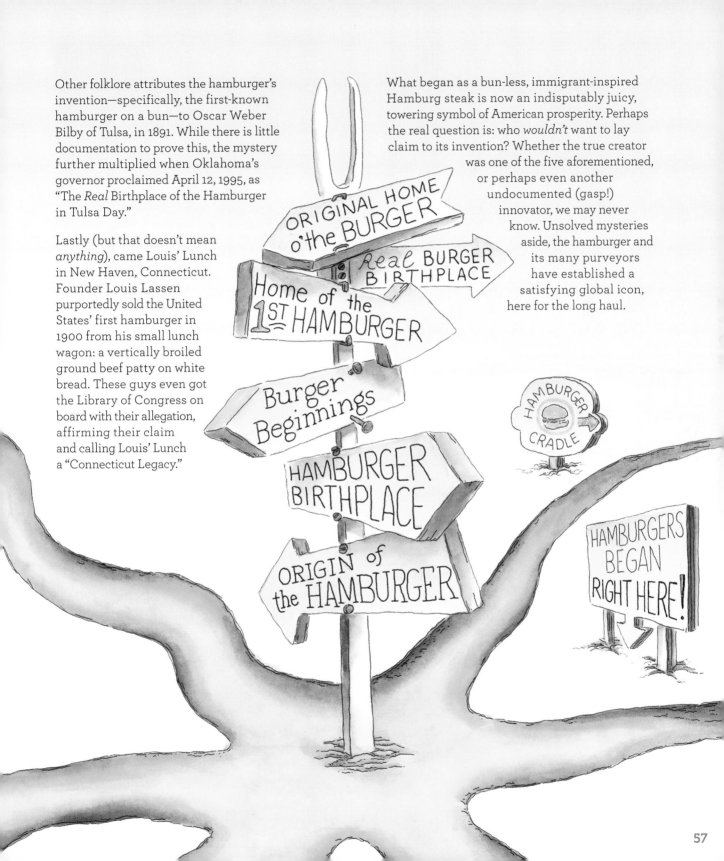

57

# BACON PORTABELLO CHEESEBURGERS

SERVES: **4** | PREP TIME: **30 MINUTES** | GRILLING TIME: **8 TO 10 MINUTES**

8 slices thick-cut bacon
¼ cup extra-virgin olive oil
4 portabello mushrooms, each about 4 inches in diameter, stems and gills removed, wiped clean
Freshly ground black pepper
1½ pounds ground chuck (80% lean)
½ teaspoon kosher salt
4 thin slices Havarti cheese
4 hamburger buns, split
Dijon mustard
4 leaves lettuce

1. In a skillet over medium heat, fry the bacon until crisp, 10 to 12 minutes, turning occasionally. Transfer the bacon to paper towels to drain. Reserve the bacon fat in the skillet and add the oil. Brush the mushrooms with the bacon fat and oil mixture and season with pepper.

2. Mix the ground chuck with the salt and ¼ teaspoon pepper, and then gently form four patties of equal size, each about ¾ inch thick. With your thumb or the back of a spoon, make a shallow indentation about 1 inch wide in the center of the patties to prevent them from forming a dome as they cook. Refrigerate the patties until ready to grill.

3. Prepare the grill for direct cooking over medium-high heat (400° to 500°F).

4. Grill the mushrooms, gill side down first, and the patties over *direct medium-high heat*, with the lid closed, until the mushrooms are tender and the patties are cooked to medium doneness (160°F), 8 to 10 minutes, turning once. During the last 30 seconds to 1 minute of grilling time, place a slice of cheese on each patty to melt, and toast the buns, cut side down, over direct heat.

5. Build each burger on a bun with mustard, a lettuce leaf, a patty, a mushroom, and two slices of bacon. Serve warm.

# PANCETTA BEEF BURGERS WITH GARLIC-ROSEMARY MAYO

SERVES: **4**  |  PREP TIME: **15 MINUTES**  |  GRILLING TIME: **9 TO 11 MINUTES**

## PATTIES

1¼ pounds ground chuck (80% lean)
4 ounces pancetta, finely diced
1½ tablespoons minced fresh Italian parsley leaves (optional)
2 garlic cloves, minced or pushed through a press

Kosher salt
Freshly ground black pepper

## MAYO

½ cup mayonnaise
2 teaspoons extra-virgin olive oil
2 teaspoons fresh lemon juice
1½ teaspoons minced fresh rosemary leaves
1 large garlic clove, minced or pushed through a press

4 sesame seed buns, split
½ cup baby arugula or mâche (lamb's lettuce)

1. Mix the patty ingredients, including ½ teaspoon salt and ¼ teaspoon pepper, and then gently form four patties of equal size, each about 1 inch thick. With your thumb or the back of a spoon, make a shallow indentation about 1 inch wide in the center of the patties to prevent them from forming a dome as they cook. Refrigerate the patties until ready to grill.

2. Prepare the grill for direct cooking over medium-high heat (400° to 500°F).

3. Combine the mayo ingredients, including ¼ teaspoon salt and ⅛ teaspoon pepper.

4. Lightly season the patties on both sides with salt and pepper, and then grill over *direct medium-high heat*, with the lid closed, until cooked to medium doneness (160°F), 9 to 11 minutes, turning once. During the last 30 seconds to 1 minute of grilling time, toast the buns, cut side down, over direct heat.

5. Build each burger on a bun with arugula, a patty, and a spoonful of garlic-rosemary mayo. Serve warm.

# SMOKED MEAT LOAF BURGERS WITH GRILLED ONION

SERVES: **4** | PREP TIME: **15 MINUTES** | GRILLING TIME: **8 TO 10 MINUTES**
SPECIAL EQUIPMENT: **2 LARGE HANDFULS MESQUITE WOOD CHIPS**

**BEEF**

## PATTIES

    8  ounces ground chuck (80% lean)
    8  ounces ground veal
    8  ounces lean ground pork
    2  large eggs, beaten
    ¾  cup dried Italian-seasoned bread crumbs
    ¼  cup freshly grated Parmigiano-Reggiano® cheese
    ½  teaspoon kosher salt
    ¼  teaspoon freshly ground black pepper

    ½  cup ketchup
    1  canned chipotle chile pepper
       in adobo sauce, minced
    1  teaspoon adobo sauce (from the can)
    1  red onion, cut crosswise into 4 slices,
       each about ½ inch thick
    2  teaspoons extra-virgin olive oil
    8  slices sourdough bread, each about ½ inch thick

1. Soak the wood chips in water for at least 30 minutes.

2. Mix the patty ingredients, and then gently form four patties of equal size, each about ¾ inch thick. With your thumb or the back of a spoon, make a shallow indentation about 1 inch wide in the center of the patties to prevent them from forming a dome as they cook. Refrigerate the patties until ready to grill.

3. Whisk the ketchup, chipotle chile pepper, and adobo sauce.

4. Prepare the grill for direct cooking over medium-high heat (400° to 500°F).

5. Brush the onion slices with the oil. Drain and add the wood chips to the charcoal or to the smoker box of a gas grill, following manufacturer's instructions, and close the lid. When the wood begins to smoke, grill the patties and onion over *direct medium-high heat*, with the lid closed, until the patties are cooked to medium doneness (160°F), 8 to 10 minutes, and the onion is tender, 6 to 8 minutes, turning once. During the last minute of grilling time, toast the bread over direct heat, turning once.

6. Build each burger on a bread slice with a patty, chipotle ketchup, a grilled onion slice, and the remaining bread slice. Serve warm.

Meat loaf, America's quintessential comfort food, is also a whatever's-in-the-pantry wonder. No bread crumbs? No problem! You can use anything from oats or cracker crumbs to rice or minced veggies as your meat loaf's obligatory binder.

# GRASS-FED BEEF BURGERS WITH CHARRED TOMATOES AND SMOKY MAYO

SERVES: **4** | PREP TIME: **20 MINUTES** | GRILLING TIME: **23 TO 30 MINUTES** | SPECIAL EQUIPMENT: **CAST-IRON SKILLET**

## PATTIES

1½ pounds ground grass-fed beef (90% lean)
1 large garlic clove, minced or pushed through a press
1 teaspoon kosher salt
1 teaspoon freshly ground black pepper

2 cups ripe grape tomatoes
1 tablespoon extra-virgin olive oil
½ teaspoon kosher salt
½ teaspoon granulated sugar

## MAYO

½ cup mayonnaise
1–2 small canned chipotle chile peppers in adobo sauce, minced
¼ teaspoon paprika
¼ teaspoon kosher salt

4 hamburger buns, split
2 cups loosely packed baby greens

1. Mix the patty ingredients, and then gently form four patties of equal size, each about ¾ inch thick. With your thumb or the back of a spoon, make a shallow indentation about 1 inch wide in the center of the patties to prevent them from forming a dome as they cook. Refrigerate the patties until ready to grill.

2. Prepare the grill for direct cooking over medium heat (350° to 450°F) and preheat a cast-iron skillet.

3. Combine the tomatoes, oil, salt, and sugar and turn to coat. Transfer to the hot cast-iron skillet and cook over *direct medium heat*, with the lid closed, until the tomatoes break down, 15 to 20 minutes, stirring occasionally. Remove the skillet from the grill and transfer the tomatoes to a bowl. Cool to room temperature.

4. Whisk the mayo ingredients.

5. Grill the patties over *direct medium heat*, with the lid closed, until cooked to medium doneness (160°F), 8 to 10 minutes, turning once. During the last 30 seconds to 1 minute of grilling time, toast the buns, cut side down, over direct heat.

6. Build each burger on a bun with the smoky mayo, greens, a patty, and charred tomatoes. Serve immediately.

Grass-fed beef is leaner than grain-fed beef. Grilling at a slightly lower temperature will prevent grass-fed patties from drying out and will accentuate their flavor.

63

# OPEN-FACED SICILIAN BURGERS WITH SPINACH AND TOMATO SALAD

SERVES: **4** | PREP TIME: **25 MINUTES** | GRILLING TIME: **9 TO 11 MINUTES**

## PATTIES

1½ pounds ground chuck
    (80% lean)
 2 tablespoons minced shallot
 2 tablespoons freshly grated
    Parmigiano-Reggiano® cheese
 2 tablespoons roughly
    chopped pine nuts
 2 garlic cloves, minced or
    pushed through a press
 ½ teaspoon dried oregano

    Kosher salt
    Freshly ground black pepper

## SALAD

1½ tablespoons extra-virgin
    olive oil
1½ teaspoons red wine vinegar
 2 cups tightly packed fresh
    baby spinach
 ¾ cup quartered ripe red and/or
    yellow cherry tomatoes
 2 teaspoons pine nuts

 4 slices Tuscan bread,
    each about ½ inch thick

1. Mix the patty ingredients, including ½ teaspoon salt and ¼ teaspoon pepper, and then gently form four patties of equal size, each about 1 inch thick. With your thumb or the back of a spoon, make a shallow indentation about 1 inch wide in the center of the patties to prevent them from forming a dome as they cook. Refrigerate the patties until ready to grill.

2. Prepare the grill for direct cooking over medium-high heat (400° to 500°F). Meanwhile, make the salad.

3. In a medium bowl whisk the oil, vinegar, ¼ teaspoon salt, and ⅛ teaspoon pepper. Add the spinach, tomatoes, and pine nuts. Do not toss.

4. Lightly season the patties on both sides with salt and pepper, and then grill over *direct medium-high heat*, with the lid closed, until cooked to medium doneness (160°F), 9 to 11 minutes, turning once. During the last minute of grilling time, toast the bread over direct heat, turning once.

5. Toss the spinach and tomato salad. Top each bread slice with a patty and an equal amount of the salad. Serve immediately.

# HUNGARIAN GOULASH BURGERS WITH GRILLED TOMATO AND SOUR CREAM

SERVES: **4** | PREP TIME: **15 MINUTES** | GRILLING TIME: **8 TO 10 MINUTES**

## PATTIES

1½ pounds ground chuck
   (80% lean)
2 tablespoons minced
   yellow onion
1 tablespoon sweet
   Hungarian paprika
1 tablespoon tomato paste
1 teaspoon caraway seed
1 teaspoon dried marjoram

   Kosher salt
⅔ cup sour cream
2 tablespoons minced fresh
   Italian parsley leaves
1 large, ripe beefsteak tomato,
   cut crosswise into 4 thick slices
2 teaspoons extra-virgin olive oil
   Freshly ground black pepper
4 hamburger buns, split

**1.** Mix the patty ingredients, including ½ teaspoon salt, and then gently form four patties of equal size, each about ¾ inch thick. With your thumb or the back of a spoon, make a shallow indentation about 1 inch wide in the center of the patties to prevent them from forming a dome as they cook. Refrigerate the patties until ready to grill.

**2.** Combine the sour cream and parsley. Cover and refrigerate until ready to use.

**3.** Prepare the grill for direct cooking over medium-high heat (400°F to 500°F).

**4.** Brush the tomato slices on both sides with oil and season evenly with salt and pepper. Grill the patties over *direct medium-high heat*, with the lid closed, until cooked to medium doneness (160°F), 8 to 10 minutes, turning once. At the same time, grill the tomatoes over *direct medium-high heat* until tender, about 5 minutes, turning once. During the last 30 seconds to 1 minute of grilling time, toast the buns, cut side down, over direct heat.

**5.** Build each burger on a bun with a patty, the sour cream mixture, and a tomato slice. Serve warm.

*Serving suggestion: Red Cabbage Slaw with Cider-Dill Vinaigrette (for recipe, see page 201).*

# CHILE-BEEF BURGERS WITH QUICK KIMCHI

SERVES: **4** | PREP TIME: **40 MINUTES** | STANDING TIME: **2 HOURS** | GRILLING TIME: **9 TO 11 MINUTES**

BEEF

## KIMCHI

- 1 small head napa or savoy cabbage, about 12 ounces, quartered and cored
- 6 scallions, ends trimmed and finely chopped
- 1 tablespoon kosher salt
- 1 small red bell pepper, finely chopped
- 1 tablespoon rice vinegar
- 2 teaspoons Asian fish sauce *or* soy sauce
- 1½ teaspoons crushed red pepper flakes *or* hot pepper sauce
- 1½ teaspoons peeled, minced fresh ginger
- 3 garlic cloves, minced or pushed through a press

## PATTIES

- 1½ pounds ground chuck (80% lean)
- 1 small shallot, minced
- 1 Thai or serrano chile pepper, stemmed, seeded, deveined, and minced (about 2 teaspoons)
- 2 garlic cloves, minced or pushed through a press

   Kosher salt
   Freshly ground black pepper
- 4 onion buns, split

1. Cut the cabbage crosswise into thin strips, and then separate the strips by hand. In a colander toss the cabbage with the scallions and salt. Let stand until the cabbage wilts, about 2 hours, tossing occasionally. Squeeze as much liquid as you can out of the cabbage. In a large bowl mix the remaining kimchi ingredients. Add the cabbage and scallions and toss to combine.

2. Mix the patty ingredients, including ½ teaspoon salt and ¼ teaspoon pepper, and then gently form four patties of equal size, each about 1 inch thick. With your thumb or the back of a spoon, make a shallow indentation about 1 inch wide in the center of the patties to prevent them from forming a dome as they cook. Refrigerate the patties until ready to grill.

3. Prepare the grill for direct cooking over medium-high heat (400° to 500°F).

4. Lightly season the patties on both sides with salt and pepper, and then grill over *direct medium-high heat*, with the lid closed, until cooked to medium doneness (160°F), 9 to 11 minutes, turning once. During the last 30 seconds to 1 minute of grilling time, toast the buns, cut side down, over direct heat.

5. Build each burger on a bun with a patty and a spoonful or two of kimchi. Serve warm.

**FUN FACT**

Packed with vitamins, minerals, and probiotics, kimchi (the national dish of Korea) is one of the world's five healthiest foods. Koreans even say "kimchi" instead of "cheese" when posing for photos. Now that's something to smile about!

# SPICY GINGER-SCALLION BURGERS WITH SESAME SPINACH

SERVES: **4** | PREP TIME: **30 MINUTES** | GRILLING TIME: **8 TO 10 MINUTES**

BEEF

## PATTIES

- 12 ounces ground chuck (80% lean)
- 12 ounces lean ground pork
- ½ cup thinly sliced scallions (white and light green parts only)
- 1 piece fresh ginger, about 2 inches long, peeled and grated
- 1 tablespoon soy sauce
- 2 teaspoons toasted sesame oil
- 2 garlic cloves, minced or pushed through a press
- ½ teaspoon kosher salt
- ½ teaspoon freshly ground black pepper

- 2 teaspoons vegetable oil
- 2 teaspoons toasted sesame oil
- 2 tablespoons plus 1 teaspoon hot chili-garlic sauce, such as Sriracha, divided
- 8 ounces fresh baby spinach
- 1 tablespoon toasted sesame seeds
- ½ cup ketchup
- 4 sesame seed buns, split

1. Mix the patty ingredients, and then gently form four patties of equal size, each about ¾ inch thick. With your thumb or the back of a spoon, make a shallow indentation about 1 inch wide in the center of the patties to prevent them from forming a dome as they cook. Refrigerate the patties until ready to grill.

2. Prepare the grill for direct cooking over medium-high heat (400° to 500°F).

3. In a large skillet over medium heat, warm the vegetable oil, sesame oil, and 1 teaspoon of the chili-garlic sauce. Gradually add the spinach by the handful and stir just until it begins to wilt, 2 to 3 minutes. Remove from the heat and add the sesame seeds.

4. Combine the ketchup with the remaining 2 tablespoons chili-garlic sauce.

5. Grill the patties over *direct medium-high heat*, with the lid closed, until cooked to medium doneness (160°F), 8 to 10 minutes, turning once. During the last 30 seconds to 1 minute of grilling time, toast the buns, cut side down, over direct heat.

6. Build each burger on a bun with chili-garlic ketchup, a patty, and sesame spinach. Serve warm.

*Serving suggestion: Corn and Black Bean Salad (for recipe, see page 219).*

# BOURBON BURGERS WITH CARAMELIZED ONIONS AND HORSERADISH DIJON

SERVES: 4 | PREP TIME: **20 MINUTES, PLUS 20 TO 22 MINUTES FOR THE ONIONS** | GRILLING TIME: **8 TO 10 MINUTES**

- 2 tablespoons extra-virgin olive oil
- 2 medium yellow onions, each cut in half and thinly sliced
   Kosher salt
   Freshly ground black pepper
- 1 teaspoon cider vinegar
- ½ teaspoon packed dark brown sugar
- ¼ cup Dijon mustard
- 1 tablespoon prepared horseradish
- 1½ pounds ground chuck (80% lean)
- 1 ounce bourbon
- 1 tablespoon Worcestershire sauce
- 4 hamburger buns, split
- 4 leaves romaine lettuce

1. In a large skillet over medium-high heat, warm the oil. Add the onions, ¼ teaspoon salt, and ¼ teaspoon pepper and cook until the onions begin to soften, about 10 minutes, stirring occasionally. Add the vinegar and brown sugar and continue cooking until tender and golden, 10 to 12 minutes more, stirring often. Remove from the heat.

2. In a small bowl combine the mustard and horseradish.

3. Mix the ground chuck, bourbon, Worcestershire sauce, ½ teaspoon salt, and ¼ teaspoon pepper, and then gently form four patties of equal size, each about ¾ inch thick. With your thumb or the back of a spoon, make a shallow indentation about 1 inch wide in the center of the patties to prevent them from forming a dome as they cook. Refrigerate the patties until ready to grill.

4. Prepare the grill for direct cooking over medium-high heat (400° to 500°F).

5. Grill the patties over *direct medium-high heat*, with the lid closed, until cooked to medium doneness (160°F), 8 to 10 minutes, turning once. During the last 30 seconds to 1 minute of grilling time, toast the buns, cut side down, over direct heat.

6. Build each burger on a bun with horseradish Dijon, a lettuce leaf, a patty, and caramelized onions. Serve warm.

# GAUCHO BURGERS WITH FRIED EGGS AND CHIMICHURRI

SERVES: **4** | PREP TIME: **20 MINUTES** | GRILLING TIME: **14 TO 18 MINUTES** | SPECIAL EQUIPMENT: **CAST-IRON SKILLET**

## PATTIES

- 1 pound ground chuck (80% lean)
- 8 ounces bulk hot Italian sausage
- 2 tablespoons minced shallot
- 2 garlic cloves, minced or pushed through a press

    Kosher salt
    Freshly ground black pepper

## CHIMICHURRI

- 1½ cups firmly packed fresh Italian parsley leaves and tender stems
- 4 garlic cloves, each quartered
- 2 tablespoons fresh oregano leaves
- ½ cup extra-virgin olive oil
- ¼ teaspoon crushed red pepper flakes

- 4 slices French or Italian bread, each about ½ inch thick
    Extra-virgin olive oil
- 1 tablespoon unsalted butter
- 4 large eggs
- 3 tablespoons white or red wine vinegar

1. Mix the patty ingredients, including ½ teaspoon salt and ¼ teaspoon pepper, and then gently form four patties of equal size, each about 1 inch thick. With your thumb or the back of a spoon, make a shallow indentation about 1 inch wide in the center of the patties to prevent them from forming a dome as they cook. Refrigerate the patties until ready to grill.

2. In a food processor fitted with a metal blade, finely chop the parsley, garlic, and oregano. Transfer to a bowl and stir in the oil, red pepper flakes, 1 teaspoon salt, and 1 teaspoon black pepper.

3. Prepare the grill for direct cooking over medium-high heat (400° to 500°F).

4. Lightly season the patties on both sides with salt and pepper, and brush the bread slices on both sides with oil. Grill the patties over *direct medium-high heat*, with the lid closed, until cooked to medium doneness (160°F), 9 to 11 minutes, turning once. Halfway into grilling time, place a cast-iron skillet on the cooking grates or on a side burner set to medium-high to preheat. Remove the patties from the grill.

5. Add the butter to the skillet. Fry the eggs sunny-side up, with the lid open, until the whites are crisp and lacy on the edges and the yolks are partially runny, 4 to 6 minutes. Toast the bread on the cooking grates over direct heat, about 1 minute, turning once.

6. Add the vinegar to the chimichurri. Mix well.

7. Top each bread slice with a patty, a fried egg, and chimichurri. Serve immediately.

---

### WHAT IS CHIMICHURRI?

Often called the "ketchup of Argentina," chimichurri is typically a green pesto-like condiment that's made from a blend of olive oil, lemon juice, and chopped fresh herbs—usually Italian parsley and oregano—and seasoned with onion, garlic, vinegar, and cayenne pepper. While chimichurri is traditionally served as a dipping sauce with grilled beef, it's also a bright, tangy flavor additive (either as a marinade or a sauce) for other meats and even grilled vegetables and tofu.

# BEEF AND VEAL PAPRIKASH BURGERS WITH ROASTED BELL PEPPERS

SERVES: **4**  |  PREP TIME: **30 MINUTES, PLUS ABOUT 25 MINUTES FOR THE RELISH**  |  GRILLING TIME: **11 TO 12 MINUTES**

## PATTIES

    8  ounces ground chuck (80% lean)
    8  ounces ground veal
    1  tablespoon minced white onion
    1  tablespoon minced fresh Italian parsley leaves
    ¾  teaspoon dried marjoram

       Kosher salt
       Freshly ground black pepper

## RELISH

    2  tablespoons vegetable oil
    2  large white onions, each cut in half and thinly sliced
    1  teaspoon paprika
    ½  teaspoon smoked paprika
    ½  teaspoon pure chile powder
    ¾  cup canned stewed tomatoes
    1  tablespoon unsalted butter, softened

    2  large green bell peppers, each cut into 8 wedges
       Vegetable oil
4 or 8 slices potato bread, each about ½ inch thick
    2  tablespoons unsalted butter, softened
    ¼  cup sour cream

1. Mix the patty ingredients, including ½ teaspoon salt and ¼ teaspoon pepper, and then gently form four patties of equal size, each about ¾ inch thick. With your thumb or the back of a spoon, make a shallow indentation about 1 inch wide in the center of the patties to prevent them from forming a dome as they cook. Refrigerate the patties until ready to grill.

2. In a large skillet over medium-low heat, warm the oil. Add the onions and sauté until golden brown, 18 to 20 minutes, stirring often. Add the paprika, smoked paprika, chile powder, and ½ teaspoon salt and stir for 2 minutes. Add the tomatoes and continue cooking until the sauce is very thick and deep red, 3 to 5 minutes, stirring occasionally. Use the back of a wooden spoon to break up any large pieces of tomato. Remove from the heat and stir in 1 tablespoon butter.

3. Prepare the grill for direct cooking over medium-high heat (400° to 500°F).

4. Lightly brush the bell pepper wedges with oil. Grill the bell peppers and patties over *direct medium-high heat*, with the lid closed, until the bell peppers are charred and softened, 11 to 12 minutes, and the patties are cooked to medium doneness (160°F), 8 to 10 minutes, turning once. During the last minute of grilling time, toast the bread over direct heat, turning once. Remove from the grill and butter each slice.

5. Top four bread slices each with a patty and relish. Serve warm with bell pepper wedges, sour cream, and another slice of bread, if desired.

Paprika, the intense red spice, has two common varieties: regular paprika has a relatively neutral flavor, whereas smoked paprika (called *pimentón* in Spain) has a rich, smoky flavor that's produced by slowly smoking red chiles over oak fires.

# GRINDING
## YOUR OWN BURGER BLEND

Some things are best left to the professionals—think electrical wiring and cage fighting. But grinding your own meat? That's a simple and worthwhile DIY endeavor. Knowing exactly what cut of meat makes up your burger and how fresh it is will yield a tastier and juicier patty with no mystery add-ins.

## WHICH MEAT?

We like chuck for its excellent flavor and ample amount of fat (around 20 percent). Grinding chuck alone will give you better results than buying ground beef from the mega-mart. To turn up the intensity of beefy taste, add some beef sirloin (for steak-like flavors) or boneless short ribs (for extra fat and juiciness) to the blend. Substituting thick-cut bacon for as much as one-quarter of all the beef will give your burgers a boost of smoke and saltiness.

## WEBER'S BURGER BLEND

SERVES: **6 TO 8**

  2  pounds boneless beef chuck
  1  pound beef sirloin *or* boneless short ribs

1. Trim off any tough gristle and remove any bones from the meat.

2. Cut the meat into chunks about 1½ inches thick and refrigerate them until ready to grind.

3. Grind the meat using one of the methods shown on the facing page.

Chuck        Beef sirloin        Flanken-style short ribs

Food grinder

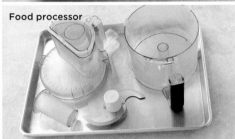

Food processor

## SELECT YOUR METHOD

Don't worry, no huge meat grinder is required. You can use a grinder attachment for a stand mixer, or you can even grind the meat in a food processor fitted with a metal blade. Because grinding meat creates friction, which could warm the meat to the point where microbes start to grow, the first step is to put all the parts of your equipment in the freezer for at least 30 minutes.

*(Top) If you are using a stand mixer, freeze the food grinder attachment, the grinding worm, grinding knife, and coarse grinding plate.*

*(Bottom) If you are using a food processor, freeze the bowl, top, and metal blade.*

## FOOD GRINDER METHOD

Set up your grinder with the coarse grinding plate. This will give the meat a nice, loose texture. Turn on the grinder and add the chunks of meat one handful at a time. You want the beef to move through the grinder constantly in a smooth, steady way. If you add too much at once, the meat will probably get stuck and friction will start to build up, so take it slow. Catch the ground meat in a bowl.

## FOOD PROCESSOR METHOD

This method produces more of a chopped texture than a ground texture, but it still works well. To avoid warming up the meat, work in small batches, about 8 ounces at a time, and pulse the chunks 8 to 10 times for a medium-fine grind. You will probably need to scrape down the side of the food processor bowl occasionally. Then transfer the meat to a bowl and process the next batch.

# BISON CHEESEBURGERS WITH BALSAMIC MUSHROOMS

SERVES: **4** | PREP TIME: **30 MINUTES** | GRILLING TIME: **7 TO 9 MINUTES**

BISON

## MUSHROOMS

- 2 tablespoons extra-virgin olive oil
- 8 ounces cremini mushrooms, cleaned, stems removed, and finely chopped
- 1½ cups finely chopped yellow onion
- 3 large garlic cloves, minced or pushed through a press
- 2 tablespoons balsamic vinegar

- Kosher salt
- Freshly ground black pepper
- 2 tablespoons finely chopped fresh chives
- 1½ pounds ground bison meat (85 to 90% lean)
- 1 package (5.2 ounces) garlic-and-herb soft cheese, coarsely crumbled
- 4 hamburger buns, split
- 4 leaves Bibb lettuce
- 1 large, ripe beefsteak tomato, cut crosswise into 4 slices

1. In a large skillet over medium-high heat, warm the oil. Add the mushrooms and onion and cook until the onion is deep golden brown, making sure that the mixture is still moist, 8 to 10 minutes, stirring frequently. Add the garlic and cook for 2 minutes, stirring occasionally. Stir in the vinegar and season with ½ teaspoon salt and ¼ teaspoon pepper. Remove from the heat. Cool to room temperature, and then stir in the chives.

2. Mix the ground bison, 1 teaspoon salt, and ½ teaspoon pepper, and then gently form four patties of equal size, each about ¾ inch thick. With your thumb or the back of a spoon, make a shallow indentation about 1 inch wide in the center of the patties to prevent them from forming a dome as they cook. Refrigerate the patties until ready to grill.

3. Prepare the grill for direct cooking over medium heat (350° to 450°F).

4. Grill the patties over *direct medium heat*, with the lid closed, until cooked to medium doneness (160°F), 7 to 9 minutes, turning once. During the last 30 seconds to 1 minute of grilling time, top each patty with an equal amount of cheese to melt slightly and toast the buns, cut side down, over direct heat.

5. Build each burger on a bun with a lettuce leaf, a tomato slice, a patty, and balsamic mushrooms. Serve immediately.

# BISON BURGERS WITH BLUE CHEESE AND HOT WING SAUCE

SERVES: **6** | PREP TIME: **20 MINUTES** | GRILLING TIME: **7 TO 9 MINUTES**

## PATTIES

- 2 pounds ground bison meat (85 to 90% lean)
- 4 ounces blue cheese, crumbled
- ½ cup minced yellow onion
- 2 garlic cloves, minced or pushed through a press
- 1 teaspoon celery seed

- 3 tablespoons unsalted butter
- ¼ cup hot wing sauce
- 6 hamburger buns, split
- 6 leaves iceberg lettuce
- 12 slices ripe tomato
- 6 very thin slices red onion

1. Mix the patty ingredients, and then gently form six patties of equal size, each about ¾ inch thick. With your thumb or the back of a spoon, make a shallow indentation about 1 inch wide in the center of the patties to prevent them from forming a dome as they cook. Refrigerate the patties until ready to grill.

2. Prepare the grill for direct cooking over medium heat (350° to 450°F).

3. In a saucepan over medium heat, melt the butter. Remove from the heat and stir in the hot wing sauce.

4. Grill the patties over *direct medium heat*, with the lid closed, until cooked to medium doneness (160°F), 7 to 9 minutes, turning once. During the last 30 seconds to 1 minute of grilling time, toast the buns, cut side down, over direct heat. Remove the patties and the buns from the grill and immediately brush the patties on both sides with the hot wing sauce mixture.

5. Build each burger on a bun with a lettuce leaf, two tomato slices, an onion slice, and a patty. Serve warm.

BISON

**FUN FACT**

Looking for a lean red meat alternative? Low in fat, low in cholesterol, and always antibiotic- and hormone-free, bison meat contains 40 percent more protein than beef. The American Heart Association even endorsed eating bison as part of a heart-healthy diet.

# JALAPEÑO LAMB BURGERS WITH GOAT CHEESE AND SALSA

SERVES: **6** | PREP TIME: **30 MINUTES** | GRILLING TIME: **7 TO 9 MINUTES**

## PATTIES

- 2 pounds ground lamb
- ¼ cup cold beer
- 3 medium jalapeño chile peppers, seeded and minced
- 2 tablespoons ketchup
- ¾ teaspoon kosher salt
- ½ teaspoon freshly ground black pepper
- 2 garlic cloves, minced or pushed through a press

## SALSA

- 1 large, ripe beefsteak tomato, cored, seeded, and finely chopped
- ½ small yellow onion, finely chopped
- 1 medium jalapeño chile pepper, seeded and minced
- 1 tablespoon finely chopped fresh mint leaves
- 2 teaspoons cider vinegar
  Finely grated zest and juice of ½ lime
- ½ teaspoon kosher salt
- ½ teaspoon granulated sugar
- 1 garlic clove, minced or pushed through a press

  Extra-virgin olive oil
- 6 ounces goat cheese, crumbled
- 6 ciabatta or telera rolls, split

1. Mix the patty ingredients, and then gently form six patties of equal size, each about ¾ inch thick. With your thumb or the back of a spoon, make a shallow indentation about 1 inch wide in the center of the patties to prevent them from forming a dome as they cook. Refrigerate the patties until ready to grill.

2. Prepare the grill for direct cooking over medium heat (350° to 450°F).

3. In a serving bowl mix the salsa ingredients.

4. Lightly brush the patties on both sides with oil, and then grill over *direct medium heat*, with the lid closed, until cooked to medium doneness (160°F), 7 to 9 minutes, turning once. During the last 30 seconds to 1 minute of grilling time, top the patties with the cheese to soften, and toast the rolls, cut side down, over direct heat.

5. Build each burger on a roll with a patty and a heaping spoonful of salsa. Serve warm with any remaining salsa on the side.

*Serving suggestion: Chili-Spiced Fries*
*(for recipe, see page 223).*

# SPICY LAMB BURGERS WITH ROASTED RED PEPPER MAYONNAISE

SERVES: **6** | PREP TIME: **20 MINUTES** | GRILLING TIME: **7 TO 9 MINUTES**

1 cup chopped roasted red bell peppers
(from a jar), patted dry
1 medium garlic clove
1 cup mayonnaise
½ teaspoon freshly ground black pepper

## PATTIES

1 tablespoon extra-virgin olive oil
½ cup finely chopped shallot
2 tablespoons finely chopped jalapeño chile peppers
2 garlic cloves, minced
½ teaspoon dried basil
2 pounds ground lamb
1½ teaspoons kosher salt
1 teaspoon ground cumin
¾ teaspoon ground coriander
½ teaspoon ground cayenne pepper

4 onion rolls, split
2 cups loosely packed baby arugula

**1.** In a food processor combine the bell peppers and garlic and blend until very finely chopped. Transfer to a bowl and stir in the mayonnaise and pepper.

**2.** In a skillet over medium heat, warm the oil. Add the shallot, jalapeños, garlic, and basil, and sauté until slightly softened, 4 to 5 minutes, stirring occasionally. Remove from the heat and cool for 5 minutes. Transfer to a bowl and mix in the remaining patty ingredients. Gently form six patties of equal size, each about ¾ inch thick. With your thumb or the back of a spoon, make a shallow indentation about 1 inch wide in the center of the patties to prevent them from forming a dome as they cook. Refrigerate the patties until ready to grill.

**3.** Prepare the grill for direct cooking over medium heat (350° to 450°F).

**4.** Grill the patties over *direct medium heat*, with the lid closed, to medium doneness (160°F), 7 to 9 minutes, turning once. During the last 30 seconds to 1 minute of grilling time, toast the rolls, cut side down, over direct heat.

**5.** Build each burger on a roll with red pepper mayonnaise (you may not need all of it), a patty, and arugula. Serve warm.

*Serving suggestion: Chopped Greek-Style Salad (for recipe, see page 209).*

# LAMB BURGERS WITH HERBED CHEESE AND RED WINE SAUCE

SERVES: **6** | PREP TIME: **20 MINUTES, PLUS 30 TO 40 MINUTES TO REDUCE THE WINE**
GRILLING TIME: **19 TO 21 MINUTES** | SPECIAL EQUIPMENT: **PERFORATED GRILL PAN**

1 bottle (750 ml) fruity red wine,
   such as cabernet sauvignon
¾ cup tomato puree
2 tablespoons honey
   Kosher salt
   Freshly ground black pepper
3 slices yellow onion, each about ½ inch thick
9 cremini mushrooms, stems removed
   Extra-virgin olive oil
2 pounds ground lamb, preferably leg of lamb
2 tablespoons finely chopped fresh
   Italian parsley leaves
2 tablespoons finely chopped fresh mint leaves
2 garlic cloves, minced or pushed through a press
6 kaiser or ciabatta rolls, split
6 tablespoons garlic-and-herb soft cheese

1. In a large skillet over medium-high heat, boil the wine until it is reduced to ¼ cup, 30 to 40 minutes (depending on the diameter of your skillet). Pour off 2 tablespoons, set aside, and allow to cool (you will use the cooled, reduced wine in the patty ingredients).

2. To the skillet with the remaining 2 tablespoons reduced wine, add the tomato puree and cook over medium heat, simmering until the mixture is thick enough to coat the back of a spoon, about 5 minutes. Stir in the honey, ½ teaspoon salt, and ½ teaspoon pepper. Pour into a serving bowl and allow to cool.

3. Prepare the grill for direct cooking over medium-high heat (400° to 500°F) and preheat a perforated grill pan.

4. Brush the onion and mushrooms with oil, and then spread them in a single layer on the grill pan. Grill over *direct medium-high heat*, with the lid closed, until browned and tender, about 10 minutes for the onion and about 6 minutes for the mushrooms, turning once or twice. Remove from the grill and finely dice.

5. Mix the onion, mushrooms, the reserved and cooled 2 tablespoons reduced wine, the lamb, parsley, mint, garlic, ½ teaspoon salt, and ¼ teaspoon pepper. Gently form six patties of equal size, each about 1 inch thick. With your thumb or the back of a spoon, make a shallow indentation about 1 inch wide in the center of the patties to prevent them from forming a dome as they cook.

6. Lightly brush the patties on both sides with oil, and then grill over *direct medium-high heat*, with the lid closed, until cooked to medium doneness (160°F), 9 to 11 minutes, turning once. During the last 30 seconds to 1 minute of grilling time, toast the rolls, cut side down, over direct heat.

7. Build each burger on a roll with 1 tablespoon of the cheese, a patty, and some red wine sauce. Serve warm with the remaining sauce on the side.

The sauce is ready when you run your fingertip down the middle of the spoon and it makes a "road."

# INDIAN LAMB BURGERS WITH MANGO CHUTNEY

LAMB

## PATTIES

- 1½ pounds ground lamb
- ¼ cup minced fresh cilantro leaves
- ¼ cup minced fresh mint leaves
- 1 jalapeño chile pepper, seeded and minced
- 2 teaspoons peeled, grated fresh ginger
- 2 teaspoons curry powder
- 1 teaspoon kosher salt
- ¼ teaspoon freshly ground black pepper
- 1 garlic clove, minced or pushed through a press

- 4 soft Italian-style round rolls, split
- 2 tablespoons extra-virgin olive oil
- ½ cup mango chutney
- 4 slices red onion

1. Mix the patty ingredients, and then gently form four patties of equal size, each about ¾ inch thick. With your thumb or the back of a spoon, make a shallow indentation about 1 inch wide in the center of the patties to prevent them from forming a dome as they cook. Refrigerate the patties until ready to grill.

2. Prepare the grill for direct cooking over medium heat (350° to 450°F).

3. Brush the cut side of the rolls with the oil. Grill the patties over *direct medium heat*, with the lid closed, until cooked to medium doneness (160°F), 7 to 9 minutes, turning once. During the last 30 seconds to 1 minute of grilling time, toast the rolls, cut side down, over direct heat.

4. Build each burger on a roll with mango chutney, a patty, and an onion slice. Serve warm.

*Serving suggestion: Sour Cream Raita (for recipe, see page 234).*

# LAMB AND GRILLED ONION BURGERS

SERVES: **4**  |  PREP TIME: **15 MINUTES**  |  GRILLING TIME: **17 TO 21 MINUTES**

## PATTIES

- 4 slices sweet onion, each about ¼ inch thick
- 1 tablespoon extra-virgin olive oil
- 14 ounces ground lamb
- 6 ounces lean ground pork
- 2 tablespoons minced fresh mint leaves
- 1 tablespoon Dijon mustard
- 1 teaspoon ground cumin
- ½ teaspoon kosher salt
- ½ teaspoon freshly ground black pepper

## SAUCE

- 3 ounces feta cheese, crumbled
- ½ cup plain Greek yogurt
- 1 tablespoon minced fresh mint leaves
- 1 teaspoon fresh lemon juice

- 4 kaiser rolls or sesame buns, split
- 2 lemons, cut into wedges

**1.** Prepare the grill for direct cooking over medium-high heat (400° to 500°F).

**2.** Brush the onion slices with the oil, and then grill over *direct medium-high heat*, with the lid closed, until golden brown and tender, 8 to 10 minutes, turning once or twice. Remove from the grill and finely chop. Set aside to cool.

**3.** Mix the onion with the remaining patty ingredients, and then gently form four patties of equal size, each about 1 inch thick. With your thumb or the back of a spoon, make a shallow indentation about 1 inch wide in the center of the patties to prevent them from forming a dome as they cook. Refrigerate the patties until ready to grill.

**4.** Combine the sauce ingredients. Cover and refrigerate until ready to serve.

**5.** Grill the patties over *direct medium-high heat*, with the lid closed, until cooked to medium doneness (160°F), 9 to 11 minutes, turning once. During the last 30 seconds to 1 minute of grilling time, toast the rolls, cut side down, over direct heat.

**6.** Build each burger on a roll with a patty and as much sauce as you like. Serve warm with lemon wedges and any remaining sauce on the side.

# SPICY JERK PORK AND BEEF BURGERS WITH PINEAPPLE SALSA

SERVES: **6** | PREP TIME: **20 MINUTES** | GRILLING TIME: **16 TO 20 MINUTES** | SPECIAL EQUIPMENT: **RUBBER GLOVES**

## PATTIES

- 1 habanero or Scotch bonnet chile pepper
- 1 pound lean ground pork
- 1 pound ground chuck (80% lean)
- ½ cup finely chopped scallions (white and light green parts only)
- 2 tablespoons packed dark brown sugar
- 1 tablespoon fresh lime juice
- 1 tablespoon soy sauce
- 1½ teaspoons minced fresh thyme leaves
- 1½ teaspoons ground allspice
- 1 teaspoon kosher salt
- ½ teaspoon ground cinnamon
- 1 garlic clove, minced or pushed through a press

## SALSA

- 4 slices ripe, fresh pineapple, each about ½ inch thick, cored
- 1 small, ripe mango, peeled and roughly chopped
- ¼ cup roughly chopped red onion
- 2 tablespoons fresh lime juice
- 2 tablespoons chopped fresh cilantro leaves
- ½ teaspoon kosher salt

  Freshly ground black pepper
- 6 brioche buns, split

1. Wearing rubber gloves (to avoid burning your skin), remove and discard the stem and seeds from the habanero. Mince the habanero and place in a large bowl. Add the remaining patty ingredients, and then gently form six patties of equal size, each about 1 inch thick. With your thumb or the back of a spoon, make a shallow indentation about 1 inch wide in the center of the patties to prevent them from forming a dome as they cook. Refrigerate the patties until ready to grill.

2. Prepare the grill for direct cooking over medium heat (350° to 450°F).

3. Grill the pineapple slices over *direct medium heat*, with the lid open, until marked and slightly softened, 6 to 8 minutes, turning once. Roughly chop the pineapple, transfer to a food processor fitted with a metal blade, and add the remaining salsa ingredients. Pulse until the salsa is finely chopped. If it seems too wet, drain in a fine-mesh strainer.

4. Generously season the patties on both sides with pepper, and then grill over *direct medium heat*, with the lid closed, until cooked to medium doneness (160°F), 10 to 12 minutes, turning once. During the last 30 seconds to 1 minute of grilling time, toast the buns, cut side down, over direct heat.

5. Build each burger on a bun with a patty and pineapple salsa. Serve immediately.

### FUN FACT

The deceivingly small, lantern-shaped habanero chile pepper packs a hint of fruity flavor and a knockout in the heat department. Vivid orange when fully ripe, the habanero can be up to 40 times spicier than its more widely available chile pepper counterpart, the jalapeño.

# FIVE-SPICE PORK BURGERS WITH SLAW

SERVES: **4** | PREP TIME: **30 MINUTES** | GRILLING TIME: **10 TO 12 MINUTES**

## PATTIES

- 1½ pounds lean ground pork
- 2 scallions, ends trimmed and finely chopped
- 1½ tablespoons minced fresh cilantro leaves
- 4 garlic cloves, minced or pushed through a press
- 1 teaspoon Chinese five spice
- ½ teaspoon kosher salt
- ¼ teaspoon freshly ground black pepper

## SLAW

- 1¾ cups finely shredded green cabbage
- ¼ red bell pepper, cut into thin strips
- 1 small carrot, grated
- 2 teaspoons fresh lime juice *or* rice vinegar
- 1 teaspoon toasted sesame oil
- ⅛ teaspoon kosher salt

- Extra-virgin olive oil
- ⅓ cup hoisin sauce
- 4 soft, slightly sweet rolls, split

Chinese five spice is an ancient but still very popular combination of ground star anise, fennel seed, cinnamon, cloves, and Szechuan or black peppercorns.

1. Mix the patty ingredients, and then gently form four patties of equal size, each about 1 inch thick. With your thumb or the back of a spoon, make a shallow indentation about 1 inch wide in the center of the patties to prevent them from forming a dome as they cook. Refrigerate the patties until ready to grill.

2. Combine the slaw ingredients.

3. Prepare the grill for direct cooking over medium heat (350° to 450°F).

4. Lightly brush the patties on both sides with olive oil, and then grill over *direct medium heat*, with the lid closed, until cooked to medium doneness (160°F), 10 to 12 minutes, turning once and then brushing with the hoisin sauce. During the last 30 seconds to 1 minute of grilling time, toast the rolls, cut side down, over direct heat.

5. Build each burger on a roll with a patty and slaw. Serve immediately.

# THAI PORK BURGERS IN LETTUCE LEAVES

SERVES: **4** | PREP TIME: **25 MINUTES** | GRILLING TIME: **10 TO 12 MINUTES**

## PATTIES

1½ pounds lean ground pork
1 stalk lemongrass
   (pale inner heart only)
   *or* 2 scallions, ends
   trimmed and minced
1 large shallot, minced
2 tablespoons minced fresh
   cilantro leaves
4 garlic cloves, minced or
   pushed through a press

   Kosher salt
   Freshly ground black pepper
4 large leaves butter lettuce
   or red leaf lettuce
   Lime wedges (optional)

1. Mix the patty ingredients, including ½ teaspoon salt and ¼ teaspoon pepper, and then gently form four patties of equal size, each about 1 inch thick. With your thumb or the back of a spoon, make a shallow indentation about 1 inch wide in the center of the patties to prevent them from forming a dome as they cook. Refrigerate the patties until ready to grill.

2. Prepare the grill for direct cooking over medium heat (350° to 450°F).

3. Lightly season the patties on both sides with salt and pepper, and then grill over *direct medium heat,* with the lid closed, until cooked to medium doneness (160°F), 10 to 12 minutes, turning once.

4. Place each patty in a lettuce leaf cup. Garnish with lime wedges, if desired. Serve warm.

*Serving suggestions: Easy Cold Noodle Salad with Peanut Sauce and Carrot (for recipe, see page 206) and Cucumber Relish (see page 234).*

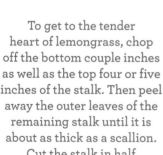

To get to the tender heart of lemongrass, chop off the bottom couple inches as well as the top four or five inches of the stalk. Then peel away the outer leaves of the remaining stalk until it is about as thick as a scallion.
Cut the stalk in half lengthwise and mince it for seasoning these burgers.

PORK

# LITTLE ITALY PORK BURGERS

SERVES: 4 | PREP TIME: **20 MINUTES** | GRILLING TIME: **48 TO 50 MINUTES**

## PATTIES

1½ pounds lean ground pork
 2 tablespoons finely chopped fresh
    Italian parsley leaves
 1 teaspoon fennel seed
 1 teaspoon paprika
 1 teaspoon crushed red pepper flakes
 ½ teaspoon granulated garlic
 ½ teaspoon dried oregano

   Kosher salt
   Freshly ground black pepper
 1 head garlic
   Extra-virgin olive oil
 ½ cup mayonnaise
 1 medium red bell pepper, cut into thin strips
 1 small yellow onion, cut in half and thinly sliced
 4 kaiser rolls, split

**1.** Mix the patty ingredients, including 1 teaspoon salt and ¼ teaspoon pepper, and then gently form four patties of equal size, each about ¾ inch thick. With your thumb or the back of a spoon, make a shallow indentation about 1 inch wide in the center of the patties to prevent them from forming a dome as they cook. Refrigerate until ready to grill.

**2.** Prepare the grill for direct and indirect cooking over medium-high heat (400° to 500°F).

**3.** Cut ½ inch off the top of the head of garlic and discard. Place the garlic head on a small sheet of aluminum foil and drizzle 1 teaspoon oil over the exposed cloves. Bring the corners of the foil together and twist to completely cover the garlic, leaving a little room in the packet for the expansion of steam. Place the garlic packet over *indirect medium-high heat*, close the lid, and cook until the garlic is soft, fragrant, and golden, about 40 minutes. When cool enough to handle, squeeze the cloves from their skins into a small bowl. Mash the garlic with a fork to form a paste. Stir in the mayonnaise, 1 teaspoon oil, ¼ teaspoon salt, and ¼ teaspoon pepper to make an aioli.

**4.** In a skillet over medium-high heat, warm 1 tablespoon oil. Add the bell pepper and onion and sauté until softened, 7 to 8 minutes, stirring occasionally. Season with ¼ teaspoon salt and ¼ teaspoon pepper and cook 3 minutes more. Remove from the heat and keep warm.

**5.** Lightly brush the patties on both sides with oil, and then grill over *direct medium-high heat*, with the lid closed, until cooked to medium doneness (160°F), 8 to 10 minutes, turning once. During the last 30 seconds to 1 minute of grilling time, toast the rolls, cut side down, over direct heat.

**6.** Build each burger on a roll with aioli, a patty, and the bell pepper–onion mixture. Serve warm.

Roasting a head of garlic in foil over indirect heat for 40 minutes or so yields sweet golden cloves that you can squeeze right out of their papery skins. Mash the roasted garlic with mayonnaise for an unusually good aioli.

# CHORIZO CHEESEBURGERS

SERVES: **4** | PREP TIME: **20 MINUTES** | GRILLING TIME: **8 TO 10 MINUTES** | SPECIAL EQUIPMENT: **INSTANT-READ THERMOMETER**

**PORK**

## PATTIES

1 pound lean ground pork
8 ounces fresh Mexican
   chorizo sausage
4 garlic cloves, minced or
   pushed through a press
1 large shallot, minced
2 tablespoons minced fresh
   Italian parsley leaves
½ teaspoon smoked paprika
½ teaspoon dried thyme
½ teaspoon ground cumin

   Kosher salt
   Freshly ground black pepper
4 sourdough rolls, split
   Extra-virgin olive oil
4 slices manchego or
   Monterey Jack cheese,
   each about 1 ounce
1 garlic clove, cut in half
8 thin slices ripe
   beefsteak tomato

The patties' centers will be slightly pink because of the chorizo. Have an instant-read thermometer on hand to be sure the pork is cooked to a safe temperature (160°F).

1. Mix the patty ingredients, including ½ teaspoon salt and ¼ teaspoon pepper, and then gently form four patties of equal size, each about ¾ inch thick. With your thumb or the back of a spoon, make a shallow indentation about 1 inch wide in the center of the patties to prevent them from forming a dome as they cook. Refrigerate the patties until ready to grill.

2. Prepare the grill for direct cooking over medium-high heat (400° to 500°F).

3. Lightly season the patties on both sides with salt and pepper. Brush the cut side of the rolls with oil. Grill the patties over *direct medium-high heat*, with the lid closed, until cooked to medium doneness (160°F), 8 to 10 minutes, turning once. During the last 30 seconds to 1 minute of grilling time, place a slice of cheese on each patty to melt, and toast the rolls, cut side down, over direct heat.

4. Rub the cut side of the toasted rolls with the cut side of the garlic half. Build each burger on a roll with two tomato slices and a patty. Serve warm.

# CUBAN PORK BURGERS

SERVES: **4** | PREP TIME: **15 MINUTES** | GRILLING TIME: **10 TO 14 MINUTES**
SPECIAL EQUIPMENT: **GRILL-PROOF GRIDDLE, SHEET PAN, 2 FOIL-WRAPPED BRICKS**

## PATTIES

- 1 pound lean ground pork
- 1 teaspoon dried oregano
- ¾ teaspoon kosher salt
- ½ teaspoon granulated garlic
- ¼ teaspoon freshly ground black pepper

- 2 tablespoons unsalted butter
- 3 garlic cloves, minced or pushed through a press
- 4 French sandwich rolls, each about 4½ inches long, split
- 2 tablespoons Dijon mustard
- 8 slices Swiss cheese, each about 1 ounce
- 8 slices Black Forest deli ham Dill pickle chips

**1.** Prepare the grill for direct cooking over medium heat (350° to 450°F) and preheat a grill-proof griddle.

**2.** Mix the patty ingredients, and then gently form four oblong patties, each about ¾ inch thick. With your thumb or the back of a spoon, make a shallow indentation about 1 inch wide and 2 inches long in the center of the patties to prevent them from forming a dome as they cook. Refrigerate the patties until ready to grill.

**3.** In a skillet over medium heat, melt the butter. Add the garlic and cook until lightly browned, 3 to 4 minutes, stirring occasionally. Remove from the heat.

**4.** Grill the patties over *direct medium heat*, with the lid closed, until cooked to medium doneness (160°F), 8 to 10 minutes, turning once. Spread the cut side of the rolls with the mustard. Top the bottom half of each roll with a slice of cheese, two ham slices, a patty, pickle chips, one more slice of cheese, and the top half of the roll. Brush the burgers on both sides with the garlic butter, place them on the griddle, and put a sheet pan on top of the burgers, weighing it down with two foil-wrapped bricks. Grill over *direct medium heat*, with the lid closed, until the rolls are toasted and the cheese is melted, 2 to 4 minutes, turning once. Serve immediately.

*Serving suggestion: Tropical Fruit Salad with Honey and Lime (for recipe, see page 217).*

# ITALIAN SAUSAGE SANDWICHES WITH BALSAMIC MAYO

SERVES: **4** | PREP TIME: **20 MINUTES** | GRILLING TIME: **8 TO 10 MINUTES**

## MAYO

- ¼ cup mayonnaise
- 1 tablespoon Dijon mustard
- 2 teaspoons balsamic vinegar
- ¼ teaspoon kosher salt
- ⅛ teaspoon freshly ground black pepper

## PATTIES

- 1 tablespoon extra-virgin olive oil
- 1 cup finely chopped yellow onion
- 3 garlic cloves, minced or pushed through a press
- 1 pound bulk Italian sausage
- 8 ounces ground beef (90% lean)
- ¼ cup finely chopped fresh Italian parsley leaves

- 4 sourdough sandwich rolls, each 6 to 7 inches long, split
- 1 cup golden pepperoncini (from a jar), sliced

1. Combine the mayo ingredients.

2. In a skillet over medium-high heat, warm the oil. Add the onion and garlic and cook until they begin to soften, 2 to 3 minutes, stirring often to prevent burning. Remove from the heat and cool for 5 minutes.

3. Mix the sausage, ground beef, parsley, and onion-garlic mixture, and then gently form four rectangular patties, each about 7 inches long and ¾ inch thick (to fit the rolls). With your thumb or the back of a spoon, make a shallow indentation about 1 inch wide and 2 inches long in the center of the patties to prevent them from forming a dome as they cook. Refrigerate the patties until ready to grill.

4. Prepare the grill for direct cooking over medium-high heat (400° to 500°F).

5. Grill the patties over *direct medium-high heat*, with the lid closed, until cooked to medium doneness (160°F), 8 to 10 minutes, turning once. During the last 30 seconds to 1 minute of grilling time, toast the rolls, cut side down, over direct heat.

6. Build each burger on a roll with balsamic mayo, a patty, and pepperoncini. Serve warm.

PORK

# LUAU PORK BURGERS WITH GRILLED PINEAPPLE AND SWEET PEPPERS

SERVES: 6 | PREP TIME: **25 MINUTES** | GRILLING TIME: **8 TO 10 MINUTES** | SPECIAL EQUIPMENT: **PERFORATED GRILL PAN**

PORK

## GLAZE

- ¾ cup packed dark brown sugar
- ¼ cup plus 2 tablespoons soy sauce
- 3 tablespoons ketchup
- 1½ tablespoons sherry vinegar
- 1½ teaspoons crushed black or Szechwan peppercorns
- 1½ teaspoons aniseed
- 1½ teaspoons kosher salt

- 2 pounds lean ground pork
- 6 slices ripe, fresh pineapple, each about ⅓ inch thick, cored and quartered
- 3 bell peppers, 1 red, 1 yellow, 1 green, each cut into ⅓-inch strips
- 6 hamburger buns, split

1. In a saucepan whisk the glaze ingredients. Bring to a simmer over medium heat, stirring until the sugar dissolves, 3 to 4 minutes. Remove from the heat and let cool. Pour ¼ cup plus 2 tablespoons of the glaze into a large bowl and pour ¼ cup into a medium bowl. Reserve the remaining glaze in the saucepan.

2. To the large bowl with the glaze add the pork and mix. Gently form six patties of equal size, each about ¾ inch thick. With your thumb or the back of a spoon, make a shallow indentation about 1 inch wide in the center of the patties to prevent them from forming a dome as they cook. Refrigerate the patties until ready to grill.

3. Prepare the grill for direct cooking over medium-high heat (400° to 500°F) and preheat a perforated grill pan.

4. To the medium bowl with the ¼ cup glaze add the pineapple and bell peppers and turn to coat evenly.

5. Spread the pineapple and bell peppers in a single layer on the grill pan and place the patties on the cooking grates. Grill over *direct medium-high heat*, with the lid closed, until the pineapple and bell peppers are tender and the patties are cooked to medium doneness (160°F), 8 to 10 minutes, turning the patties once and the pineapple and bell peppers occasionally. During the last 30 seconds to 1 minute of grilling time, toast the buns, cut side down, over direct heat. Remove from the grill and generously brush the patties with the remaining glaze in the saucepan. Build each burger on a bun with a patty and the pineapple-bell pepper mixture.

# THREE-PORK BURGERS STUFFED WITH FETA

SERVES: **4** | PREP TIME: **30 MINUTES** | GRILLING TIME: **10 TO 12 MINUTES**

## PATTIES

- 12 ounces lean ground pork
- 10 ounces hot or mild Italian sausage (if purchased in casings, remove casings)
- 2 ounces minced prosciutto
- 1 large shallot, minced
- 2 teaspoons minced fresh oregano leaves *or* ½ teaspoon dried oregano
- 4 garlic cloves, minced or pushed through a press
- ½ teaspoon kosher salt
- ¼ teaspoon freshly ground black pepper

- 4 ounces cold feta cheese, drained and cut into 4 squares
- 4 or 8 slices Italian or French bread, each about ½ inch thick Extra-virgin olive oil
- 1 garlic clove, cut in half
- 1 cup tightly packed fresh spinach leaves, divided

1. Mix the patty ingredients, and then gently form eight patties of equal size, each about ½ inch thick. Place four of the patties on a work surface. Cut each feta square in half horizontally, creating two thinner blocks. Center two blocks of the feta side by side on the top of each of the four patties. Center the remaining four patties over the top and press down until each double patty is about 1 inch thick. Pinch the edges together to seal in the cheese. Refrigerate the patties until ready to grill.

2. Prepare the grill for direct cooking over medium heat (350° to 450°F).

3. Brush the bread on both sides with oil. Grill the patties over *direct medium heat*, with the lid closed, until cooked to medium doneness (160°F), 10 to 12 minutes, turning once. During the last minute of grilling time, toast the bread over direct heat, turning once. Remove the patties and bread from the grill and let the patties rest for 2 to 3 minutes. Rub the bread with the cut side of the garlic half.

4. Top four bread slices with half of the spinach, a patty, and the remaining spinach. Serve warm, open-faced or with a second piece of bread.

# CAROLINA BARBECUE PORK BURGERS

SERVES: **6** | PREP TIME: **20 MINUTES** | GRILLING TIME: **8 TO 10 MINUTES**

## MOP

- ½ cup cider vinegar
- 2 tablespoons spicy brown mustard
- 2 tablespoons packed light brown sugar
- 2 teaspoons paprika
- 2 teaspoons hot pepper sauce
- 1 teaspoon kosher salt
- ½ teaspoon freshly ground black pepper
- ¼ teaspoon ground allspice

## COLESLAW

- 1 bag (8 ounces) shredded coleslaw mix
- 3 tablespoons mayonnaise
- 2 tablespoons mop (from the recipe above)
- 1 tablespoon sweet orange marmalade

## PATTIES

- 2 pounds lean ground pork
- ¼ cup grated yellow onion
- ¼ teaspoon kosher salt
- ¼ teaspoon freshly ground black pepper

- 6 hamburger buns, split

1. Whisk the mop ingredients.

2. Combine the coleslaw ingredients.

3. Mix the patty ingredients, and then gently form six patties of equal size, each about ¾ inch thick. With your thumb or the back of a spoon, make a shallow indentation about 1 inch wide in the center of the patties to prevent them from forming a dome as they cook. Refrigerate the patties until ready to grill.

4. Prepare the grill for direct cooking over medium-high heat (400° to 500°F).

5. Grill the patties over *direct medium-high heat*, with the lid closed, until cooked to medium doneness (160°F), 8 to 10 minutes, turning once. During the last 30 seconds to 1 minute of grilling time, toast the buns, cut side down, over direct heat. Remove the patties and the buns from the grill and generously brush the patties with the remaining mop.

6. Build each burger on a bun with a patty and coleslaw. Serve warm.

*Serving suggestion: Pickled Okra (for recipe, see page 234).*

# BURGER GEOGRAPHY

From sea to shining sea, the burger is America's culinary calling card.
Just as dramatic as the changes in landscape are the regional preferences
for the classic beef patty so near and dear to our hearts and mouths.
While this list is by no means exhaustive, it does give us a taste (ahem)
of our collective creativity between the bun. Behold, America the Burgerful.

### CALIFORNIA BURGER

*California*

Californians are a lucky group:
they've got the weather, the
landscape, and all those avocados.
So when in the Golden State of
mind, do as the locals do, and throw
a couple slices of ripe avocado on
your burger right before serving.
A dollop of citrusy-spicy
guacamole qualifies, too.

### PASTRAMI BURGER

*Salt Lake City, Utah*

When a standard burger simply isn't
meaty enough, Utah doubles down.
Slices of pastrami, the brined and
smoked deli staple, are piled atop a
beef patty with a special Thousand
Island–esque sauce, American
cheese, shredded lettuce, tomato,
and onions, all on a sesame seed
bun. Vegetarians, look away.

### GREEN CHILE CHEESEBURGER

*Santa Fe, New Mexico*

The Southwest is known for
its heat, both out of doors and
on the plate. New Mexicans
pile their beloved green chiles,
roasted, fried, or whirred into
salsa, atop cheeseburgers to
scorching effect. The cheese
is a must, since dairy can
cool torched taste buds.

## BEAN BURGER

### San Antonio, Texas

Forget the Alamo—remember the bean burger. The original version combines some of America's more eclectic culinary traditions, all with a Tex-Mex twist: a beef patty topped with diced onions, refried beans, crushed corn chips, and, yep, processed cheese sauce.

## THETA BURGER

### Oklahoma

You've got to love college kids and their ingenuity. Rumor has it that a late-night food order made by a University of Oklahoma sorority to a nearby restaurant inspired this saucy creation. A patty is topped with thick grated cheddar, mayo, dill pickle slices, and barbecue or "hickory" sauce on a sesame bun. Consider us pledges.

## JUCY LUCY

### Minneapolis, Minnesota

It's what's inside that counts, which is why some crafty Minnesotans put cheese *in* the burger rather than on it. (Maybe they took the "i" out of "juicy" to make room for more cheese.) A slice of American is laid between two thin burger patties, which are then pinched shut and grilled.

## GUBERBURGER

### Sedalia, Missouri

Opposites attract, and this burger's ingredients are gooey proof. First peddled at a drive-in nearly 100 miles southeast of Kansas City, the Guberburger is comprised of a thin chuck patty topped with lettuce, tomato, mayo, and—get this—creamy melted peanut butter. Grab extra napkins.

## SLUGBURGER

### Northeast Mississippi

Stretching a dollar is a tasty endeavor in Mississippi, where we found this Depression-era holdout. Ground beef is mixed with flour, grits, crackers, or soy meal; formed into patties; and cooked on a griddle. They got their name because you could once buy one for a nickel, known as a "slug" way back when.

## PIMENTO CHEESE BURGER

### Columbia, South Carolina

Pardon our drool, but we like our burgers with a drawl. Pimento cheese is grated cheddar that is mixed with mayonnaise, diced pimento (or pimiento) peppers, salt, and pepper until chunky and spreadable. It's yummy, period, but when zapped with a little radiant heat from a piping-hot burger, the flavors come alive.

# THANKSGIVING BURGERS WITH BRIE AND CRANBERRY MAYO

SERVES: **4** | PREP TIME: **20 MINUTES** | GRILLING TIME: **8 TO 10 MINUTES**

POULTRY

## PATTIES

1½  pounds ground turkey, preferably thigh meat
  1  tablespoon minced fresh sage leaves
  1  tablespoon minced fresh rosemary leaves
  2  teaspoons minced fresh thyme leaves
  2  teaspoons minced garlic

   Kosher salt
   Freshly ground black pepper
  ¼  cup mayonnaise
  ¼  cup whole-berry cranberry sauce
   Extra-virgin olive oil
  ½  teaspoon fresh lemon juice
1½  cups slivered fresh Swiss chard or kale
   (remove tough stems before cutting),
   leaves cut crosswise into ¼-inch strips
  8  ounces Brie cheese, cut into 8 slices
  4  potato buns, split

1. Mix the patty ingredients, including 1 teaspoon salt and ½ teaspoon pepper, and then gently form four patties of equal size, each about ¾ inch thick. With your thumb or the back of a spoon, make a shallow indentation about 1 inch wide in the center of the patties to prevent them from forming a dome as they cook. Refrigerate the patties until ready to grill.

2. Prepare the grill for direct cooking over medium-high heat (400° to 500°F).

3. Combine the mayonnaise, cranberry sauce, ¼ teaspoon salt, and ¼ teaspoon pepper.

4. Whisk 2 teaspoons oil, the lemon juice, and a pinch of salt and pepper. Add the Swiss chard and toss to combine.

5. Brush the patties on both sides with oil, and then grill over *direct medium-high heat*, with the lid closed, until fully cooked (165°F), 8 to 10 minutes, turning once. During the last 30 seconds to 1 minute of grilling time, place two slices of cheese on each patty to soften and toast the buns, cut side down, over direct heat.

6. Build each burger on a bun with a patty, cranberry mayo, and dressed Swiss chard.

**FUN FACT**

Thanksgiving wouldn't be the same without it: the sweet, tangy goodness of canned cranberry. In fact, Americans consume roughly 5,062,500 gallons each holiday season—that's enough sauce to fill nearly 50 Macy's Thanksgiving Day Parade balloons!

# LEMON AND DILL TURKEY BURGERS

SERVES: **4** | PREP TIME: **20 MINUTES** | GRILLING TIME: **11 TO 13 MINUTES**

POULTRY

## PATTIES

- 2 tablespoons extra-virgin olive oil
- 1 small yellow onion, finely chopped
- 1 garlic clove, minced or pushed through a press
- 1½ pounds ground turkey, preferably thigh meat
- 2 tablespoons minced fresh dill
  Finely grated zest of 1 lemon
- 1 tablespoon fresh lemon juice
- 1 teaspoon kosher salt
- ¼ teaspoon freshly ground black pepper

  Extra-virgin olive oil
- 4 hamburger buns, split
- ¼ cup mayonnaise
- 4 leaves butter lettuce
- 2 roasted red bell peppers (from a jar), each cut in half

1. In a medium skillet over medium heat, warm the oil. Add the onion and garlic and sauté until tender, about 5 minutes, stirring occasionally. Remove from the heat and let cool for at least 5 minutes. Combine the onion and garlic with the remaining patty ingredients, and then gently form four patties of equal size, each about 1 inch thick. With your thumb or the back of a spoon, make a shallow indentation about 1 inch wide in the center of the patties to prevent them from forming a dome as they cook. Refrigerate the patties until ready to grill.

2. Prepare the grill for direct cooking over medium heat (350° to 450°F).

3. Brush the patties on both sides with oil, and then grill over *direct medium heat*, with the lid closed, until fully cooked (165°F), 11 to 13 minutes, turning once. During the last 30 seconds to 1 minute of grilling time, toast the buns, cut side down, over direct heat.

4. Build each burger on a bun with mayonnaise, a lettuce leaf, a roasted bell pepper half, and a patty. Serve immediately.

# CURRIED TURKEY BURGERS WITH APPLE CHUTNEY

SERVES: **4** | PREP TIME: **20 MINUTES, PLUS 20 TO 25 MINUTES FOR THE CHUTNEY** | GRILLING TIME: **11 TO 13 MINUTES**

### PATTIES

- 1½ pounds ground turkey, preferably thigh meat
- 2 tablespoons finely chopped white or yellow onion
- 2 teaspoons curry powder
- 1½ teaspoons Worcestershire sauce
- 1 teaspoon kosher salt
- ¼ teaspoon freshly ground black pepper

### CHUTNEY

- 2 Granny Smith apples, peeled, cored, and diced
- 1 cup golden raisins
- ½ cup roughly chopped walnuts
- ½ cup white wine vinegar
- ¼ cup granulated sugar
- ¼ cup fresh orange juice
- 1 cinnamon stick
- ¼ teaspoon kosher salt

   Extra-virgin olive oil
- 4 whole-wheat buns, split

1. Mix the patty ingredients, and then gently form four patties of equal size, each about 1 inch thick. With your thumb or the back of a spoon, make a shallow indentation about 1 inch wide in the center of the patties to prevent them from forming a dome as they cook. Refrigerate the patties until ready to grill.

2. In a heavy saucepan combine the chutney ingredients and stir until the sugar is dissolved. Bring to a simmer over medium heat and cook, uncovered, until most of the liquid is gone, 20 to 25 minutes. Transfer to a bowl and let cool slightly. Discard the cinnamon stick.

3. Prepare the grill for direct cooking over medium heat (350° to 450°F).

4. Brush the patties on both sides with oil, and then grill over *direct medium heat*, with the lid closed, until fully cooked (165°F), 11 to 13 minutes, turning once. During the last 30 seconds to 1 minute of grilling time, toast the buns, cut side down, over direct heat.

5. Build each burger on a bun with a patty and apple chutney. Serve warm.

# GREEK TURKEY BURGERS WITH TOMATO VINAIGRETTE

SERVES: **6** | PREP TIME: **20 MINUTES** | GRILLING TIME: **8 TO 10 MINUTES**

## PATTIES

- 1 tablespoon extra-virgin olive oil
- 1 package (10 ounces) frozen chopped spinach, thawed and squeezed dry
- 1 garlic clove, minced or pushed through a press
- 6 kalamata olives, coarsely chopped
- 2 pounds ground turkey, preferably thigh meat
- 4 ounces feta cheese, crumbled
- 2 tablespoons apple butter
- ½ teaspoon poultry seasoning
- ½ teaspoon kosher salt
- ¼ teaspoon freshly ground black pepper

## VINAIGRETTE

- 1 cup tomato puree
- ¼ cup extra-virgin olive oil
- 2 tablespoons red wine vinegar
- 1 tablespoon finely chopped fresh oregano leaves
- 1 tablespoon finely chopped fresh Italian parsley leaves
- ½ teaspoon kosher salt
- ¼ teaspoon freshly ground black pepper

  Extra-virgin olive oil
- 4 hamburger buns, split

1. In a large skillet over medium heat, warm the oil. Add the spinach and garlic and cook until the spinach is dry, stirring occasionally. Remove from the heat and stir in the olives. Allow to cool.

2. Combine the spinach mixture with the remaining patty ingredients, and then gently form six patties of equal size, each about ¾ inch thick. With your thumb or the back of a spoon, make a shallow indentation about 1 inch wide in the center of the patties to prevent them from forming a dome as they cook. Refrigerate the patties until ready to grill.

3. Prepare the grill for direct cooking over medium-high heat (400° to 500°F).

4. Whisk the vinaigrette ingredients.

5. Brush the patties on both sides with oil, and then grill over *direct medium-high heat*, with the lid closed, until fully cooked (165°F), 8 to 10 minutes, turning once. During the last 30 seconds to 1 minute of grilling time, toast the buns, cut side down, over direct heat.

6. Build each burger on a bun with a patty and as much tomato vinaigrette as you like. Serve warm with any remaining vinaigrette on the side.

---

Ground turkey is often bland and dry. It needs help to become a succulent burger, which is why turkey burgers usually have a lot more ingredients in them than burgers made from beef or pork. The secret to this one is apple butter, which gives the turkey a darker color and adds spices that make the meat taste much richer.

---

# TURKEY CHEESEBURGERS

SERVES: **4** | PREP TIME: **20 MINUTES** | GRILLING TIME: **8 TO 10 MINUTES**

## PATTIES

1½ pounds ground turkey, preferably thigh meat

2 scallions, ends trimmed and finely chopped

1 rib celery, ends trimmed and finely chopped

2 teaspoons hot pepper sauce

1 teaspoon minced garlic

1 teaspoon kosher salt

½ teaspoon freshly ground black pepper

Extra-virgin olive oil

4 slices Havarti cheese, each about 1 ounce

4 brioche buns, split

4 leaves crisp lettuce

8 slices ripe tomato

1. Mix the patty ingredients, and then gently form four patties of equal size, each about ¾ inch thick. With your thumb or the back of a spoon, make a shallow indentation about 1 inch wide in the center of the patties to prevent them from forming a dome as they cook. Refrigerate the patties until ready to grill.

2. Prepare the grill for direct cooking over medium-high heat (400° to 500°F).

3. Brush the patties on both sides with oil, and then grill over *direct medium-high heat,* with the lid closed, until fully cooked (165°F), 8 to 10 minutes, turning once. During the last 30 seconds to 1 minute of grilling time, place a slice of cheese on each patty to melt, and toast the buns, cut side down, over direct heat.

4. Build each burger on a bun with a patty, a lettuce leaf, and two tomato slices. Serve warm.

*Serving suggestion: Weber's Secret Sauce (for recipe, see page 237).*

# PEPPER JACK TURKEY BURGERS WITH JALAPEÑO MAYO

SERVES: **4** | PREP TIME: **25 MINUTES** | GRILLING TIME: **11 TO 13 MINUTES**

## PATTIES

- 1½ pounds ground turkey, preferably thigh meat
- ¼ small green bell pepper, finely chopped
- ¼ small red bell pepper, finely chopped
- 3 tablespoons finely chopped onion
- 2 tablespoons minced fresh cilantro leaves
- 2 garlic cloves, minced or pushed through a press
- ½ teaspoon dried oregano
- ½ teaspoon pure chile powder

  Kosher salt
  Freshly ground black pepper
  Ground cumin

## MAYO

- ½ cup mayonnaise
- 1 jalapeño chile pepper, seeded and minced
- 1 tablespoon finely grated lime zest
- 1 tablespoon fresh lime juice
- 1 garlic clove, minced or pushed through a press

  Extra-virgin olive oil
- 4 thick slices pepper jack cheese
- 4 kaiser rolls, split
- 4 leaves crisp lettuce

1. Mix the patty ingredients, including 1 teaspoon salt, ½ teaspoon pepper, and ¼ teaspoon cumin, and then gently form four patties of equal size, each about 1 inch thick. With your thumb or the back of a spoon, make a shallow indentation about 1 inch wide in the center of each patty to prevent them from forming a dome as they cook. Refrigerate the patties until ready to grill.

2. Prepare the grill for direct cooking over medium heat (350° to 450°F).

3. In a small bowl whisk the mayo ingredients, including ¼ teaspoon salt, ¼ teaspoon pepper, and ¼ teaspoon cumin.

4. Brush the patties on both sides with oil, and then grill over *direct medium heat*, with the lid closed, until fully cooked (165°F), 11 to 13 minutes, turning once. During the last 30 seconds to 1 minute of grilling time, place a slice of cheese on each patty to melt, and toast the rolls, cut side down, over direct heat.

5. Build each burger on a roll with jalapeño mayo, a patty, and a lettuce leaf. Serve warm.

# TURKEY BURGERS WITH CORN AND PEPPER RELISH

SERVES: **4** | PREP TIME: **15 MINUTES** | GRILLING TIME: **21 TO 28 MINUTES**

**POULTRY**

## PATTIES

1½ pounds ground turkey, preferably thigh meat
1½ teaspoons Worcestershire sauce
3 garlic cloves, minced or pushed through a press
1 teaspoon pure chile powder
1 teaspoon dried oregano
½ teaspoon ground cumin

Kosher salt

## RELISH

2 ears fresh corn, husked
2 tablespoons extra-virgin olive oil
1½ teaspoons white wine vinegar
½ teaspoon Dijon mustard
½ teaspoon finely grated lime zest
1 tablespoon fresh lime juice
½ small red bell pepper, cut into ¼-inch dice
4 scallions (white and light green parts only), thinly sliced
¼ teaspoon paprika

Extra-virgin olive oil
Freshly ground black pepper
4 whole-wheat buns, split

1. Mix the patty ingredients, including 1 teaspoon salt, and then gently form four patties of equal size, each about 1 inch thick. With your thumb or the back of a spoon, make a shallow indentation about 1 inch wide in the center of the patties to prevent them from forming a dome as they cook. Refrigerate the patties until ready to grill.

2. Prepare the grill for direct cooking over medium heat (350° to 450°F).

3. Grill the corn over *direct medium heat*, with the lid closed, until browned in spots and tender, 10 to 15 minutes, turning occasionally. When cool enough to handle, cut the kernels off the cobs. In a medium bowl whisk 2 tablespoons oil, the vinegar, mustard, lime zest, and lime juice. Add the corn and the remaining relish ingredients. Season with ¼ teaspoon salt. Toss to coat.

4. Brush the patties on both sides with oil and lightly season with salt and pepper. Grill the patties over *direct medium heat*, with the lid closed, until fully cooked (165°F), 11 to 13 minutes, turning once. During the last 30 seconds to 1 minute of grilling time, toast the buns, cut side down, over direct heat.

5. Build each burger on a bun with a patty and corn and pepper relish. Serve warm.

*Serving suggestion: Grilled Avocado and Jalapeño Guacamole (for recipe, see page 230).*

# CHICKEN POPEYE SLIDERS WITH MOZZARELLA AND PESTO

SERVES: **6** | PREP TIME: **20 MINUTES** | GRILLING TIME: **18 TO 22 MINUTES**

## PATTIES

1½  pounds ground chicken thigh meat
 1  package (10 ounces) frozen chopped spinach, thawed and squeezed dry
 4  ounces mozzarella cheese, grated
 ¼  cup dried bread crumbs
 ¼  cup finely chopped yellow onion
 2  tablespoons balsamic vinegar
 1  teaspoon kosher salt
 2  garlic cloves, minced or pushed through a press
 ½  teaspoon freshly ground black pepper

 2  medium red bell peppers
    Extra-virgin olive oil
12  slices mozzarella cheese, trimmed to roughly the size of the sliders
12  slider buns, split
    Store-bought pesto

**1.** Mix the patty ingredients, and then gently form 12 patties of equal size, each about ½ inch thick (roughly the size of the buns). Refrigerate the patties until ready to grill.

**2.** Prepare the grill for direct cooking over medium heat (350° to 450°F).

**3.** Grill the bell peppers over *direct medium heat*, with the lid closed, until blackened and blistered all over, 10 to 12 minutes, turning occasionally. Place the peppers in a bowl and cover with plastic wrap to trap the steam. Let stand for about 10 minutes. Remove and discard the charred skin, stem, and seeds, and cut each pepper into 6 strips.

**4.** Brush the patties on both sides with oil, and then grill over *direct medium heat*, with the lid closed, until fully cooked (165°F), 8 to 10 minutes, turning once. During the last 30 seconds to 1 minute of grilling time, place a slice of cheese on each patty to melt, and toast the buns, cut side down, over direct heat.

**5.** Build each slider on a bun with a thin layer of pesto, a bell pepper strip, and a patty. Serve immediately.

**FUN FACT**

In the 1930s, Popeye, the lovable, roughneck comic strip and cartoon character, was best known for consuming massive amounts of canned spinach, which gave him superhuman strength and instantaneous talents. During this time, spinach growers credited the sailor man with increasing American spinach consumption by more than a third—even briefly slotting spinach as the third most popular kids' food, after ice cream and turkey.

# SPICY CHICKEN SLIDERS WITH BLUE CHEESE DRESSING

SERVES: **4** | PREP TIME: **15 MINUTES** | GRILLING TIME: **8 TO 10 MINUTES**

POULTRY

## DRESSING

    2  ounces blue cheese, crumbled
    ¼  cup sour cream
    ¼  cup mayonnaise
    2  teaspoons white wine vinegar
    ¼  teaspoon kosher salt
    ⅛  teaspoon freshly ground
       black pepper
    ½  cup finely chopped celery

## PATTIES

 1½  pounds ground chicken
      thigh or mixed thigh
      and breast meat
    ½  cup dried bread crumbs
 1–2  tablespoons hot pepper sauce
    1  teaspoon prepared chili powder
    ¾  teaspoon smoked paprika
    ¼  teaspoon ground
       cayenne pepper
    ½  teaspoon kosher salt

    2  tablespoons unsalted
       butter, melted
    8  slider buns, split

**1.** Combine all the dressing ingredients except for the celery, and mash well with a fork. Stir in the celery.

**2.** Mix the patty ingredients, and then gently form eight patties of equal size, each about ½ inch thick (roughly the size of the buns). Refrigerate the patties until ready to grill.

**3.** Prepare the grill for direct cooking over medium heat (350° to 450°F).

**4.** Brush the patties on both sides with the butter, and then grill over *direct medium heat*, with the lid closed, until fully cooked (165°F), 8 to 10 minutes, turning once. During the last 30 seconds to 1 minute of grilling time, toast the buns, cut side down, over direct heat.

**5.** Build each slider on a bun with a patty and blue cheese dressing. Serve warm.

*Serving suggestion: Classic Creamy Slaw (for recipe, see page 200).*

### FUN FACT

The term "sliders" probably originated in the US Navy in the 1930s or '40s, when it referred to hamburgers so greasy that they slid across the galley grill during heavy seas—though some sailors say the term refers to the way those burgers slid right down your gullet. Now chefs use the term to describe small burgers of any kind that are slipped inside little buns.

# CHICKEN BURGERS WITH GRILLED PINEAPPLE AND HULI HULI SAUCE

SERVES: **4** | PREP TIME: **20 MINUTES, PLUS ABOUT 15 MINUTES FOR THE SAUCE** | GRILLING TIME: **8 TO 10 MINUTES**

## SAUCE
- ½ cup ketchup
- ⅓ cup packed dark brown sugar
- ¼ cup soy sauce
- 2 tablespoons sherry vinegar
- 1 teaspoon peeled, grated fresh ginger
- 2 garlic cloves, minced or pushed through a press

- 1¼ pounds ground chicken, preferably thigh meat
- ½ cup panko bread crumbs
- 4 slices ripe, fresh pineapple, each about ⅓ inch thick, cored
- 4 hamburger buns, split
- 4 leaves lettuce
- 4 thin slices red onion

1. In a saucepan combine the sauce ingredients. Bring to a boil over medium-high heat, and then reduce the heat to medium. Simmer gently until the sauce is thickened and reduced to about ⅔ cup, about 15 minutes, stirring frequently. Remove from the heat and cool to room temperature.

2. Combine ⅓ cup of the sauce with the ground chicken and bread crumbs, and then gently form four patties of equal size, each about ¾ inch thick. With your thumb or the back of a spoon, make a shallow indentation about 1 inch wide in the center of the patties to prevent them from forming a dome as they cook. Refrigerate the patties until ready to grill.

3. Prepare the grill for direct cooking over medium-high heat (400°F to 500°F).

4. Grill the patties and pineapple slices over *direct medium-high heat*, with the lid closed, until the patties are fully cooked (165°F), 8 to 10 minutes, and the pineapple slices are well marked, 4 to 6 minutes, turning once. During the last 2 to 3 minutes of grilling time, brush the patties and pineapple slices with the remaining sauce. During the last 30 seconds to 1 minute of grilling time, toast the buns, cut side down, over direct heat.

5. Build each burger on a bun with a lettuce leaf, an onion slice, a patty, and a pineapple slice. Serve warm.

# CHEESE, IF YOU PLEASE

## AMERICAN

This no-frills standby is the best for pleasing a crowd. Many of us were reared on these individual slices of cheese ease.

**PROS:** Good melter; in-expensive; easy to find; mild flavor; will please the pickiest eaters

**CONS:** Can taste metallic or synthetic; lacks depth and nuance; can be melty to the point of messy

**BEST USES:** With all-American (that's no coincidence) burgers and hot dogs to be served at large gatherings

## CHEDDAR

The only thing sharper than a good aged cheddar is the knife you'll need to cut it. This reliable cheese is frequently our first choice to top a burger.

**PROS:** Easy to find; universally liked; versatile; a great grater

**CONS:** The generic stuff can be waxy and flavorless; overheating or reheating makes it rubbery

**BEST USES:** With beef burgers; with any items that have Latin or South-western undertones

## SWISS

Nutty and sophisticated, this holey favorite is mild enough to delight the masses.

**PROS:** Great when baked or broiled; affordable; widely available; tones down big flavors; a nice alternative to American and cheddar

**CONS:** Some mass-produced types are flavorless; can be stubborn melters

**BEST USES:** With pork, poultry, or lamb burgers; with German-influenced hot dog and sausage varieties

## MOZZARELLA

Don't you get fresh ... unless we're talking mozzarella. Mild and chewy, it's unmatched in its ability to melt.

**PROS:** The authentic stuff is a delicacy worth the price tag; melts beautifully; shredded varieties are easy to find

**CONS:** The mass-produced stuff is flavorless and chalky, as are low-fat versions; the real deal is expensive

**BEST USES:** With anything Italian; with tomatoes or tomato sauce; alongside bold flavors

Now here's a topic that really makes us melt. A little dose of dairy can make beef taste beefier, spice tamer, and lean meats more luxurious. As with much in life, you get what you pay for, so shelling out a few more bucks for quality leads to superior results. There are really no bad cheese choices in our book, but below are a few of our favorites.

## PROVOLONE

This Italian *formaggio* can take the heat, and likes it. Aged varieties can be quite sharp, while supermarket styles are much milder.

PROS: Soft and subtle flavors; great complement to bold meats and spices

CON: Can taste bland and forgettable

BEST USES: With dried Italian sausages; anything with "pizza" flavors (it's a good change-up from the typical mozzarella choice)

## PEPPER JACK

Is it hot in here, or is it just the cheese? Studded with hot pepper flakes, the assertive, spicy pepper jack melts in an instant.

PROS: Packs a flavor punch; widely available; good melter

CON: May overpower subtler flavors

BEST USES: With any burger or sausage under the south-of-the-border influence; with leaner poultry burgers that lack flavor on their own

## BLUE CHEESE

Pungent and piquant, this mold-injected variety can get the party started, or clear a room.

PROS: Loaded with flavor; varieties vary from sweet to knock-you-on-your-behind strong; complex, creamy, crumbly, and a darling of cheese aficionados

CONS: Can be over-powering; the good stuff is pricey; doesn't melt well

BEST USE: With beef burgers

## BRIE

This wheel of creamy dreaminess is as indulgent as it gets for cheese lovers. The French long ago dubbed it "King of Cheeses."

PROS: An instant statement-maker; mild and approachable, but still flavorful; very soft and melts with little effort

CONS: Difficult to slice; usually needs the rind left on to hold its shape, which might be unappealing to some; a little too ooey-gooey at times

BEST USES: On veggie burgers with walnuts; on poultry patties topped with a compote or chutney

# CHICKEN PATTY MELTS

SERVES: **4** | PREP TIME: **30 MINUTES** | GRILLING TIME: **10 TO 14 MINUTES**

POULTRY

## ONIONS

    2 tablespoons extra-virgin olive oil
    2 yellow onions, about 1 pound total,
      each cut in half and thinly sliced
    ½ teaspoon dried thyme
    ¼ teaspoon kosher salt
    ⅛ teaspoon freshly ground black pepper

## PATTIES

1½ pounds ground chicken, preferably thigh meat
    ⅓ cup dried bread crumbs
    1 teaspoon ground cumin
    1 teaspoon kosher salt
    ½ teaspoon freshly ground black pepper

    3 tablespoons unsalted butter, softened
    8 slices rye bread, each about ½ inch thick
    8 slices sharp cheddar cheese, each about 1 ounce
      Ketchup

1. In a large skillet over medium-high heat, warm the oil. Add the onions, thyme, salt, and pepper, and cook until the onions are tender and golden, about 20 minutes, stirring often. Remove from the heat.

2. Mix the patty ingredients, and then gently form four patties, each slightly larger than the bread slices and about ¾ inch thick. With your thumb or the back of a spoon, make a shallow indentation about 1 inch wide in the center of the patties to prevent them from forming a dome as they cook. Refrigerate the patties until ready to grill.

3. Prepare the grill for direct cooking over medium-high heat (400° to 500°F).

4. Butter one side of each bread slice. Place four slices on a work surface, buttered side down, and top each with one slice of cheese and one-fourth of the onions.

5. Grill the patties over *direct medium-high heat*, with the lid closed, until fully cooked (165°F), 8 to 10 minutes, turning once. Transfer the patties to the prepared bread on top of the onions. Top the patties with the remaining cheese and bread slices, buttered side up. Grill the patty melts over *direct medium-high heat*, with the lid closed, until the bread is toasted and the cheese is melted, 2 to 4 minutes, carefully turning once. Serve hot with ketchup.

Making up more than 80 percent of our total onion crop, yellow onions are the most popular onion in the United States. This is likely due to their nice balance of astringency and sweetness—and they get even sweeter and nuttier as they cook, making them excellent for recipes like this one. White onions are sharper and more astringent, and the crop is much smaller (just 5 percent of the total). We like them in bold-tasting salsas, though we often rinse the chopped onions in a fine-mesh strainer under cold water to take off some of their harshness.

# CHICKEN BURGERS WITH GUACAMOLE

SERVES: **4** | PREP TIME: **20 MINUTES** | GRILLING TIME: **11 TO 13 MINUTES**

### PATTIES

1½ pounds ground chicken, preferably thigh meat
1½ teaspoons Worcestershire sauce
1½ teaspoons minced garlic
 1 teaspoon kosher salt
 ½ teaspoon hot pepper sauce
 ½ teaspoon dried oregano

### GUACAMOLE

 1 large or 2 small, ripe Hass avocados, diced
 1 tablespoon minced red onion
 1 tablespoon minced fresh cilantro leaves
 1 tablespoon fresh lime juice, or to taste
 ¼ teaspoon hot pepper sauce, or to taste

 Kosher salt
 Freshly ground black pepper
 Extra-virgin olive oil
 4 whole-wheat buns, split
 4 thick slices ripe tomato
 4 thin slices red onion

1. Mix the patty ingredients, and then gently form four patties of equal size, each about 1 inch thick. With your thumb or the back of a spoon, make a shallow indentation about 1 inch wide in the center of the patties to prevent them from forming a dome as they cook. Refrigerate the patties until ready to grill.

2. Prepare the grill for direct cooking over medium heat (350° to 450°F).

3. Mash the guacamole ingredients and season with salt and pepper.

4. Brush the patties on both sides with oil and lightly season with salt and pepper. Grill the patties over *direct medium heat*, with the lid closed, until fully cooked (165°F), 11 to 13 minutes, turning once. During the last 30 seconds to 1 minute of grilling time, toast the buns, cut side down, over direct heat.

5. Build each burger on a bun with a tomato slice, an onion slice, a patty, and a mound of guacamole. Serve warm.

# CHICKEN-APPLE BURGERS WITH CELERY SALAD

SERVES: **4** | PREP TIME: **20 MINUTES** | GRILLING TIME: **11 TO 13 MINUTES**

## PATTIES

1½ pounds ground chicken, preferably thigh meat
1 large Granny Smith apple, peeled and finely diced
1 large shallot, minced
¾ teaspoon ground cumin

Kosher salt
Freshly ground black pepper

## SALAD

¼ cup mayonnaise
1 tablespoon fresh lemon juice
6 ribs celery, preferably from the heart, trimmed and cut into thin slices
⅓ cup roughly chopped walnuts
1½ tablespoons finely chopped red onion
1 tablespoon minced fresh Italian parsley leaves
½ teaspoon prepared horseradish

Extra-virgin olive oil
8 slices walnut bread, each about ½ inch thick
*or* 4 whole-wheat buns, split
4 teaspoons Dijon mustard

1. Mix the patty ingredients, including 1 teaspoon salt and ½ teaspoon pepper, and then gently form four patties of equal size, each about 1 inch thick. With your thumb or the back of a spoon, make a shallow indentation about 1 inch wide in the center of the patties to prevent them from forming a dome as they cook. Refrigerate the patties until ready to grill.

2. Prepare the grill for direct cooking over medium heat (350° to 450°F).

3. Whisk the mayonnaise and lemon juice, and then fold in the remaining salad ingredients. Season with ½ teaspoon salt and ¼ teaspoon pepper.

4. Brush the patties on both sides with oil and lightly season with salt and pepper. Grill the patties over *direct medium heat*, with the lid closed, until fully cooked (165°F), 11 to 13 minutes, turning once. During the last minute of grilling time, toast the bread over direct heat, turning once.

5. Build each burger on a bread slice with mustard, a patty, a spoonful of celery salad, and the remaining bread slice. Serve immediately.

117

# SMOKED CHICKEN BURGERS WITH BACON AND BLUE CHEESE

SERVES: **4** | PREP TIME: **25 MINUTES** | GRILLING TIME: **8 TO 10 MINUTES**
SPECIAL EQUIPMENT: **2 LARGE HANDFULS HICKORY WOOD CHIPS**

## PATTIES

- 4 slices bacon
- ½ medium onion, finely chopped
- ½ teaspoon minced fresh thyme leaves
- 1¼ pounds ground chicken, preferably thigh meat
- ½ teaspoon kosher salt
- ¼ teaspoon freshly ground black pepper

## SAUCE

- ½ cup mayonnaise
- 1 tablespoon cider vinegar
- 1 teaspoon prepared horseradish
- ½ teaspoon granulated sugar
- ¼ teaspoon kosher salt
- ¼ teaspoon freshly ground black pepper

- 4 hamburger buns, split
- 4 ounces blue cheese, crumbled
- 12 sweet pickle chips

**FUN FACT**

Did you know that the bluish-green veins running through the white, crumbly wheels and wedges of blue cheese are actually mold? But it's not just any old mold—it's a harmless, pungent, mouthwatering mold, said to have been gleefully discovered by early cheese makers who aged their cheeses in the naturally dark, damp, cool environment of caves.

1. Soak the wood chips in water for at least 30 minutes.

2. In a skillet over medium heat, fry the bacon until crisp, 10 to 12 minutes, turning occasionally. Transfer the bacon to paper towels to drain. Pour off all but 1 tablespoon of bacon fat. Return the skillet over medium heat and add the onion and thyme. Cook until the onion starts to soften, 2 to 3 minutes, stirring occasionally. Crumble the bacon. Mix the bacon, onion mixture, ground chicken, salt, and pepper, and then gently form four patties of equal size, each about ¾ inch thick. With your thumb or the back of a spoon, make a shallow indentation about 1 inch wide in the center of the patties to prevent them from forming a dome as they cook. Refrigerate the patties until ready to grill.

3. Prepare the grill for direct cooking over medium-high heat (400° to 500°F).

4. Whisk the sauce ingredients.

5. Drain and add the wood chips to the charcoal or to the smoker box of a gas grill, following manufacturer's instructions, and close the lid. When smoke appears, cook the patties over *direct medium-high heat*, with the lid closed, until fully cooked (165°F), 8 to 10 minutes, turning once. During the last 30 seconds to 1 minute of grilling time, toast the buns, cut side down, over direct heat.

6. Build each burger on a bun with sauce, a patty, blue cheese, and pickle chips. Serve warm.

# SURF AND TURF BURGERS WITH PESTO

SERVES: **4** | PREP TIME: **15 MINUTES** | CHILLING TIME: **30 MINUTES TO 2 HOURS**
GRILLING TIME: **8 TO 9 MINUTES** | SPECIAL EQUIPMENT: **PERFORATED GRILL PAN**

## PATTIES

- 12 ounces shrimp, peeled and deveined
- 12 ounces ground chicken, preferably thigh meat
- 6-8 tablespoons panko bread crumbs
- 3 tablespoons finely chopped red bell pepper
- 1 large egg, lightly beaten
- 1 tablespoon Dijon mustard
- 1 tablespoon mayonnaise
- ½ teaspoon granulated garlic
- ½ teaspoon pure chile powder
- ¼ teaspoon kosher salt
- ¼ teaspoon freshly ground black pepper

- 8 teaspoons store-bought pesto
  Extra-virgin olive oil
- 4 whole-wheat buns, split
- 4 leaves butter lettuce
- 8 thin slices ripe tomato

1. Wrap the shrimp in paper towels and squeeze out the excess moisture. Roughly chop the shrimp into chunks of ¼ inch or less. Mix the shrimp with the remaining patty ingredients, starting with 6 tablespoons panko. Gently squeeze a bit of the mixture to see if it clumps; if not, add up to two additional tablespoons panko. Freeze for 5 minutes. Form eight patties of equal size, each about ½ inch thick.

2. Place four patties on a work surface and spread 2 teaspoons of pesto on top of each, leaving a ½-inch border. Center the remaining four patties over the tops, and press down until each double patty is about 1 inch thick.

Pinch the edges together tightly, sealing in the pesto. Cover and refrigerate for 30 minutes to 2 hours.

3. Prepare the grill for direct cooking over high heat (450° to 550°F) and preheat a perforated grill pan.

4. Brush the patties with oil, place on the grill pan over *direct high heat*, close the lid, and grill for 4 minutes (do not move the patties). Turn the patties over and continue cooking until golden and firm, 4 to 5 minutes more. During the last 30 seconds to 1 minute of grilling time, toast the buns on the cooking grates, cut side down, over direct heat.

5. Build each burger on a bun with a lettuce leaf, two tomato slices, and a patty. Serve warm.

After you fill the patties with pesto, making sure that it doesn't spill out the sides, refrigerate the patties for about 30 minutes to make them firmer and easier to handle on the grill.

# SHRIMP AND SCALLION BURGERS WITH CRISPY PANCETTA

SERVES: **4** | PREP TIME: **30 MINUTES** | CHILLING TIME: **30 MINUTES TO 2 HOURS**
GRILLING TIME: **12 TO 16 MINUTES** | SPECIAL EQUIPMENT: **GRILL-PROOF GRIDDLE**

## MAYONNAISE

- ¼ cup mayonnaise
  Finely grated zest of 1 lemon
- 1 teaspoon fresh lemon juice
- 1 teaspoon prepared horseradish
- ⅛ teaspoon kosher salt

## PATTIES

- 1¼ pounds shrimp,
  peeled and deveined
- 6–8 tablespoons panko
  bread crumbs
- 3 scallions, ends trimmed
  and finely chopped
- 1 large egg, lightly beaten
- 1 tablespoon Dijon mustard
- 1 tablespoon mayonnaise
  Finely grated zest of 1 lemon
- ½ teaspoon kosher salt
- ⅛ teaspoon freshly ground
  black pepper

- 8 thin slices pancetta
- 4 English muffins, split
  Extra-virgin olive oil
- 2 tablespoons finely chopped
  scallion greens

Squeezing water out of the raw shrimp is an important first step; otherwise, the patties will be too wet and will steam rather than char on the grill. You must have *some* moisture in the patties, which should come from ingredients like mayonnaise and mustard (they taste a lot better than shrimp water).

1. Mix the mayonnaise ingredients. Refrigerate until ready to use.

2. Wrap the shrimp in paper towels and squeeze out the excess moisture. In a food processor fitted with a metal blade, pulse the shrimp until roughly chopped. Mix the shrimp with the remaining patty ingredients, starting with 6 tablespoons panko. Gently squeeze a bit of the mixture to see if it clumps; if not, add up to two additional tablespoons panko. Freeze for 5 minutes. Form four patties of equal size, each about ¾ inch thick. Cover and refrigerate for 30 minutes to 2 hours.

3. Prepare the grill for direct cooking over medium heat (350° to 450°F) and preheat a grill-proof griddle.

4. Cook the pancetta on the griddle until crisp, 6 to 8 minutes, turning occasionally. Drain on paper towels. Increase the temperature of the grill to high heat (450° to 550°F). Keep the griddle on the cooking grates.

5. Brush the patties on both sides with oil. Place the patties on the griddle and cook over *direct high heat*, with the lid closed, until golden and firm, 6 to 8 minutes, turning once. During the last 30 seconds to 1 minute of grilling time, toast the English muffins on the cooking grates, cut side down, over direct heat.

6. Build each burger on an English muffin with a patty, lemon mayonnaise, pancetta, and scallions. Serve warm.

# SHRIMP BURGERS WITH RÉMOULADE

SERVES: **4** | PREP TIME: **30 MINUTES** | CHILLING TIME: **30 MINUTES TO 2 HOURS**
GRILLING TIME: **6 TO 8 MINUTES** | SPECIAL EQUIPMENT: **GRILL-PROOF GRIDDLE**

### RÉMOULADE

- ¼ cup mayonnaise
- 3 scallions, ends trimmed and finely chopped
- 2 tablespoons finely chopped fresh Italian parsley leaves
- 1½ tablespoons fresh lemon juice
- 1½ tablespoons finely chopped celery heart
- 1 tablespoon whole-grain mustard
- 1 tablespoon ketchup
- 1 tablespoon prepared horseradish
- ¾ teaspoon Worcestershire sauce
- 1 garlic clove, minced or pushed through a press
- ¼ teaspoon paprika
- ⅛ teaspoon hot pepper sauce, or to taste

  Kosher salt
  Freshly ground black pepper

### PATTIES

- 1¼ pounds shrimp, peeled and deveined
- 6–8 tablespoons panko bread crumbs
- 1 large egg, lightly beaten
- 3 scallions, ends trimmed and finely chopped
- 2 tablespoons chopped celery heart
- 1 tablespoon mayonnaise
  Finely grated zest of 1 lemon

  Extra-virgin olive oil
- 2 tablespoons unsalted butter, softened
- 4 slices challah, each about ½ inch thick

1. Whisk the rémoulade ingredients until smooth, including ¼ teaspoon salt and ⅛ teaspoon pepper. Cover and refrigerate until ready to serve.

2. Wrap the shrimp in paper towels and squeeze out the excess moisture. Put the shrimp in a food processor fitted with a metal blade, and pulse about six times until roughly chopped (pieces should be about ¼ inch or less). Combine the shrimp, 6 tablespoons panko, the egg, scallions, celery, mayonnaise, lemon zest, ½ teaspoon salt, and ¼ teaspoon pepper. Blend well with a fork. Gently squeeze a bit of the mixture to see if it clumps; if not, add up to two additional tablespoons panko. Freeze for 5 minutes. Form four patties of equal size, each about ¾ inch thick. Cover and refrigerate for 30 minutes to 2 hours.

3. Prepare the grill for direct cooking over medium heat (350° to 450°F) and preheat a grill-proof griddle.

4. Lightly brush the patties on both sides with oil. Spread the butter on both sides of the challah. Place the patties on the griddle and cook over *direct medium heat*, with the lid closed, until golden and firm, 6 to 8 minutes, carefully turning once. During the last minute of grilling time, toast the challah on the cooking grates over direct heat, turning once.

5. Place a patty on a slice of challah and top with rémoulade. Serve warm.

---

To grill shrimp patties without sticking problems,
make sure the grill is hot and the food is cold.
It also helps to have a grill-proof griddle and the
patience to wait until the patties have browned
on the first side before trying to turn them.

# SMOKED SALMON BURGERS WITH FRIED EGGS AND SCALLION CREAM CHEESE

SERVES: **6** | PREP TIME: **30 MINUTES** | CHILLING TIME: **1 HOUR**
GRILLING TIME: **6 TO 8 MINUTES** | SPECIAL EQUIPMENT: **GRILL-PROOF GRIDDLE**

**SEAFOOD**

## PATTIES

1½ pounds skinless salmon fillets, pin bones removed, cut into 1-inch pieces
8 ounces lox-style smoked salmon, finely chopped
½ cup panko bread crumbs
3 tablespoons finely chopped yellow onion
3 tablespoons minced fresh chives
1 tablespoon minced garlic
1 teaspoon kosher salt

Freshly ground black pepper
3 ounces cream cheese, softened
3 scallions (white and light green parts only), finely chopped
1 tablespoon extra-virgin olive oil
6 English muffins, split
1 tablespoon unsalted butter
6 large eggs
Microgreens or sprouts

1. In a food processor fitted with a metal blade, pulse the salmon fillet pieces 8 to 10 times until coarsely chopped but not pasty; transfer to a bowl. Add the remaining patty ingredients to the bowl, including ¼ teaspoon pepper, and stir gently to combine. Form six patties of equal size, each about ¾ inch thick. Cover and refrigerate the patties for 1 hour.

2. Prepare the grill for direct cooking over medium heat (350° to 450°F) and preheat a grill-proof griddle.

3. Mix the cream cheese and scallions until well blended. Refrigerate until ready to grill the patties.

4. Brush the patties on both sides with the oil. Place the patties on the griddle and cook over *direct medium heat*, with the lid closed, until fully cooked but still juicy, 6 to 8 minutes, carefully turning once. During the last 30 seconds to 1 minute of grilling time, toast the English muffins on the cooking grates, cut side down, over direct heat.

5. In a skillet over medium-high heat, melt the butter. Fry the eggs until the whites are set to your desired doneness.

6. Spread the scallion cream cheese on both sides of the toasted English muffins. Place a patty on each muffin bottom and top with an egg and a small handful of microgreens. Season with pepper. Serve warm with the muffin tops on the side.

*Serving suggestion: Tropical Fruit Salad with Honey and Lime (for recipe, see page 217).*

One key to great salmon burgers is evenly chopped fish, which is easy to get with a big food processor. However, if the bowl of your processor has a diameter of less than seven inches, process the fish in two batches with quick pulses until you get a coarsely chopped consistency in each batch.

# LEMON-CAPER SALMON BURGERS WITH PESTO MAYO

SERVES: **4** | PREP TIME: **20 MINUTES** | CHILLING TIME: **1 HOUR** | GRILLING TIME: **6 TO 8 MINUTES**

SEAFOOD

## PATTIES

1½ pounds skinless salmon
    fillets, pin bones removed,
    cut into 1-inch pieces
¼ cup minced shallots
¼ cup minced fresh
    Italian parsley leaves
1 large egg, beaten
    Finely grated zest of 1 lemon
1 tablespoon fresh lemon juice
½ cup fresh white or
    egg bread crumbs
1½ tablespoons capers,
    drained and chopped
¾ teaspoon kosher salt
½ teaspoon freshly ground
    black pepper

⅓ cup store-bought pesto
¼ cup mayonnaise
2 or 4 focaccia squares, each about
    4½ inches in diameter, split
    Extra-virgin olive oil
8 slices ripe tomato
4 leaves butter lettuce

1. In a food processor fitted with a metal blade, pulse the salmon pieces 8 to 10 times until coarsely chopped but not pasty. Add the shallots, parsley, egg, lemon zest, and lemon juice. Pulse a few times until just blended, being careful to leave some texture. Transfer to a bowl and gently stir in the remaining patty ingredients. Form four patties of equal size, each about ¾ inch thick. Cover and refrigerate for 1 hour.

2. Combine the pesto and mayonnaise. Cover and refrigerate until ready to use.

3. Prepare the grill for direct cooking over medium heat (350° to 450°F).

4. Brush the patties on both sides with oil, and then grill over *direct medium heat*, with the lid closed, until fully cooked but still juicy, 6 to 8 minutes, carefully turning once. During the last 30 seconds to 1 minute of grilling time, toast the focaccia, cut side down, over direct heat.

5. Top four focaccia halves with pesto mayo, two tomato slices, a lettuce leaf, and a patty. Serve warm topped with another focaccia half, if desired.

# OPEN-FACED SALMON BURGERS WITH PINEAPPLE-GINGER SALSA

SERVES: **6** | PREP TIME: **45 MINUTES** | CHILLING TIME: **1 HOUR** | GRILLING TIME: **16 TO 18 MINUTES**

## PATTIES

 2 pounds skinless salmon
   fillets, pin bones removed,
   cut into 1-inch pieces
 ½ cup panko bread crumbs
 1 scallion (white and green
   parts only), finely chopped
   Finely grated zest and
   juice of 1 lime
 2 tablespoons soy sauce
 ½ teaspoon hot pepper sauce
 ¼ teaspoon freshly ground
   black pepper

## SALSA

 ½ cup finely chopped ripe,
   fresh pineapple
 ½ cup finely chopped ripe tomato
 2 teaspoons peeled, grated
   fresh ginger
 ½ small jalapeño chile pepper,
   seeded and minced
 ½ teaspoon kosher salt
 ⅛ teaspoon freshly ground
   black pepper
 1 large sweet onion, cut
   crosswise into ⅓-inch slices

   Vegetable oil
 6 slices sourdough bread,
   each about ⅓ inch thick
 ¼ cup plus 2 tablespoons
   mayonnaise
 6 leaves Bibb lettuce

**1.** In a food processor fitted with a metal blade, pulse the salmon pieces 8 to 10 times until coarsely chopped but not pasty; transfer to a bowl. Add the remaining patty ingredients to the bowl and stir gently to combine. Form six patties of equal size, each about ¾ inch thick. Cover and refrigerate for 1 hour.

**2.** Prepare the grill for direct cooking over medium heat (350° to 450°F).

**3.** Combine all the salsa ingredients except for the onion. Brush the onion slices on both sides with oil, and then grill over *direct medium heat*, with the lid closed, until well marked and tender, about 10 minutes, turning once or twice. Finely chop the onion and add it to the salsa. Mix well.

**4.** Brush the patties on both sides with oil, and then grill over *direct medium heat*, with the lid closed, until fully cooked but still juicy, 6 to 8 minutes, carefully turning once. During the last minute of grilling time, toast the bread over direct heat, turning once.

**5.** Spread one tablespoon mayonnaise on each bread slice and top with a lettuce leaf, a patty, and pineapple-ginger salsa. Serve warm.

# CEDAR-PLANKED SALMON BURGERS WITH MAPLE MUSTARD

SERVES: **4** | PREP TIME: **25 MINUTES** | CHILLING TIME: **1 HOUR** | GRILLING TIME: **12 TO 14 MINUTES**
SPECIAL EQUIPMENT: **1 UNTREATED CEDAR PLANK, 12 TO 15 INCHES LONG AND ABOUT 7 INCHES WIDE**

**SEAFOOD**

## PATTIES

- 1½ pounds skinless salmon fillets, pin bones removed, cut into 1-inch pieces
- ½ cup panko bread crumbs
- 3 tablespoons finely chopped scallions (white and light green parts only)
- 1 large egg, beaten
- 2 tablespoons finely chopped fresh Italian parsley leaves
- 2 teaspoons Dijon mustard
- 1 teaspoon hot pepper sauce
- 1 teaspoon kosher salt
- ½ teaspoon freshly ground black pepper

## MUSTARD

- 3 tablespoons Dijon mustard
- 1½ tablespoons maple syrup
- ¼ teaspoon kosher salt
- ¼ teaspoon freshly ground black pepper

- 1 tablespoon extra-virgin olive oil
- 4 ciabatta rolls, split
- 1 small red onion, thinly sliced
- 2 cups baby greens

1. Soak the cedar plank in water for at least 1 hour.

2. In a food processor fitted with a metal blade, pulse the salmon pieces 8 to 10 times until coarsely chopped but not pasty; transfer to a bowl. Add the remaining patty ingredients to the bowl and stir gently to combine. Form four patties of equal size, each about ¾ inch thick. Cover and refrigerate for 1 hour.

3. Whisk the mustard ingredients.

4. Prepare the grill for direct cooking over medium heat (350° to 450°F).

5. Lightly brush the patties on both sides with the oil. Place the soaked cedar plank over *direct medium heat* and close the lid. After 5 to 10 minutes, when the plank begins to smoke and char, turn the plank over. Place the patties in a single layer on the plank. Grill over *direct medium heat*, with the lid closed, until the patties are fully cooked but still juicy, 12 to 14 minutes, carefully turning once. During the last 30 seconds to 1 minute of grilling time, toast the rolls on the cooking grates, cut side down, over direct heat.

6. Build each burger on a roll with a patty, maple mustard, onion, and baby greens. Serve warm.

Char one side of the plank over direct heat before turning it over and placing the salmon patties on top. In other words, the plank should be smoking before you start cooking the patties.

# SALMON BURGERS WITH LEMON SALSA VERDE

SERVES: **4** | PREP TIME: **20 MINUTES**
CHILLING TIME: **1 HOUR** | GRILLING TIME: **6 TO 8 MINUTES**

## PATTIES

1¼ pounds skinless salmon fillets, pin bones removed, cut into 1-inch pieces
½ cup panko bread crumbs
¼ cup mayonnaise
3 tablespoons finely chopped shallot
2 tablespoons finely chopped fresh basil leaves

　Kosher salt
　Freshly ground black pepper

## SALSA

¼ cup extra-virgin olive oil
¼ cup finely chopped fresh basil leaves
1½ tablespoons capers, drained and finely chopped
　Finely grated zest of 1 lemon
1 tablespoon fresh lemon juice

　Extra-virgin olive oil
4 hamburger buns, split
4 leaves lettuce
8 slices ripe plum tomato

1. In a food processor fitted with a metal blade, pulse the salmon pieces 8 to 10 times until coarsely chopped but not pasty; transfer to a bowl. Add the remaining patty ingredients to the bowl, including ½ teaspoon salt and ¼ teaspoon pepper, and stir gently to combine. Form four patties of equal size, each about ¾ inch thick. Cover and refrigerate for 1 hour.

2. Mix the salsa ingredients and season with salt and pepper. Set aside at room temperature.

3. Prepare the grill for direct cooking over medium heat (350° to 450°F).

4. Brush the patties on both sides with oil, and then grill over *direct medium heat*, with the lid closed, until fully cooked but still juicy, 6 to 8 minutes, carefully turning once. During the last 30 seconds to 1 minute of grilling time, toast the buns, cut side down, over direct heat.

5. Build each burger on a bun with a lettuce leaf, two tomato slices, a patty, and lemon salsa verde. Serve warm.

# YELLOWTAIL BURGERS WITH WASABI MAYO AND PICKLED VEGETABLES

SERVES: **6** | PREP TIME: **30 MINUTES** | CHILLING TIME: **AT LEAST 30 MINUTES**
GRILLING TIME: **6 TO 8 MINUTES** | SPECIAL EQUIPMENT: **PERFORATED GRILL PAN**

## PATTIES

2 pounds boneless, skinless yellowtail fillet
½ cup finely chopped scallions
  (white and light green parts only)
½ cup panko bread crumbs
3 tablespoons chopped pickled sushi ginger
2 tablespoons canola oil
1½ tablespoons soy sauce
2 teaspoons toasted sesame oil
1 teaspoon wasabi paste
2 garlic cloves, minced or pushed through a press
½ teaspoon kosher salt
¼ teaspoon freshly ground black pepper

2 medium, ripe Hass avocados, finely diced
¼ cup finely diced red radishes
2 tablespoons rice vinegar
1 tablespoon mirin (sweet rice wine)
2 teaspoons toasted sesame oil, divided
⅓ cup mayonnaise
1 teaspoon wasabi paste
  Vegetable oil
6 ciabatta rolls, split

**1.** Cut the yellowtail fillet into small pieces, and place in a food processor. Pulse 8 to 10 times until coarsely chopped but not pasty; transfer to a bowl. Add the remaining patty ingredients and stir gently to combine. Form six patties of equal size, each about ¾ inch thick. Cover and refrigerate the patties for at least 30 minutes.

**2.** In a bowl combine the avocados, radishes, vinegar, mirin, and 1 teaspoon of the sesame oil.

**3.** In another bowl whisk the mayonnaise, wasabi, and the remaining 1 teaspoon sesame oil.

**4.** Prepare the grill for direct cooking over medium heat (350° to 450°F) and preheat a perforated grill pan.

**5.** Brush the patties on both sides with vegetable oil. Grill the patties on the grill pan over *direct medium heat*, with the lid closed, until fully cooked but still juicy, 6 to 8 minutes, turning once. During the last 30 seconds to 1 minute of grilling time, toast the rolls on the cooking grates, cut side down, over direct heat.

**6.** Build each burger on a roll with wasabi mayo, a patty, and pickled vegetables. Serve warm.

# TUNA PATTIES WITH CREAMY GINGER SLAW

SERVES: **4** | PREP TIME: **40 MINUTES** | FREEZING TIME: **2 HOURS** | CHILLING TIME: **1 TO 2 HOURS**
GRILLING TIME: **5 TO 6 MINUTES** | SPECIAL EQUIPMENT: **GRILL-PROOF GRIDDLE**

## PATTIES

- 3 skinless ahi tuna steaks, each about 6 ounces and 1 inch thick
- 6–8 tablespoons panko bread crumbs
- 3 tablespoons cottage cheese
- 1 large egg
- 2 large egg yolks
- 1 medium shallot, minced
- 2 teaspoons peeled, grated fresh ginger
  Finely grated zest of 1 lime
- ½ teaspoon kosher salt
- ⅓ teaspoon freshly ground black pepper

## DRESSING

- ¼ cup mayonnaise
- ¼ cup pickled sushi ginger, drained
- 2½ tablespoons rice vinegar
- 2 tablespoons toasted sesame oil
- 1 small shallot, thinly sliced
- 1½ tablespoons mirin (sweet rice wine) (optional)
- 6–7 fresh basil leaves
- 1 tablespoon low-sodium soy sauce
- 1 tablespoon granulated sugar
- 2 large garlic cloves, thinly sliced

- 1 small head savoy cabbage, cored and very thinly sliced
- 1 fennel bulb, trimmed, quartered, cored, and very thinly sliced
- 3 scallions, ends trimmed and finely chopped
  Extra-virgin olive oil
- 4 small, ripe tomatoes, each cut in half
- 2 tablespoons roughly chopped fresh Italian parsley leaves

1. Freeze the tuna steaks for 2 hours (this will make it easier to chop them).

2. Finely chop the tuna. Pat dry. Combine all of the patty ingredients, starting with 6 tablespoons panko. Blend well with a fork. Gently squeeze a bit of the mixture to see if it clumps; if not, add up to two additional tablespoons panko. Form four patties of equal size, each about 1 inch thick. Cover and refrigerate for 1 to 2 hours. Leave the patties in the refrigerator until right before grilling.

3. Prepare the grill for direct cooking over high heat (450° to 550°F) and preheat a grill-proof griddle.

4. Meanwhile, in a food processor fitted with a metal blade, combine the dressing ingredients and process until smooth. In a large bowl toss the cabbage and fennel with the dressing. Just before serving, fold in the scallions.

5. Brush the patties on both sides with oil. Grill the patties on the griddle over *direct high heat*, with the lid closed, until firm but still pink in the center, 5 to 6 minutes, carefully turning once after 4 minutes. During the last minute of grilling time, warm the tomato halves on the cooking grates, cut side down, over direct heat.

6. Serve the patties warm with creamy ginger slaw and tomato halves. Garnish with parsley.

Panko bread crumbs are the preferred binder for all kinds of seafood burgers, because they have a coarser texture than traditional bread crumbs. In fact, they are more like jagged flakes than crumbs, meaning that they don't soak up as much moisture and turn dense. They maintain a certain airiness that makes the burgers themselves wonderfully light.

# WHAT'S THE DILL?

Consider their longevity: Aristotle praised pickles' healing powers, Cleopatra credited them as a beauty aid, and George Washington was such a fan that he had a collection of more than 400 varieties. From Biblical and Shakespearean references to a hitched ride on Christopher Columbus's voyages, the humble cured cuke sure has gotten a lot of press. But it doesn't stop there.

Today's modern pickle is more popular than ever. According to Pickle Packers International, Inc., Americans consume more than 20 billion pickles each year—that's about nine pounds of pickles per person. It makes sense, then, that half of the United States' cucumber crop is specifically grown for pickle production.

You may be thinking: *There's no way that I eat nine pounds of pickles each year ... oh wait. You mean fried pickles, too? Yep, make that 10 pounds.* These crisp, tangy, easy-to-eat little treats are delicious fresh or fried, on burgers and sandwiches, in salads and dips, and, of course, on their own. Plus, pickles are fat free and low in calories—when served in their original form.

From chips to spears to sandwich slices, dill to half-sour to sweet, and relish to salad cubes to pickled peppers, there are literally hundreds of pickle varieties. It only seems fair to begin with the daddy of them all, the world's most popular pickle: the Grand Dillmeister. Even within the dill division, you'll find dozens of types, including genuine, overnight, and kosher, to name a few. Highly acidic, and some say sour, genuine dills are processed and fermented slowly with dill weed; whereas, the crunchy, bright green overnight dills are brined quickly and are *always* refrigerated. Robust and flavorful, kosher dills, while not always truly "kosher" by rabbinic standards, are fermented and distinctly garlic flavored.

Occupying the opposite end of the pickle spectrum, sweet pickles are classically packed in sugar, spices, and vinegar. Sweet and slightly tangy, the perennial favorite bread-and-butter pickle supposedly got its name in the 1920s from a man whose family had fallen on hard times. His solution? Selling cucumbers pickled with onions and peppers on the street corner. His quick pickle fix was successful enough to put bread and butter on his own table—and his bread-and-butter brainchildren on relish trays throughout the United States.

But what about the brine? For many, pickle brine is both a curative and culinary commodity. Some athletes swear by drinking pickle juice for its scientifically proven, electrolyte-restoring prowess in preventing post-workout muscle cramps. It's hailed by others as a hangover remedy (and prevention) and a heartburn cure. And with its complex flavor, it's a tasty addition to salad dressings and soups, marinades and Bloody Marys. Plus, pickle juice is a great weed killer. Cramp-free, pickle cocktail in hand, overlooking a picture perfect lawn—who's laughing now?

We're now in a bit of a pickle renaissance, with boutique brands made from locally sourced heirloom cucumber varieties popping up at markets regularly. Are pickles the next big thing in food, or are they just getting their due? Definitely the latter. Pickles are the real dill.

135

# MAHIMAHI BURGERS WITH MISO MAYO

SERVES: **4** | PREP TIME: **20 MINUTES** | CHILLING TIME: **6 TO 8 HOURS**
GRILLING TIME: **6 TO 8 MINUTES** | SPECIAL EQUIPMENT: **GRILL-PROOF GRIDDLE**

SEAFOOD

1¼ pounds skinless mahimahi fillets, pin bones
removed, patted dry, and cut into 1-inch pieces
1 large egg, beaten
3 tablespoons white miso paste, divided
¼ teaspoon toasted sesame oil
⅓ cup panko bread crumbs, toasted in a dry skillet
1 tablespoon sesame seeds, toasted in a dry skillet
¼ teaspoon kosher salt
½ cup mayonnaise
1 tablespoon vegetable oil
4 sesame seed buns, split
1 medium, ripe beefsteak tomato, cut crosswise
into 4 slices
1 cup thinly sliced English cucumber

Most seafood patties
are so delicate that it
is best to cook them
on a grill-proof griddle.

1. In a food processor fitted with a metal blade, pulse the mahimahi pieces 8 to 10 times until coarsely chopped but not pasty. Add the egg, 1 tablespoon of the miso paste, and the sesame oil. Pulse a few times until just blended, being careful to leave some texture. Transfer to a bowl and gently stir in the panko, sesame seeds, and salt. Form four patties of equal size, each about ¾ inch thick. Cover and refrigerate for 6 to 8 hours.

2. Prepare the grill for direct cooking over medium heat (350° to 450°F) and preheat a grill-proof griddle.

3. Whisk the mayonnaise and the remaining 2 tablespoons miso paste. Cover and refrigerate until ready to use.

4. Drizzle the vegetable oil on the griddle. Place the patties on the griddle and cook over *direct medium heat*, with the lid closed, until fully cooked but still moist, 6 to 8 minutes, turning once. During the last 30 seconds to 1 minute of grilling time, toast the buns on the cooking grates, cut side down, over direct heat.

5. Build each burger on a bun with miso mayo, a patty, a tomato slice, and cucumber slices. Serve immediately.

# RED BEAN AND MUSHROOM BURGERS WITH CHILE MAYO

SERVES: **4** | PREP TIME: **20 MINUTES** | CHILLING TIME: **30 MINUTES**
GRILLING TIME: **6 TO 8 MINUTES** | SPECIAL EQUIPMENT: **GRILL-PROOF GRIDDLE**

VEGETARIAN

## PATTIES

   2 tablespoons extra-virgin olive oil
   4 ounces button or cremini mushrooms,
     cleaned, stems removed, and finely chopped
   2 tablespoons minced jalapeño chile pepper
     (without seeds)
   2 garlic cloves, minced or pushed through a press
   1 can (15 ounces) low-sodium pinto beans,
     rinsed and drained
   ½ cup panko bread crumbs
   1 large egg, beaten
   ¾ teaspoon kosher salt
   ½ teaspoon ground cumin

   ⅓ cup mayonnaise
   1½ teaspoons minced canned chipotle chile pepper
     in adobo sauce
     Extra-virgin olive oil
   4 hamburger buns, split
   4 large leaves crisp lettuce
   8 slices ripe tomato

1. In a skillet over medium-high heat, warm the oil. Add the mushrooms and cook until tender, about 3 minutes, stirring occasionally. Add the jalapeño and garlic and cook until lightly browned, 2 to 3 minutes. Transfer to a food processor fitted with a metal blade, add the remaining patty ingredients, and pulse several times until coarsely chopped. Form four patties of equal size, each about ½ inch thick. Refrigerate the patties for 30 minutes.

2. Prepare the grill for direct cooking over medium heat (350° to 450°F) and preheat a grill-proof griddle.

3. Combine the mayonnaise and chipotle chile pepper.

4. Generously brush the patties on both sides with oil. Place the patties on the griddle and cook over *direct medium heat*, with the lid closed, until browned, 6 to 8 minutes, turning once. During the last 30 seconds to 1 minute of grilling time, toast the buns on the cooking grates, cut side down, over direct heat.

5. Build each burger on a bun with chile mayo, a lettuce leaf, two tomato slices, and a patty. Serve immediately.

# BLACK BEAN CHEESEBURGERS WITH AVOCADO

SERVES: **4** | PREP TIME: **20 MINUTES** | CHILLING TIME: **1 TO 4 HOURS**
GRILLING TIME: **6 TO 8 MINUTES** | SPECIAL EQUIPMENT: **PERFORATED GRILL PAN**

1 can (15 ounces) black beans, rinsed and drained
¼ cup fresh cilantro or Italian parsley leaves
1 shallot, thinly sliced
2 garlic cloves, thinly sliced
¾ teaspoon pure chile powder
½ teaspoon dried oregano
  Extra-virgin olive oil
  Kosher salt
  Freshly ground black pepper
1 large egg
1 large egg white
¾ cup panko bread crumbs
4 thin slices pepper jack cheese
4 whole-wheat buns, split
¼ cup mayonnaise
4 leaves romaine lettuce
2 small, ripe Hass avocados, cut into thin slices

Bean burgers lend themselves to lots of variations. Use chickpeas or kidney beans instead. Choose different herbs. Substitute a cooked grain like quinoa or brown rice for an equal amount of the beans. But always pay special attention to the texture: it should be moist (yet not wet) when you shape the patties.

**1.** In a food processor fitted with a metal blade, combine the beans, cilantro, shallot, garlic, chile powder, oregano, 1 tablespoon oil, ½ teaspoon salt, and ¼ teaspoon pepper and pulse 15 to 20 times to form a thick, slightly chunky paste. Transfer to a large bowl. In a small bowl whisk the egg and egg white until blended. Add the eggs and panko to the large bowl and combine thoroughly. The mixture should be quite thick. Form four compact patties of equal size, each about ¾ inch thick. Cover and refrigerate the patties for 1 to 4 hours.

**2.** Prepare the grill for direct cooking over medium-high heat (400° to 500°F) and preheat a perforated grill pan.

**3.** Brush the patties on both sides with oil and season evenly with salt and pepper. Place the patties on the grill pan and cook over *direct medium-high heat*, with the lid closed, until browned and warm throughout, 6 to 8 minutes, carefully turning once. During the last 30 seconds to 1 minute of grilling time, place a slice of cheese on each patty to melt, and toast the buns on the cooking grates, cut side down, over direct heat.

**4.** Build each burger on a bun with mayonnaise, a lettuce leaf, a patty, and avocado slices. Serve warm.

# CURRIED RED LENTIL BURGERS WITH MANGO CHUTNEY

SERVES: **4**  |  PREP TIME: **25 MINUTES**  |  CHILLING TIME: **2 TO 4 HOURS**
GRILLING TIME: **5 TO 7 MINUTES**  |  SPECIAL EQUIPMENT: **GRILL-PROOF GRIDDLE**

½ cup red lentils, sorted, rinsed in a fine-mesh strainer, and drained
2 cups water
1 can (15 ounces) chickpeas (garbanzo beans), rinsed and drained
¾ cup roasted, salted peanuts
2 teaspoons curry powder
2 teaspoons ground cumin
½ teaspoon kosher salt
¼ teaspoon freshly ground black pepper
½ cup panko bread crumbs
½ cup plain Greek yogurt
2 large eggs, beaten
2 tablespoons minced fresh cilantro leaves
1 tablespoon vegetable oil
4 large pita pockets
2 cups shredded butter lettuce
1 cup thinly sliced English cucumber
½ cup mango chutney

**1.** In a saucepan combine the lentils and water. Bring to a boil. Skim off any foam that rises to the top. Reduce the heat to medium-low and simmer until tender, 10 to 20 minutes. Drain well, rinse briefly, and let cool.

**2.** In a food processor fitted with a metal blade, pulse the lentils, chickpeas, peanuts, curry powder, cumin, salt, and pepper to form a thick, slightly chunky paste. Transfer to a bowl and fold in the panko, yogurt, eggs, and cilantro until combined. Form four gently packed patties, each about ¾ inch thick. The patties will be quite wet. Cover and refrigerate the patties for 2 to 4 hours.

**3.** Prepare the grill for direct cooking over medium-high heat (400° to 500°F) and preheat a grill-proof griddle.

**4.** Coat the griddle lightly with the oil. Place the patties on the griddle and cook over *direct medium-high heat*, with the lid closed, until firm and nicely marked, 5 to 7 minutes, carefully turning once. During the last minute of grilling time, warm the pitas on the cooking grates over direct heat, turning once.

**5.** Cut the pitas and patties in half. Place a patty half inside each pita half. Divide the lettuce, cucumber, and mango chutney among the pitas, tucking the ingredients inside. Serve immediately.

VEGETARIAN

# CHICKPEA PATTIES WITH LEMON PICKLED ONION

SERVES: **6** | PREP TIME: **45 MINUTES** | CHILLING TIME: **3 TO 4 HOURS**
GRILLING TIME: **6 TO 8 MINUTES** | SPECIAL EQUIPMENT: **GRILL-PROOF GRIDDLE**

2 cans (each 15 ounces) chickpeas (garbanzo beans),
  rinsed and drained, divided
2 garlic cloves, chopped
1 large egg, lightly beaten
¼ cup tahini
½ cup fresh lemon juice, divided
1 teaspoon ground cumin
1 teaspoon ground coriander
½ teaspoon freshly ground black pepper
¼ teaspoon ground cayenne pepper
  Kosher salt
½ cup whole milk plain Greek yogurt
½ cup panko bread crumbs
¼ cup finely chopped fresh cilantro leaves
2 tablespoons minced red jalapeño chile pepper
  (without seeds)
1 medium red onion, cut in half and thinly sliced
½ teaspoon granulated sugar

## SAUCE

¾ cup whole milk plain Greek yogurt
2 tablespoons fresh lemon juice
1 tablespoon tahini
2 teaspoons harissa *or* hot pepper sauce
⅛ teaspoon granulated sugar

  Extra-virgin olive oil
1 tablespoon finely chopped fresh
  Italian parsley leaves
1 tablespoon finely chopped fresh mint leaves
  Chopped ripe tomato
  Harissa *or* hot pepper sauce

1. Place half of the chickpeas in a food processor fitted with a metal blade. Add the garlic, egg, tahini, ¼ cup of the lemon juice, the cumin, coriander, black pepper, cayenne pepper, and 1 teaspoon salt. Process to blend.

Add the remaining chickpeas, the yogurt, panko, cilantro, and jalapeño. Pulse for 10 to 15 one-second bursts to coarsely blend. Gently form six patties, each about ¾ inch thick. Place on a sheet pan lined with wax paper. Cover and refrigerate the patties for 3 to 4 hours. Meanwhile, prepare the pickled onion.

2. Place the onion in a heatproof bowl. Pour in boiling water to cover the onion and let stand for 5 minutes. Rinse under cold water and drain. Blot dry. In a medium bowl whisk the lemon juice, sugar, and ¼ teaspoon salt until the sugar and salt are dissolved. Add the onion and toss to combine. Set aside at room temperature for 1 hour, stirring once or twice.

3. Prepare the grill for direct cooking over medium heat (350° to 450°F) and preheat a grill-proof griddle.

4. Whisk the sauce ingredients, including ½ teaspoon salt.

5. Brush the tops of the patties with oil. Place the patties on the griddle, oiled side down, and remove the wax paper. Cook over *direct medium heat*, with the lid closed, for 3 to 4 minutes. Oil the tops of the patties, turn them over, and continue cooking until browned and heated through, 3 to 4 minutes more.

6. Add the parsley and mint to the pickled onion. Top the patties with sauce, pickled onion, tomato, and harissa. Serve warm.

Rather than lifting fragile patties with your hands alone, cut the wax paper underneath them, and use the paper to support the patties as you take them to the grill.

# QUINOA AND PINTO BEAN BURGERS WITH YOGURT SAUCE

SERVES: **6** | PREP TIME: **50 MINUTES** | CHILLING TIME: **1 TO 3 HOURS**
GRILLING TIME: **8 TO 10 MINUTES** | SPECIAL EQUIPMENT: **GRILL-PROOF GRIDDLE**

## SAUCE

- ½ cup plain Greek yogurt
- 3 tablespoons finely chopped fresh cilantro leaves
- 1 garlic clove, minced or pushed through a press

  Kosher salt
  Freshly ground black pepper

## PATTIES

- ½ cup yellow or red quinoa, rinsed in a fine-mesh strainer, drained
- 1 cup water
  Extra-virgin olive oil
- 1 cup finely chopped red onion
- ¾ cup finely chopped red bell pepper
- 2 garlic cloves, minced or pushed through a press
- 1 can (15 ounces) pinto beans, rinsed and drained
- 1 cup fresh or thawed frozen corn kernels
- 1 cup panko bread crumbs
- 1 large egg, lightly beaten
- 3 tablespoons plain Greek yogurt
- 3 tablespoons coarsely chopped fresh cilantro leaves
- 1 teaspoon finely grated lime zest
- 1 tablespoon fresh lime juice
- ½ teaspoon hot chili-garlic sauce, such as Sriracha

- 6 hamburger buns, split
- 1 cup tightly packed baby arugula
- 2 medium, ripe plum tomatoes, each cut crosswise into 6 slices

1. Mix the sauce ingredients and season with salt and pepper. Refrigerate until ready to use.

2. In a saucepan over medium-high heat, bring the quinoa, water, and 1 teaspoon salt to a boil. Cover the saucepan and reduce the heat to low. Simmer until the quinoa is tender and the water is almost absorbed, 18 to 20 minutes. Remove from the heat, keep covered, and let stand for 5 minutes. Drain the quinoa in a fine-mesh strainer to remove any excess water. Let cool completely.

3. In a skillet over medium heat, warm 1 tablespoon oil. Add the onion, bell pepper, and garlic. Cook until tender, about 8 minutes, stirring occasionally. Remove from the heat and cool completely.

4. In a food processor fitted with a metal blade, combine the quinoa, the onion mixture, and the remaining patty ingredients, including 1 teaspoon salt. Pulse until well combined and the corn is coarsely chopped.

5. Generously oil a rimmed sheet pan. Transfer one-sixth of the quinoa mixture to the sheet pan and form into a 3-inch patty, ½ to ¾ inch thick. Repeat with the remaining quinoa mixture. Cover and refrigerate the patties for 1 to 3 hours.

6. Prepare the grill for direct cooking over medium heat (350° to 450°F) and preheat a grill-proof griddle.

7. Brush the tops of the patties with oil and drizzle 1 tablespoon oil on the griddle. Place the patties on the griddle, oiled side down, and cook over *direct medium heat*, with the lid closed, until the undersides are golden brown, 4 to 5 minutes. Brush the tops of the patties with oil, turn them over, and continue cooking until the other side is golden brown, 4 to 5 minutes more. During the last 30 seconds to 1 minute of grilling time, toast the buns on the cooking grates, cut side down, over direct heat.

8. Build each burger on a bun with arugula, two tomato slices, a patty, and a dollop of yogurt sauce. Serve immediately.

# FARRO AND CANNELLINI BURGERS WITH GRILLED RADICCHIO SLAW

SERVES: **4** | PREP TIME: **35 MINUTES, PLUS 20 TO 25 MINUTES FOR THE FARRO** | CHILLING TIME: **1 TO 3 HOURS**
GRILLING TIME: **12 TO 16 MINUTES** | SPECIAL EQUIPMENT: **GRILL-PROOF GRIDDLE**

VEGETARIAN

## PATTIES

- 1¼ cups water
- ½ cup semi-pearled or pearled farro
- 1½ teaspoons kosher salt, divided
- ½ cup chopped scallions
  (white and light green parts only)
- 2 garlic cloves, roughly chopped
- ½ teaspoon crushed red pepper flakes
- 1 can (15 ounces) cannellini beans, rinsed and drained
- 2 large eggs
- ½ cup fresh bread crumbs
- ½ cup freshly grated Parmigiano-Reggiano® cheese
- 2 tablespoons chopped fresh basil leaves
- 1 tablespoon red wine vinegar

  Extra-virgin olive oil

## SLAW

- 1 small head radicchio, 6 to 7 ounces,
  cut lengthwise in half
- 2 cups thinly sliced butter or romaine lettuce
- ¼ cup thinly slivered fresh basil leaves
- 1 teaspoon balsamic vinegar
- ½ teaspoon kosher salt
- ¼ teaspoon freshly ground black pepper

- 8 slices crusty Italian bread, each about ¼ inch thick
- ⅓ cup mayonnaise

**1.** In a saucepan over medium heat, bring the water, farro, and ½ teaspoon of the salt to a boil. Cover and reduce the heat to medium-low. Simmer until the farro is tender and almost all of the water is absorbed, 20 to 25 minutes. Drain, rinse under cold water, and drain again. Cool completely.

**2.** In a food processor fitted with a metal blade, first add the scallions, garlic, and red pepper flakes, then add the farro, the remaining 1 teaspoon salt, the beans, eggs, bread crumbs, cheese, basil, and vinegar. Pulse until the mixture is combined and the farro is coarsely chopped.

**3.** Generously oil a sheet pan. Transfer one-fourth of the farro mixture to the sheet pan and, with oiled hands, form into a 3-inch oval patty (to fit the bread slices). Repeat with the remaining farro mixture. Cover and refrigerate the patties for 1 to 3 hours.

**4.** Prepare the grill for direct cooking over medium heat (350° to 450°F) and preheat a grill-proof griddle.

**5.** Brush the radicchio halves with oil, place them on the cooking grates, and grill over *direct medium heat*, with the lid closed, until lightly browned on the outside but still raw inside, 4 to 6 minutes, turning once. Remove from the grill and let cool. Cut out the core, and cut the radicchio crosswise into ¼-inch strips. In a bowl toss the radicchio, lettuce, and basil with 1 tablespoon oil and the vinegar. Season with the salt and pepper.

**6.** Brush the patties on both sides with oil and drizzle 1 tablespoon oil on the griddle. Place the patties on the griddle and cook over *direct medium heat*, with the lid closed, until golden brown, 8 to 10 minutes, carefully turning once. During the last 30 seconds of grilling time, toast the bread slices on the cooking grates over direct heat, one side only.

**7.** Brush the un-grilled side of four slices of the bread with mayonnaise, and top with the patties, radicchio slaw, and the remaining bread slices. Serve immediately.

*Serving suggestion: Tomato and Avocado Salad with Lemon-Caper Vinaigrette (for recipe, see page 208).*

Shaping these patties right on an oiled sheet pan is the simplest way to handle the sticky farro-and-bean mixture.

# GREEK EGGPLANT SLIDERS WITH CREAMY FETA SAUCE

SERVES: **6 TO 8 (MAKES 12 SLIDERS)** | PREP TIME: **30 MINUTES** | CHILLING TIME: **30 MINUTES**
GRILLING TIME: **13 TO 15 MINUTES** | SPECIAL EQUIPMENT: **GRILL-PROOF GRIDDLE**

### SAUCE
4½ ounces feta cheese, crumbled
¼ cup plain Greek yogurt
1 tablespoon mayonnaise
1 tablespoon fresh lemon juice
½ teaspoon paprika

Freshly ground black pepper

### PATTIES
2 globe eggplants, about 2½ pounds total,
   ends trimmed, cut crosswise into ½-inch slices
   Extra-virgin olive oil
   Kosher salt
1½ cups panko bread crumbs
1 cup finely grated Asiago cheese
1 large egg, lightly beaten
¼ cup finely chopped yellow onion
¼ cup finely chopped fresh Italian parsley leaves
½ teaspoon dried oregano
2 garlic cloves, minced or pushed through a press
¼ teaspoon ground cayenne pepper

12 slider buns, split
24 large fresh basil leaves
12 thin slices red onion

Eggplant sliders are at their best when their
texture is a little chunky, not completely
smooth. Grill the slices first and then
pulse them just until coarsely chopped.

1. In a food processor fitted with a metal blade, combine the sauce ingredients, including ½ teaspoon pepper, and process until smooth. Transfer to a small bowl.

2. Prepare the grill for direct cooking over medium heat (350° to 450°F).

3. Brush the eggplant slices on both sides with oil and season evenly with ¾ teaspoon salt. Grill over *direct medium heat*, with the lid closed, until charred and soft, 8 to 10 minutes, turning once or twice. Remove from the grill and cool slightly, and then cut each slice into quarters. Place the eggplant in the food processor and pulse 8 to 10 times until blended but not completely smooth. Transfer to a large bowl. Add the remaining patty ingredients, including 1 teaspoon salt and ½ teaspoon pepper, and stir to combine. Gently form 12 patties of equal size, each about ½ inch thick. Cover and refrigerate the patties for 30 minutes.

4. Preheat a grill-proof griddle over *direct medium heat*. Add 2 tablespoons oil to the griddle. Place the patties on the griddle and cook over *direct medium heat*, with the lid closed, until browned on both sides and heated through, about 5 minutes, turning once. During the last 30 seconds to 1 minute of grilling time, toast the buns on the cooking grates, cut side down, over direct heat.

5. Build each slider on a bun with creamy feta sauce, a patty, two basil leaves, and an onion slice. Serve warm.

# CAPRESE BURGERS

SERVES: **4** | PREP TIME: **20 MINUTES** | GRILLING TIME: **11 TO 15 MINUTES**

## PESTO

- 1 garlic clove
- 3 tablespoons toasted pine nuts
- 1½ cups tightly packed fresh basil leaves
- ⅓ cup extra-virgin olive oil
- ⅓ cup freshly grated Parmigiano-Reggiano® cheese
- ¼ teaspoon kosher salt
- ⅛ teaspoon freshly ground black pepper

<br>

- 1 large red onion, cut crosswise into four ½-inch slices
- 1 ripe beefsteak tomato, cut crosswise into four ½-inch slices
- 2 tablespoons extra-virgin olive oil
- ½ teaspoon kosher salt
- ¼ teaspoon freshly g=round black pepper
- 4 focaccia squares, each about 4½ inches in diameter, split
- 2 tablespoons balsamic vinegar
- 8 ounces fresh mozzarella cheese, cut into 8 slices, at room temperature

To toast pine nuts, heat them in a preheated skillet over medium heat until light golden, about 3 minutes, shaking the skillet occasionally and watching carefully to prevent burning.

**1.** Prepare the grill for direct and indirect cooking over medium heat (350° to 450°F).

**2.** In a food processor fitted with a metal blade, puree the garlic. Add the pine nuts and pulse until finely chopped. Add the basil and process to a coarse puree. With the motor running, add the oil through the feed tube and process until almost smooth. Add the cheese, salt, and pepper and process until just combined. Transfer to a bowl.

**3.** Brush the onion and tomato slices with the oil and season evenly with the salt and pepper. Grill the vegetables over *direct medium heat*, with the lid closed, until tender and nicely marked, turning once. The onion will take 8 to 12 minutes, and

the tomato will take 2 to 4 minutes. During the last 30 seconds to 1 minute of grilling time, toast the focaccia, cut side down, over direct heat.

**4.** Brush the toasted side of the focaccia with the vinegar. Top each bottom half with one onion slice, one tomato slice, and two mozzarella slices. Spread the top halves of the focaccia with the pesto (you may not need all of it) and place pesto side down on top of the mozzarella. Grill the burgers over *indirect medium heat*, with the lid closed, until the cheese melts slightly and the bread is hot, 3 to 5 minutes (do not turn). Serve immediately.

# PORTABELLO BURGERS WITH CHEDDAR AND GRILLED RED PEPPERS

SERVES: **4** | PREP TIME: **25 MINUTES** | MARINATING TIME: **20 MINUTES** | GRILLING TIME: **10 TO 15 MINUTES**

## MARINADE

- ¼ cup plus 2 tablespoons extra-virgin olive oil
- 2 tablespoons balsamic vinegar
- 2 tablespoons finely chopped shallots
- 1 tablespoon soy sauce
- ½ tablespoon honey
- 1 teaspoon Dijon mustard
- 1 garlic clove, minced or pushed through a press

- 4 large portabello mushrooms, each 4 to 5 inches in diameter, stems and gills removed, wiped clean
- 1 red onion, cut crosswise into four ½-inch slices
- 2 medium red bell peppers, each cut into 4 planks
- ¾ teaspoon kosher salt
- ¼ teaspoon freshly ground black pepper
- 4 slices mild cheddar cheese
- 4 hamburger buns, split
- 20 small fresh basil leaves

**1.** Whisk the marinade ingredients. Reserve ⅓ cup of the marinade in a separate bowl for basting the mushrooms and brushing the buns.

**2.** Prepare the grill for direct cooking over medium heat (350° to 450°F).

**3.** Generously brush the mushrooms and onion slices with the remaining marinade. Let stand at room temperature for 20 minutes.

**4.** Season the vegetables evenly with the salt and pepper. Grill the mushrooms, gill side down first, over *direct medium heat,* with the lid closed, until tender when pierced with the tip of a knife,

8 to 12 minutes, basting with half of the reserved marinade and turning occasionally. At the same time, grill the bell peppers and onion over *direct medium heat* until tender, 8 to 12 minutes, turning occasionally. During the last 30 seconds to 1 minute of grilling time, place one slice of cheese on the gill side of each mushroom to melt, and toast the buns, cut side down, over direct heat.

**5.** Brush the cut side of the buns with the remaining reserved marinade. Build each burger on a bun with two bell pepper planks, one mushroom, an onion slice, and five basil leaves. Serve immediately.

# WINE COUNTRY MUSHROOM BURGERS WITH GOAT CHEESE

SERVES: **4** | PREP TIME: **20 MINUTES** | MARINATING TIME: **30 MINUTES TO 1 HOUR** | GRILLING TIME: **10 TO 12 MINUTES**

## MARINADE
- ¼ cup full-bodied red wine
- 1 tablespoon chopped fresh rosemary leaves
- 2 garlic cloves, minced or pushed through a press
- 1 teaspoon kosher salt
- ½ teaspoon freshly ground black pepper
- ⅓ cup extra-virgin olive oil

- 4 large portabello mushrooms, each 4 to 5 inches in diameter, stems and gills removed, wiped clean

## ONIONS
- 1 tablespoon extra-virgin olive oil
- 2 large yellow onions, thinly sliced (about 3 cups)
- 1 tablespoon finely chopped fresh rosemary leaves
- ½ teaspoon kosher salt
- ¼ teaspoon granulated sugar
- 2 tablespoons full-bodied red wine
- ¼ teaspoon freshly ground black pepper

- 4 ounces fresh goat cheese, crumbled
- 4 ciabatta rolls, halved
- 2 cups mixed baby greens

1. Whisk the wine, rosemary, garlic, salt, and pepper. Add the oil in a steady stream, whisking constantly to emulsify. Arrange the mushrooms in a single layer on a rimmed sheet pan. Liberally brush the mushrooms on all sides with the marinade, and marinate at room temperature for 30 minutes to 1 hour. Meanwhile, prepare the onions.

2. In a skillet over medium heat, warm the oil. Add the onions, rosemary, salt, and sugar. Cook until the onions turn golden brown, about 20 minutes, stirring occasionally. Add the wine and cook until the liquid evaporates, about 2 minutes, stirring once or twice. Remove from the heat and season with the pepper.

3. Prepare the grill for direct cooking over medium heat (350° to 450°F).

4. Grill the mushrooms, gill side down first, over *direct medium heat*, with the lid closed, until juicy and tender, 10 to 12 minutes, turning once or twice and basting with any juices from the sheet pan. During the last 2 minutes of grilling time, turn the mushrooms to remove any collected juice in their caps, arrange them gill side up, and sprinkle the cavities with an equal amount of the cheese. During the last 30 seconds to 1 minute of grilling time, toast the rolls, cut side down, over direct heat.

5. Build each burger on a roll with greens, a mushroom, and onions. Serve immediately.

Mushrooms dry out quickly, so brush them with the leftover marinade once or twice to keep them moist.

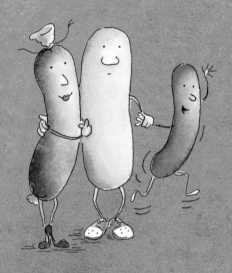

# HOT DOGS,
# SAUSAGES
# & BRATS

# HOT DOG GEOGRAPHY

If you want to know where someone is from, listen to how they talk. If you *really* want to know where they're from, listen to them talk about their hot dogs. About as big a source of regional pride (and competitiveness) as our sports allegiances, Americans' take on hot dogs is as inventive and diverse as we are. Whether they are steamed in a cart, drenched in chili, or doused in cheese, we're passionately linked to our links. Take a taste of some regional traditions.

**SEATTLE DOG**

*Seattle, Washington*

For those who like a schmear: hear, hear. Inside a toasted bun lined with cream cheese lies a hot dog or Polish sausage that is grilled, split, and topped with grilled onions and cabbage, jalapeños, and any variety of other toppings and sauces.

**SONORAN DOG**

*Arizona*

This meaty number comprises a bacon-wrapped hot dog tucked into a soft Mexican *bolillo* roll and topped with chopped tomatoes and onions, pinto beans, jalapeño salsa, mustard, and mayonnaise. *Ay, caramba!* (For recipe, see page 160.)

**REUBEN DOG**

*Kansas City, Missouri*

This is the frank of choice at Kauffman Stadium, where the Royals play. Here, hot dogs are done the deli way: with melted Swiss, sauerkraut, caraway seeds, and Thousand Island dressing. Is there such a thing as a rye bun? There ought to be.

### CHICAGO-STYLE HOT DOG

*Chicago, Illinois*

Purists demand an all-beef frank on a poppy seed bun, and toppings *must* include the following: diced onions, sliced tomatoes, super green sweet pickle relish, spicy pickled green sport peppers, a dill pickle spear, yellow mustard, and a dusting of celery salt—no substitutions, and *never* ketchup. (For recipe, see page 159.)

### DETROIT CONEY DOG

*Detroit, Michigan*

This petite hot dog in a steamed bun is topped with no-bean chili, mustard, onions, and—if you ask for it "loaded"—grated cheddar. Did we mention the chili ought to be made with beef heart? Don't say we didn't warn you.

### SLAW DOG

*West Virginia*

Here we've got a three-course meal on a steamed bun, and a common sight on menus all over the South. A frank is blanketed in spicy chili and capped with mayo-based coleslaw, creating that hot-spicy-cool-crunchy-creamy sensation that can really only be found when chili and slaw meet on a hot dog.

### NEW YORK DOG

*New York, New York*

Visualize a quick lunch for a harried New Yorker: an all-beef frank is plucked from a warm water bath in a street cart, dressed with a couple squirts of brown mustard, sauerkraut, or onions stewed in tomato paste, and eaten tie-over-shoulder while heading to a power meeting. Or so we imagine. (For recipe, see page 166.)

### ITALIAN DOG

*Newark, New Jersey*

How to make a hot dog more indulgent in three easy steps: (1) deep-fry your frank; (2) stuff it into a half-moon of pizza bread or an Italian roll; and (3) top with fried or grilled onions, peppers, and fried potatoes. All that is left to do is *mangia*, New Jersey–style.

### NEW YORK SYSTEM HOT WIENER

*Providence, Rhode Island*

And you may ask yourself, why "New York" if this is Rhode Island? Supposedly, the creators were New Yorkers before heading to the Ocean State. Small, griddled "wieners" in natural casings are topped with ground beef sauce, mustard, diced onions, and a dash of celery salt. Skilled purveyors can line up a dozen on the inside of a forearm for easy serving.

# CALIFORNIA HOT DOGS WITH AVOCADO, ARUGULA, AND BASIL CREMA

SERVES: **4** | PREP TIME: **20 MINUTES** | GRILLING TIME: **4 TO 5 MINUTES**

## CREMA

- ½ cup sour cream
- ¼ cup roughly chopped fresh basil leaves
- 1 scallion, trimmed and roughly chopped
- ½ teaspoon fresh lemon juice
- ¼ teaspoon kosher salt
- 1 small garlic clove, chopped
- ⅛ teaspoon hot pepper sauce, or to taste

- 4 best-quality all-beef hot dogs
- 4 hot dog buns, split
- 1 large, ripe Hass avocado, cut into thin slices
- ½ cup baby arugula, roughly chopped
- ½ cup grated carrots
- ½ cup diced English cucumber
- ¼ cup fresh or thawed frozen corn kernels

1. Prepare the grill for direct cooking over medium heat (350° to 450°F).

2. In a food processor fitted with a metal blade, combine the crema ingredients and process until smooth.

3. Cut a few shallow slashes in each hot dog. Grill the hot dogs over *direct medium heat,* with the lid closed, until hot all the way to the center, 4 to 5 minutes, turning occasionally. During the last 30 seconds to 1 minute of grilling time, toast the buns, cut side down, over direct heat.

4. Place each hot dog in a bun and top with avocado, arugula, carrots, cucumber, corn, and basil crema. Serve immediately.

**FUN FACT**

Did you know that avocados don't ripen on the tree? They must be picked to initiate ripening, which is why many times the supermarket shelves are piled high with this rock-hard fruit. To speed up the ripening process, place your avocado in a paper bag with an apple or a banana; these fruits emit ethylene gas, which will soften the avocado in just a few days.

# CHILI DOGS WITH CRUMBLED CORN CHIPS

SERVES: **6 TO 8** | PREP TIME: **15 MINUTES, PLUS ABOUT 1 HOUR FOR THE CHILI** | GRILLING TIME: **4 TO 5 MINUTES**

**CHILI**

- 1 tablespoon extra-virgin olive oil
- 8 ounces ground chuck (80% lean)
- 1 small onion, finely chopped
- 1 can (15 ounces) diced tomatoes in juice
- 1 cup tomato juice
- 1½ teaspoons ground cumin
- 1 teaspoon ancho chile powder
- 1 teaspoon dried oregano
- ½ teaspoon hot pepper sauce, or to taste
- ¼ teaspoon kosher salt
- ¼ teaspoon freshly ground black pepper
- 1 can (15 ounces) red kidney beans, drained

- 6–8 best-quality all-beef hot dogs
- 6–8 hot dog buns, split
- 1 cup grated cheddar cheese
- 1 cup corn chips, crumbled

1. In a medium skillet over medium-high heat, warm the oil. Add the ground chuck and onion and sauté for 4 to 6 minutes, stirring occasionally and breaking up the meat with a spoon. Stir in the diced tomatoes, tomato juice, cumin, chile powder, oregano, hot pepper sauce, salt, and pepper and bring to a strong simmer. Simmer over medium heat, partially covered, until very thick, about 20 minutes, stirring occasionally to keep the mixture from scorching. Stir in the beans and cook for 10 minutes more. Remove from the heat and set aside for up to 30 minutes; rewarm before serving.

2. Prepare the grill for direct cooking over medium heat (350° to 450°F).

3. Cut a few shallow slashes in each hot dog, and then grill over *direct medium heat*, with the lid closed, until hot all the way to the center, 4 to 5 minutes, turning occasionally. During the last 30 seconds to 1 minute of grilling time, toast the buns, cut side down, over direct heat.

4. Place each hot dog in a bun and top with warm chili, cheese, and corn chips.

# CHICAGO-STYLE HOT DOGS

SERVES: **8**  |  PREP TIME: **10 MINUTES**  |  GRILLING TIME: **4 TO 5 MINUTES**

8  slices ripe tomato, each about ¼ inch thick
8  best-quality all-beef hot dogs with natural casings
    (slightly longer than the buns)
8  poppy seed hot dog buns, split
16  pickled sport peppers
2  dill pickles, each cut into 4 spears
½  cup finely chopped white onion, rinsed in
    a fine-mesh strainer under cold water
½  cup super green sweet pickle relish
    Yellow mustard
    Celery salt

1. Prepare the grill for direct cooking over medium heat
(350° to 450°F).

2. Cut each tomato slice in half to make half-moons.

3. Cut a few shallow slashes in each hot dog, and then
grill over *direct medium heat*, with the lid closed,
until hot all the way to the center, 4 to 5 minutes,
turning occasionally.

4. Place each hot dog in a bun and add two tomato
half-moons, two peppers, one pickle spear, onion,

and relish. Add mustard to taste, and finish with a dash
of celery salt. Serve warm.

### WHERE DID THE WORD "FRANKFURTER" COME FROM?

Who's the father of this ... frankfurter? While
Germany may seem like the obvious answer, as
"frankfurter" means "of Frankfurt," there are
always two sides to every story—even behind
the birth of our beloved frank. The Germans
claim to have first created the Frankfurter
Würstchen (its official name), even enacting
a law to reserve the term "frankfurter" for
sausages actually made in or around the city
of Frankfurt. The second story credits the
Austrians: Johann Georg Lahner, a Frankfurt-
area butcher, allegedly moved to Vienna,
Austria, and sold sausages, which he called the
"frankfurter." Hmm ... so, Germany or a German
emigrant? Either way you spin it, it seems that,
sorry, Austria: you are not the father.

# SONORAN HOT DOGS

SERVES: **4** | PREP TIME: **15 MINUTES** | GRILLING TIME: **ABOUT 8 MINUTES**

4 best-quality all-beef hot dogs
4 slices bacon (not thick cut)
4 torpedo rolls, split
(don't cut all the way through)
¼ cup mayonnaise
1 cup grated Monterey
Jack cheese
1 cup canned pinto beans,
rinsed and drained
1 large, ripe tomato, cored,
seeded, and roughly chopped
1 cup roughly chopped
crisp lettuce
1 small, ripe Hass avocado, diced
⅓ cup sliced pickled jalapeño
chile peppers (from a jar),
well drained

1. Prepare the grill for direct cooking over low heat (250° to 350°F).

2. Wrap each hot dog with a slice of bacon, winding it around in a spiral. Open the rolls and spread the cut side evenly with the mayonnaise.

3. Grill the hot dogs over *direct low heat*, with the lid closed, until the bacon is nicely browned and crispy on the outside and the hot dogs are hot all the way to the center, about 8 minutes, turning three times. During the last 30 seconds to 1 minute of grilling time, toast the buns, mayo side down, over direct heat.

4. Place each hot dog in a bun and top with cheese, beans, tomato, lettuce, avocado, and pickled jalapeños. Serve immediately.

# SPICY BUFFALO HOT DOGS WITH CELERY RELISH AND BLUE CHEESE

SERVES: **4** | PREP TIME: **20 MINUTES** | GRILLING TIME: **4 TO 5 MINUTES**

## RELISH
- ¼ cup finely chopped shallots
- 1 tablespoon white wine vinegar
- 4 ribs celery, ends trimmed and cut into small dice
- 1 cup diced English cucumber
- 2 tablespoons extra-virgin olive oil
- 1 tablespoon mayonnaise
- 1 tablespoon finely chopped fresh dill
- ½ teaspoon kosher salt
- ¼ teaspoon freshly ground black pepper
- ¼ teaspoon celery salt

- 4 best-quality all-beef hot dogs
- 4 poppy seed hot dog buns, split
- 4 ounces blue cheese, crumbled
  Hot wing sauce

1. In a bowl combine the shallots and vinegar and let stand for 20 minutes. Place the diced celery in a fine-mesh strainer and bring 3 cups of water to a boil. Holding the strainer over the sink, pour the water slowly over the celery; drain thoroughly. Add the celery and the remaining relish ingredients to the bowl and fold until evenly blended.

2. Prepare the grill for direct cooking over medium heat (350° to 450°F).

3. Cut a few shallow slashes in each hot dog, and then grill over *direct medium heat*, with the lid closed, until hot all the way to the center, 4 to 5 minutes, turning occasionally. During the last 30 seconds to 1 minute of grilling time, toast the buns, cut side down, over direct heat.

4. Spread an even layer of celery relish on the bottom half of each bun (you may not need all of it), and top each with a hot dog, blue cheese, and hot wing sauce. Serve immediately.

**FUN FACT**

Few can resist the fiery orange goodness of buffalo wing sauce: thus, its sweeping adoption in non-wing dishes like buffalo chicken salads and dips, and meatless dishes like buffalo fries and even deviled eggs. In this recipe, we continue to expand the saucy trend to dress up the all-American hot dog.

HOT DOGS

# THE NEW ENGLAND–STYLE TOP-LOADING
# WONDER BUN

Does your hot dog suffer from soggy bun syndrome? Does your bun split before you even get a chance to take that first bite, causing an awkward wiener-wrangling moment? Do your condiments weep and run off to the side, making for a less-than-desirable presentation? If the answer is "yes" to any of these questions, then we're here to tell you: there is life outside the basic side-split bun.

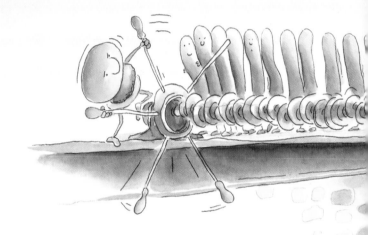

Enter the New England–style hot dog bun— also known as the "top-sliced," "top-loading," or "frankfurter" roll. This Texas toast–like Northeastern summertime staple, prized as much for its satisfying crunch as for its form and function, has flat, crustless sides that make the perfect surface for buttering and toasting on the grill. And unlike the two-piece rounded rolls that are common across most of the country, this V-shaped bun's flat bottom provides a stable seat and a neat presentation for everything from hot dogs to lobster salad. No more runny condiments: this guy can stand up (literally) to its standard side-split competition any day.

Developed in Massachusetts in the mid- to late 1940s, the New England–style bun came about thanks to America's first franchised restaurant chain: Howard Johnson's. The orange-roofed landmark's owners had originally approached Maine's J.J. Nissen Baking Company about creating a special bun for its fried clam strip sandwich. The restaurant chain specifically wanted top-sliced rolls that would stand upright and, thus, would be easier to assemble, serve, and devour. And so, the quintessential "New England–style" bun was born.

This top-loading wonder bun remains true to its namesake, rarely available anywhere outside of the Northeast. From fish shacks to backyard barbecues, the New England–style bun is also a home-team concessions staple at America's oldest ballpark. Cubs fans have their Chicago-Style Hot Dogs in poppy seed buns and Milwaukee fans, their Brewers Bratwurst served in crusty rolls, but Red Sox rooters enjoy a favorite found exclusively at Boston's famed Fenway Park— the Fenway Frank, a slightly smoky, garlicky hot dog, traditionally topped with mustard, onions, and relish, then tucked into the classic top-sliced bun.

For those of you New Englanders who have fled the coop and lust for your beloved split-top rolls but can't find them in your regional grocery stores or restaurants, consider getting crafty and creating your own out of a basic hot dog bun. To make your own top-loaders, start with fresh, unsliced hot dog buns from your local bakery. Simply slice each bun vertically from the top, trim off the sides to create two flat surfaces for grilling, toast them up, stuff with creamy lobster salad or sizzling sausage, and let the nostalgia begin.

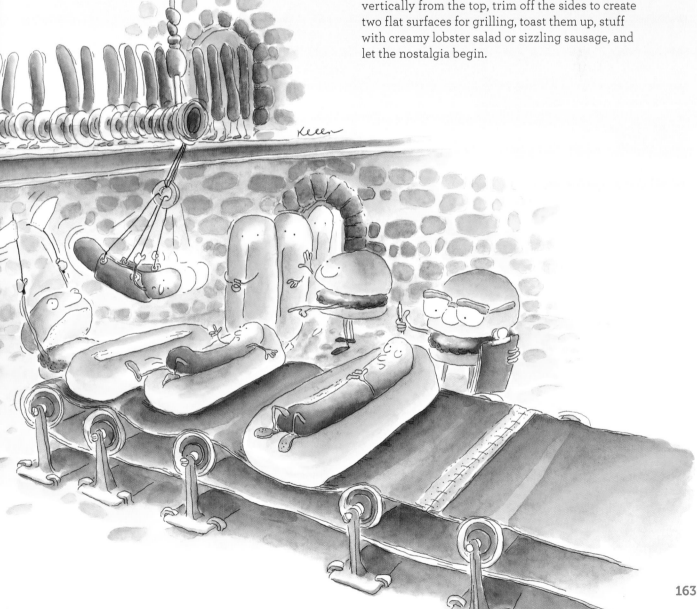

# WARM AND CHEESY BALLPARK FRANKS

SERVES: **4** | PREP TIME: **5 MINUTES** | GRILLING TIME: **5 TO 7 MINUTES**

4 top-split New England–style hot dog buns
⅔ cup finely grated cheddar cheese
4 best-quality all-beef hot dogs
¼ cup ketchup
¼ cup yellow "ballpark" mustard
¼ cup sweet pickle relish

1. Prepare the grill for direct and indirect cooking over medium heat (350° to 450°F).

2. Gently open the buns a little bit to make room for the cheese. Sprinkle an equal amount of the cheese inside each bun. Cut a few shallow slashes in each hot dog.

3. Grill the cheese-filled buns over *indirect medium heat*, with the lid closed, until the cheese is melted and the buns are lightly toasted, 5 to 7 minutes. At the same time, grill the hot dogs over *direct medium heat* until hot all the way to the center, 4 to 5 minutes, turning occasionally.

4. Place each hot dog in a bun, being careful to keep the two halves of each bun in once piece, and top with your choice of ketchup, mustard, and/or relish. Serve immediately.

What is "ballpark" mustard, you ask? This bright yellow mustard found in most American ballparks (and supermarkets) has just enough spice and tartness to be noticed, but there is no honey here, no coarse brown seeds, and no French accent. We are talking classic American mustard—that so proudly we hail.

# PATAGONIAN HOT DOGS WITH AVOCADO MAYO

SERVES: **4 TO 8** | PREP TIME: **20 MINUTES** | GRILLING TIME: **4 TO 5 MINUTES**

## MAYO

- 1 ripe Hass avocado, roughly chopped
- ⅓ cup mayonnaise
- ½ jalapeño chile pepper, seeded and chopped
- 1 tablespoon chopped shallot
- 1 tablespoon fresh lemon juice
- 1 garlic clove, minced or pushed through a press
- ¼ teaspoon kosher salt
- ¼ teaspoon freshly ground black pepper

- 8 best-quality all-beef hot dogs
- 8 hot dog buns, split
- 1 jar or bag (1 pound) sauerkraut, drained
- 1 pound ripe tomatoes, cored, seeded, and chopped
- ¼ cup roughly chopped fresh cilantro leaves
- ¼ cup finely chopped red onion

1. In a food processor fitted with a metal blade, combine the mayo ingredients and puree until smooth.

2. Prepare the grill for direct cooking over medium heat (350° to 450°F).

3. Cut a few shallow slashes in each hot dog, and then grill over *direct medium heat*, with the lid closed, until hot all the way to the center, 4 to 5 minutes, turning occasionally. During the last 30 seconds to 1 minute of grilling time, toast the buns, cut side down, over direct heat.

4. Generously spread the avocado mayo inside each bun (you will not need all of it). Then add a hot dog, sauerkraut, tomatoes, cilantro, and onion. Serve warm.

At the southern end of South America, hot dog fanatics in Patagonia, Argentina, like a colorful variation that involves copious amounts of sauerkraut, chopped tomatoes, and a creamy avocado mayo.

# NEW YORK HOT DOGS WITH SWEET ONIONS

SERVES: 4 | PREP TIME: **20 MINUTES, PLUS ABOUT 40 MINUTES FOR THE ONIONS** | GRILLING TIME: **4 TO 5 MINUTES**

## ONIONS

⅔ cup water
1 teaspoon cornstarch
1 tablespoon store-bought barbecue sauce
1 tablespoon tomato paste
1 tablespoon balsamic vinegar
1 teaspoon Dijon mustard
1 teaspoon packed light brown sugar
1 teaspoon caraway seed
½ teaspoon hot pepper sauce
2 tablespoons vegetable oil
2 large red onions, each cut in half and thinly sliced
¼ teaspoon kosher salt
1 teaspoon minced garlic

4 best-quality all-beef hot dogs
4 soft hot dog buns, split
  Spicy brown mustard
  Kosher dill pickle spears

1. Combine the water and cornstarch and whisk until smooth. Whisk in the barbecue sauce, tomato paste, vinegar, mustard, brown sugar, caraway seed, and hot pepper sauce.

2. In a skillet over medium heat, warm the oil. Add the onions and salt, partially cover the skillet, and cook until the onions are softened but not at all brown, 10 to 12 minutes, stirring occasionally. Add the garlic and cook for 1 minute more. Add the cornstarch mixture and stir to blend. Adjust the heat to low, cover the skillet, and cook until the onions are juicy and glossy but not wet, 20 to 25 minutes, stirring occasionally and checking to make sure the onions don't scorch. Add another tablespoon of water, if needed. Remove from the heat.

3. Prepare the grill for direct cooking over medium heat (350° to 450°F).

4. Cut a few shallow slashes in each hot dog, and then grill over *direct medium heat*, with the lid closed, until hot all the way to the center, 4 to 5 minutes, turning occasionally. During the last 30 seconds to 1 minute of grilling time, toast the buns, cut side down, over direct heat.

5. Spread a little mustard on each bun, add a hot dog, and top with plenty of onions. Serve with the pickles.

# DELUXE HOT DOGS WITH PROSCIUTTO AND RED ONION RELISH

SERVES: **4** | PREP TIME: **20 MINUTES, PLUS 20 TO 24 MINUTES FOR THE RELISH** | GRILLING TIME: **3 TO 4 MINUTES**

**HOT DOGS**

### RELISH

- 2 tablespoons extra-virgin olive oil
- 2 large red onions, finely chopped
- 1 cup fruity red wine, such as zinfandel
- 2 tablespoons red wine vinegar
- 1 tablespoon packed brown sugar
- 2 ounces prosciutto, trimmed of perimeter fat, finely chopped
- 2 tablespoons finely chopped fresh basil leaves
- ½ teaspoon kosher salt
- ¼ teaspoon freshly ground black pepper

- 4 best-quality all-beef hot dogs, each cut lengthwise in half (don't cut all the way through)
- 4 rectangles focaccia bread, each about 1 inch thick and 2½ inches wide, split
  Extra-virgin olive oil
- 2 tablespoons whole-grain mustard

1. In a skillet over medium heat, warm the oil. Add the onions and sauté until very tender, 10 to 12 minutes, stirring occasionally. Add the wine, vinegar, and brown sugar, and continue cooking until most of the liquid is absorbed but the mixture is still juicy, 10 to 12 minutes more, stirring occasionally. Remove from the heat and stir in the prosciutto, basil, salt, and pepper.

2. Prepare the grill for direct cooking over medium heat (350° to 450°F).

3. Cut a few shallow slashes in each hot dog. Lightly brush the cut side of the focaccia with oil. Grill the hot dogs over *direct medium heat*, with the lid closed, until hot, 3 to 4 minutes, turning once. During the last 30 seconds to 1 minute of grilling time, toast the focaccia, cut side down, over direct heat, until lightly golden but still soft.

4. Spread the focaccia generously with mustard and top each with a hot dog and a mound of relish. Serve immediately.

167

# CHORIZO QUESADILLAS WITH MANGO SALSA

SERVES: **4; 8 TO 10 AS AN APPETIZER** | PREP TIME: **20 MINUTES** | GRILLING TIME: **30 TO 38 MINUTES**

SAUSAGES

### SALSA

- 1 large, ripe mango, peeled and finely chopped
- 1 small red bell pepper, finely chopped
- ¼ cup finely chopped red onion
- 2 tablespoons finely chopped fresh cilantro leaves
- 1 tablespoon fresh lime juice
- ¼ teaspoon kosher salt

- 4 serrano chile peppers
- 1 pound fresh chorizo sausages, pierced several times with a fork
- 2 ripe Hass avocados, diced
- 2 teaspoons fresh lime juice
- 8 flour tortillas (8 inches)
- 4 cups grated Monterey Jack cheese
  Sour cream

1. Prepare the grill for direct and indirect cooking over medium heat (350° to 450°F).

2. Mix the salsa ingredients.

3. Grill the chiles over *direct medium heat*, with the lid closed, until blackened and blistered, 6 to 7 minutes, turning occasionally. Transfer to a bowl and cover with plastic wrap to trap the steam. Let stand for about 10 minutes.

4. Grill the sausages over *indirect medium heat*, with the lid closed, until fully cooked (160°F), 20 to 25 minutes, turning occasionally. Remove from the grill and cut the sausages at an angle into ½-inch slices.

5. Decrease the temperature of the grill to low heat (250° to 350°F).

6. Remove the peppers from the bowl and peel away and discard the skin, seeds, and stems. Finely chop the peppers and place them in a bowl. Add the avocados and 2 teaspoons lime juice, and then mash with a fork until the mixture is fairly smooth.

7. Assemble the quesadillas by spreading the avocado mixture evenly over one half of each tortilla, then ¼ cup cheese, an equal amount of sausage slices, and another ¼ cup cheese. Fold the empty side of the tortillas over the filling.

8. Grill the quesadillas over *direct low heat*, with the lid closed, until golden on both sides, 4 to 6 minutes, turning once. Cut the quesadillas into wedges and serve warm with mango salsa and sour cream.

Don't be afraid to blacken the chiles' skins. You will scrape away most of the skin later, leaving the tender flesh for spicing up the avocado filling of these fabulous quesadillas.

# GARLIC SAUSAGE BRUSCHETTA WITH CORN AND WATERCRESS

SERVES: **8 AS AN APPETIZER** | PREP TIME: **15 MINUTES** | GRILLING TIME: **9 TO 11 MINUTES**

1 bunch watercress, thick stems removed and leaves roughly chopped (about 2 cups)
1½ cups fresh corn kernels
1 large shallot, minced
Finely grated zest of 1 lemon
1½ tablespoons fresh lemon juice
1 teaspoon minced garlic
1 teaspoon Dijon mustard
Extra-virgin olive oil
Kosher salt
Freshly ground black pepper
8 slices French or sourdough bread, each about 3 by 5 inches and ½ inch thick
1 pound precooked garlic sausages, each cut lengthwise in half

1. Prepare the grill for direct cooking over medium heat (350° to 450°F).

2. Combine the watercress, corn, shallot, lemon zest and juice, garlic, mustard, ⅓ cup oil, ½ teaspoon salt, and ¼ teaspoon pepper. Toss to blend. Lightly coat the bread slices with oil and season with a little salt and pepper.

3. Grill the sausages over *direct medium heat*, with the lid closed, until nicely browned and heated through, 8 to 10 minutes, turning once. Remove from the grill and cut crosswise into ½-inch slices. Add the sausage slices to the large bowl with the corn mixture and toss to blend.

4. Grill the bread slices over *direct medium heat* until golden and crusty on the outside, but not crisp, about 1 minute, turning once. Place a slice of bread on each plate and top evenly with the sausage-corn mixture. Serve warm.

# POLENTA CROSTINI WITH SAUSAGE-TOMATO RAGOUT

SERVES: **4 TO 6; 8 TO 10 AS AN APPETIZER**
PREP TIME: **20 MINUTES, PLUS ABOUT 25 MINUTES FOR THE RAGOUT** | GRILLING TIME: **4 TO 6 MINUTES**

## RAGOUT

8 ounces fresh Italian sausage, hot or mild, casings removed
Extra-virgin olive oil
½ small yellow onion, finely chopped
2 large garlic cloves, finely chopped
1 can (14½ ounces) diced plum tomatoes in juice
Kosher salt
Freshly ground black pepper
¼ cup finely chopped fresh basil leaves, divided

2 tubes (each 1 pound) precooked polenta, ends trimmed, cut into ½-inch slices
4 ounces Parmigiano-Reggiano® cheese, at room temperature, shaved into pieces with a vegetable peeler

Polenta tends to stick to the cooking grates, unless you brush the rounds generously with oil and use high heat. Then you should be able to turn them easily.

1. Prepare the grill for direct cooking over high heat (450° to 550°F).

2. Warm a skillet over medium heat. Add the sausage and cook until no trace of pink remains, 5 to 8 minutes, stirring and breaking up the meat with a spoon. Tip the skillet and spoon off all but about 1 tablespoon of the fat, if necessary. If there is no liquid fat in the skillet, add 1 tablespoon oil. Add the onion and garlic and sauté until softened, about 5 minutes. Add the tomatoes, ½ teaspoon salt, and ¼ teaspoon pepper, and bring to a simmer. Cook until the liquid is evaporated and the mixture is quite thick, about 10 minutes, stirring occasionally. Stir in half of the basil and keep the ragout warm while you grill the polenta.

3. Generously brush the polenta slices on both sides with oil, season with salt and pepper, and grill over *direct high heat*, with the lid closed, until nicely marked by the grill, 4 to 6 minutes, turning once. Transfer to a platter and immediately top each slice with a little cheese and a spoonful of ragout. Garnish with the remaining basil and serve immediately.

171

# WHITE WINE–STEAMED CLAMS WITH CHORIZO

SERVES: **4** | PREP TIME: **15 MINUTES** | GRILLING TIME: **ABOUT 30 MINUTES**
SPECIAL EQUIPMENT: **GRILL-PROOF DUTCH OVEN OR LARGE CAST-IRON SKILLET**

12 ounces fully cooked Spanish chorizo sausage
 1 baguette, about 16 inches long,
    cut on a diagonal into 32 slices
    Extra-virgin olive oil
 3 tablespoons unsalted butter
 1 medium yellow onion, finely chopped
 6 garlic cloves, thinly sliced
 1 tablespoon finely chopped fresh oregano leaves
 2 teaspoons finely chopped fresh thyme leaves
 1 cup dry white wine
 3 dozen littleneck clams, scrubbed under cold
    running water (discard any clams that won't close)
 1 large garlic clove, cut in half

1. Prepare the grill for direct cooking over medium heat (350° to 450°F).

2. Grill the sausage over *direct medium heat*, with the lid closed, until browned, about 8 minutes, turning occasionally. Cut each sausage lengthwise in half, and then cut the halves crosswise into ½-inch pieces.

3. Lightly brush the baguette slices on both sides with oil.

4. Place a grill-proof Dutch oven or a large cast-iron skillet over *direct medium heat* and preheat for 10 minutes. To the Dutch oven add 2 tablespoons oil and the butter. When the butter is melted and begins to foam, add the onion, sliced garlic, oregano, and thyme. Continue cooking until the onion softens, about 5 minutes, stirring occasionally. Pour in the wine, bring to a boil, close the grill lid, and cook for 2 minutes more.

5. Arrange the clams and sausage pieces in the Dutch oven and cover with the pot lid. Cook over *direct medium heat*, with the grill lid closed, for 10 minutes. Carefully lift the lid off the Dutch oven and check to see if the clams are open. If not, replace the lid and cook for 3 to 5 minutes more. Wearing insulated barbecue mitts or gloves, carefully remove the Dutch oven from the grill. Discard any unopened clams.

6. Grill the baguette slices over *direct medium heat*, with the lid open, until lightly toasted, about 1 minute, turning once or twice. Remove from the grill and rub the bread with the cut side of the garlic clove.

7. Spoon equal amounts of sausage, clams, and juice into deep bowls. Serve with the bread for dipping.

**FUN FACT**

Much like a tree, you can tell a clam's age by counting the rings on its shell. In 2007, scientists pulled an adult littleneck clam from the icy Arctic waters off Iceland's northern coast that reportedly had 507 annual growth rings—now known as the world's oldest animal.

**SAUSAGES**

# MERGUEZ SAUSAGE PIZZAS WITH MOZZARELLA, PEPPERS, AND FETA

SERVES: 4 | PREP TIME: 25 MINUTES | GRILLING TIME: 24 TO 35 MINUTES

SAUSAGES

4 scallions, ends trimmed
   Extra-virgin olive oil
1 medium red bell pepper, cut into 4 planks
8 ounces fresh merguez sausage
1 pound premade pizza dough, at room temperature
3 cups grated fresh mozzarella cheese
1 cup crumbled feta cheese
3 tablespoons finely chopped fresh mint leaves
3 tablespoons thinly sliced fresh basil leaves

1. Prepare the grill for direct cooking over medium heat (350° to 450°F).

2. Lightly brush the scallions with oil. Grill the bell pepper planks over *direct medium heat*, with the lid closed, until tender, 8 to 10 minutes, turning occasionally. At the same time, grill the scallions over *direct medium heat* until wilted, 2 to 3 minutes, turning once. Cut the bell pepper planks into ⅓-inch strips. Finely chop the scallions.

3. Grill the sausage over *direct medium heat*, with the lid closed, until fully cooked (160°F), 12 to 15 minutes, turning occasionally. Cut the sausage into ¼-inch slices.

4. Divide the dough into four equal pieces. Lightly brush four 9-inch squares of parchment paper on one side with oil. Roll or press each piece of dough on the oiled side of the paper into an 8-inch circle about ⅓ inch thick. Lightly brush the tops with oil. Allow the dough to stand at room temperature for 10 minutes.

5. Grill the dough, paper side facing up, over *direct medium heat*, with the lid closed, until well marked and firm on the underside, 2 to 5 minutes, rotating as needed for even cooking. Discard the parchment paper. Transfer the crusts to a work surface with the grilled side facing up.

6. Top each pizza with equal amounts of the cheeses, sausage, bell pepper, and scallions, leaving a ¼-inch border. Return the pizzas to the grill and cook over *direct medium heat*, with the lid closed, until the cheese is melted and the bottoms of the crusts are crisp, 2 to 5 minutes, rotating the pizzas occasionally. Transfer to a cutting board. Top the pizzas with mint and basil and cut into wedges. Serve warm.

# BRUNCH PIZZAS

SERVES: **4**  |  PREP TIME: **30 MINUTES**  |  GRILLING TIME: **14 TO 20 MINUTES**

12 ounces fully cooked chicken-apple sausage links
1 medium red onion, cut into ½-inch wedges
1 large red bell pepper
　　Extra-virgin olive oil
2 teaspoons balsamic vinegar
1½ teaspoons finely chopped fresh rosemary leaves
½ teaspoon kosher salt
½ teaspoon freshly ground black pepper
1 pound premade pizza dough, at room temperature
2 cups coarsely grated Monterey Jack cheese
½ cup freshly grated Parmigiano-Reggiano® cheese

You can use either a gas or a charcoal grill for making pizzas, but there is something really special about the way pizza dough picks up the smokiness of a charcoal grill. It is reminiscent of great thin-crusted pizzas cooked in a wood-fired oven.

1. Prepare the grill for direct cooking over medium heat (350° to 450°F).

2. Brush the sausages, onion, and bell pepper with oil and grill them over *direct medium heat*, with the lid closed, until grill marks appear, turning once. The sausages and bell pepper will take about 6 minutes, and the onion will take about 10 minutes. Chop into ½-inch pieces. Transfer to a bowl and add the vinegar, rosemary, salt, and pepper.

3. To prepare the dough and grill the first side, follow steps 4 and 5 for the Merguez Sausage Pizzas (see recipe on facing page).

4. Top each pizza with equal amounts of the Monterey Jack cheese, sausage mixture, and Parmigiano-Reggiano cheese, leaving a ¼-inch border. Return the pizzas to the grill and cook over *direct medium heat*, with the lid closed, until the cheese is melted and the bottoms of the crusts are crisp, 2 to 5 minutes, rotating the pizzas occasionally. Transfer to a cutting board and cut into wedges. Serve warm.

SAUSAGES

# FRESH CHORIZO AND TEX-MEX POTATO SALAD

SERVES: **4 TO 6** | PREP TIME: **15 MINUTES** | GRILLING TIME: **20 TO 25 MINUTES** | SPECIAL EQUIPMENT: **PERFORATED GRILL PAN**

¼ cup finely chopped fresh cilantro leaves
2 tablespoons fresh lime juice
1 teaspoon Dijon mustard
½ teaspoon ground cumin
Kosher salt
Freshly ground black pepper
Extra-virgin olive oil
½ teaspoon granulated garlic
2½ pounds small red and white new potatoes, 1½ to 2 inches in diameter, each cut in half
3 fresh chorizo sausages, each about 4 ounces, pierced several times with a fork
1 medium red bell pepper, cut into thin strips
1 medium red onion, cut into very thin slices

With your grill set up for both direct and indirect heat, you can grill the potatoes and roast the sausages at the same time.

1. Prepare the grill for direct and indirect cooking over medium heat (350° to 450°F) and preheat a perforated grill pan over direct heat.

2. Whisk the cilantro, lime juice, mustard, cumin, ½ teaspoon salt, ¼ teaspoon pepper, and ¼ cup oil to make a vinaigrette.

3. In a large bowl whisk 2 tablespoons oil, ¼ teaspoon salt, ¼ teaspoon pepper, and the granulated garlic. Add the potatoes and turn to coat. Spread the potatoes in a single layer on the grill pan and cook over *direct medium heat*, with the lid closed, until golden brown and tender, 20 to 25 minutes, turning occasionally. At the same time, grill the sausages on the cooking grates over *indirect medium heat* until fully cooked (160°F), 20 to 25 minutes, turning occasionally. Cut each potato half in half, and cut the sausages into ¼-inch slices.

4. Combine the potatoes, sausages, bell pepper, and onion. Drizzle with the vinaigrette and gently toss. Season with salt and pepper. Serve warm or at room temperature.

# CHICKEN SAUSAGE SKEWERS WITH NECTARINES AND HONEY-LIME GLAZE

SERVES: 4 | PREP TIME: **25 MINUTES** | GRILLING TIME: **6 TO 8 MINUTES** | SPECIAL EQUIPMENT: **10 METAL OR BAMBOO SKEWERS**

## GLAZE

- 1 teaspoon finely grated lime zest
- ¼ cup fresh lime juice
- ¼ cup honey
- 2 tablespoons finely chopped fresh cilantro leaves
- 1 tablespoon low-sodium soy sauce
- ½ teaspoon kosher salt

- 4 medium, ripe nectarines
- 1 tablespoon extra-virgin olive oil
- 10 fully cooked spicy jalapeño chicken sausages, 1¼ to 1½ pounds total, each cut into 4 pieces
  Hot cooked rice (optional)

Whenever you have a sweet glaze like this one, wait until the final 3 to 5 minutes of grilling time to apply it. Otherwise, it might burn.

1. If using bamboo skewers, soak them in water for at least 30 minutes.

2. Prepare the grill for direct cooking over medium heat (350° to 450°F).

3. In a small bowl whisk the glaze ingredients.

4. Cut each nectarine into 10 chunks about the same size as the sausage pieces. In a medium bowl combine the oil with the nectarines and stir to coat. Thread the sausages and nectarines onto skewers, alternating the pieces and arranging them so they are touching but not crammed together. You can also thread them separately on their own skewers.

5. Grill the skewers over *direct medium heat*, with the lid closed, until the sausages are heated through and the nectarines are marked in spots, 6 to 8 minutes, turning every 2 minutes and brushing with the glaze during the last 4 minutes of grilling time. Remove from the grill and serve immediately with rice, if desired.

# KIELBASA, ONION, AND PEPPER SPIEDINI
## WITH GRILLED GARLIC BREAD

SERVES: **4** | PREP TIME: **20 MINUTES** | GRILLING TIME: **8 TO 10 MINUTES** | SPECIAL EQUIPMENT: **8 METAL OR BAMBOO SKEWERS**

SAUSAGES

4 teaspoons fresh lemon juice
1 tablespoon finely chopped shallot
1 teaspoon Dijon mustard
  Kosher salt
  Freshly ground black pepper
  Extra-virgin olive oil
2 large red bell peppers
2 medium yellow onions
1 package (14 ounces) Polska kielbasa,
  cut crosswise into 16 pieces
4 slices country-style bread, each about ½ inch thick
1 garlic clove, cut in half
8 cups baby arugula

1. If using bamboo skewers, soak them in water for at least 30 minutes.

2. Prepare the grill for direct cooking over medium heat (350° to 450°F).

3. Whisk the lemon juice, shallot, mustard, ½ teaspoon salt, and ¼ teaspoon pepper. Slowly add ⅓ cup oil, whisking constantly until the vinaigrette is emulsified.

4. Cut each bell pepper into 8 one-inch squares. Quarter each onion and separate each quarter into two leaves (discard the very small leaves from the center of the onion). Using four skewers, thread the vegetables through their centers, alternating the ingredients and arranging them so they are touching but not crammed together. Thread the kielbasa separately onto four skewers. Brush the vegetables and kielbasa with 3 tablespoons of the vinaigrette. Lightly brush the bread slices on both sides with oil.

5. Grill the skewers over *direct medium heat*, with the lid closed, until the vegetables are lightly charred and the kielbasa is nicely browned and heated through, 8 to 10 minutes, turning occasionally. During the last minute of grilling time, toast the bread over direct heat, turning once. Remove everything from the grill. Rub one side of each bread slice with the cut side of the garlic clove. Place a slice of bread, garlic side up, on each of four serving plates.

6. In a bowl toss the arugula with the remaining vinaigrette, and divide among the four bread slices. Set one vegetable skewer and one kielbasa skewer on top of the arugula and serve immediately.

Run the flat, cut side of a clove of garlic across a warm piece of toast for instant garlic bread. *Delizioso!*

# A GUIDE TO UNDERSTANDING
# SAUSAGES

**For about as long as humans have been on the hunt, sausages have been on the menu.**

Tasty and efficient (they were designed to use all parts of an animal, but don't dwell on that), cured and smoked meats kept our pre-fridge ancestors well fed. No doubt they would be amazed at how far sausage makers have taken this craft. We have so many types to choose from that it can be hard to know which is which. Here, then, is a little primer on four broad categories of sausages and how to cook them.

## FRESH

The ground meat in these sausage casings is uncooked.

**EXAMPLES (SHOWN LEFT TO RIGHT):** Hot or sweet Italian sausage, fresh poultry sausage, Mexican chorizo

**COOKING:** Mandatory. Grill directly over low to medium heat, or roast them over indirect heat until no pink remains.

## COLD SMOKED

These sausages have been smoked with some type of wood and are usually completely cooked.

**EXAMPLES (SHOWN LEFT TO RIGHT):** Andouille, linguica, kielbasa

**COOKING:** Not always necessary, but a quick grilling to warm the meat and get a good char will only make them better.

## PRECOOKED

These have been made with fresh, blended meat and were then cooked prior to packaging and distribution.

**EXAMPLES (SHOWN LEFT TO RIGHT):** Hot dog, pork bratwurst, veal bratwurst, mortadella

**COOKING:** Not required, but certainly recommended to boost flavor.

## CURED

Here we have sausages that have been salted and air-dried for weeks. They enjoy long shelf lives.

**EXAMPLES (SHOWN LEFT TO RIGHT):** Spanish chorizo, salami, Landjäger

**COOKING:** Your call. They're designed to be delicious as is but can be great cooked, too.

# ITALIAN SAUSAGES WITH PEPPERS, ONIONS, AND PROVOLONE

SERVES: **4** | PREP TIME: **20 MINUTES** | GRILLING TIME: **8 TO 10 MINUTES** | SPECIAL EQUIPMENT: **PERFORATED GRILL PAN**

Extra-virgin olive oil
Kosher salt
Freshly ground black pepper
2 medium bell peppers, 1 red and 1 green,
  cut into ⅓-inch-wide strips
1 medium yellow onion, cut crosswise
  into ⅓-inch slices
4 fresh Italian sausages, any combination of sweet
  and hot, each about 5 ounces, each cut lengthwise
  in half (don't cut all the way through)
2 tablespoons red wine vinegar
1 garlic clove, minced or pushed through a press
1 baguette, about 8 ounces and 2 feet long,
  cut lengthwise in half
4 strips provolone cheese, each
  about ½ ounce and 6 inches long
1 tablespoon roughly chopped fresh
  Italian parsley leaves

1. Prepare the grill for direct cooking over medium heat (350° to 450°F) and preheat a perforated grill pan.

2. In a medium bowl whisk 2 tablespoons oil, ½ teaspoon salt, and ¼ teaspoon pepper. Add the bell peppers and onion and turn to coat.

3. Lightly brush the sausages all over with oil.

4. Whisk the vinegar, garlic, 2 tablespoons oil, ¼ teaspoon salt, and ¼ teaspoon pepper to make a vinaigrette. Brush the cut side of the baguette with oil.

5. Spread the bell peppers and onion in a single layer on the grill pan, and place the sausages on the cooking grates. Grill over *direct medium heat*, with the lid closed, until the vegetables are tender and the sausages are browned and fully cooked (160°F), 8 to 10 minutes, turning occasionally. During the last 30 seconds to 1 minute of grilling time, place a strip of cheese inside each sausage slit to melt, and toast the baguette, cut side down, over direct heat.

6. Transfer the vegetables to a bowl, add the parsley, and toss to combine.

7. Cut the baguette into four 6-inch pieces. Place each sausage in a baguette piece, and top with the vegetables and a tablespoon of the vinaigrette. Serve warm.

By splitting sausages open and exposing more of the meat to the fire, you can develop more charred and smoky flavors. Just be sure to watch for flare-ups.

# SAUSAGE MIXED GRILL OVER CREAMY POLENTA

SERVES: **8** | PREP TIME: **15 MINUTES** | GRILLING TIME: **15 TO 20 MINUTES**

**SAUSAGES**

## DRESSING
¼ cup finely chopped fresh basil leaves
2 tablespoons white balsamic vinegar
2 tablespoons finely chopped shallot

Kosher salt
Freshly ground black pepper
Extra-virgin olive oil

## POLENTA
5 cups milk
1 cup water
1½ cups quick-cooking polenta
4 ounces cream cheese, softened
½ cup grated Pecorino Romano cheese

1 ring fresh sweet luganiga sausage, about 1 pound, pierced a few times with a fork
3 fresh hot Italian sausages, about 8 ounces total
1 package (14 ounces) Polska kielbasa

1. Prepare the grill for indirect cooking over medium heat (350° to 450°F).

2. Whisk the dressing ingredients, including ½ teaspoon salt and ¼ teaspoon pepper. Slowly add ⅓ cup oil, whisking constantly until the dressing is emulsified. Set aside.

3. In a saucepan combine the milk, water, 1½ teaspoons salt, and ¼ teaspoon pepper. Bring to a boil over medium-high heat, and then whisk in the polenta in a slow and steady stream. Reduce the heat to medium and cook until the polenta is thick, 4 to 5 minutes, stirring constantly. Remove from the heat and add the cream cheese and Romano cheese, stirring constantly until the cheeses are melted. Keep warm over low heat, stirring occasionally to prevent scorching.

4. Grill the luganiga and Italian sausages over *indirect medium heat*, with the lid closed, until fully cooked (160°F), 15 to 20 minutes, turning occasionally. At the same time, grill the kielbasa over *indirect medium heat* until nicely browned and heated through, 12 to 15 minutes, turning occasionally. If desired, during the last 3 to 5 minutes of grilling time, brown the luganiga and Italian sausages over direct heat, turning once. Remove all the sausages from the grill and cut them into bite-sized pieces.

5. Spread the polenta in a thick layer on a large serving platter. Top with the sausage pieces. Whisk the dressing again and spoon it over the sausages. Serve immediately.

Luganiga is a thin ring of sweet sausage that tends to be milder than traditional Italian sausage and is often flavored with parsley and cheese. It can be found in most supermarkets.

SAUSAGES

# LITTLE SAUSAGES WITH ONIONS, FLAT BREAD, AND MUSTARD

SERVES: **6** | PREP TIME: **40 MINUTES** | GRILLING TIME: **8 TO 10 MINUTES**

1 teaspoon finely grated lemon zest
2 tablespoons fresh lemon juice
2 teaspoons granulated sugar
Extra-virgin olive oil
Kosher salt
Freshly ground black pepper
2 medium red onions, each cut in half and
very thinly sliced

## SAUSAGES

1½ pounds lean ground pork
8 ounces ground beef (90% lean)
⅓ cup finely chopped fresh Italian parsley leaves
6 garlic cloves, minced or pushed through a press
1 tablespoon smoked paprika
1½ teaspoons fennel seed
1 teaspoon ground cumin
¾ teaspoon dried thyme
¼ teaspoon saffron threads, crushed (optional)

Flat bread
Spicy brown mustard

1. Whisk the lemon zest and juice, sugar, 1 tablespoon oil, ½ teaspoon salt, and ¼ teaspoon pepper. Stir in the onions and set aside.

2. Mix the sausage ingredients, including 2 tablespoons oil, 1½ teaspoons salt, and 1 teaspoon pepper, and then form into 24 sausages, each about 3 inches long and 1 inch thick, slightly compressing each sausage so they will hold together on the grill. Refrigerate the sausages until ready to grill.

3. Prepare the grill for indirect cooking over medium heat (350° to 450°F).

4. Grill the sausages over *indirect medium heat*, with the lid closed, until cooked to medium doneness (160°F), 8 to 10 minutes, turning once or twice. During the last minute of grilling time, warm the flat bread over direct heat, turning once.

5. Serve the sausages warm with the onions, flat bread, and mustard.

# TURKEY-CILANTRO SAUSAGE TACOS

SERVES: **4** | PREP TIME: **20 MINUTES** | GRILLING TIME: **8 TO 10 MINUTES**

## SAUSAGES

- 2 pounds ground turkey, preferably thigh meat, very cold
- ½ cup finely chopped fresh cilantro leaves
- ¼ cup finely chopped canned chipotle chile peppers in adobo sauce (include some of the sauce)
- ¾ teaspoon dried oregano, preferably Mexican
- ½ teaspoon freshly ground black pepper
- ½ teaspoon garlic powder
- ½ teaspoon ground cumin
- ½ teaspoon ground coriander
- ½ teaspoon kosher salt

- 8 flour tortillas (6 inches)
  Extra-virgin olive oil
- 1 cup grated cheddar cheese
- 1 cup quartered ripe cherry tomatoes
- 1 cup shredded romaine lettuce

1. Mix the sausage ingredients, and then form 16 torpedo-shaped sausages, each about 3 inches long, compacting the meat gently. Refrigerate the sausages until ready to grill.

2. Prepare the grill for direct and indirect cooking over medium heat (350° to 450°F).

3. Wrap the tortillas in an aluminum foil packet. Brush the sausages with oil, and then grill over *direct medium heat*, with the lid closed, until fully cooked (165°F), 8 to 10 minutes, turning once. At the same time, warm the tortilla packet over *indirect medium heat*.

4. Place two sausages inside each tortilla. Divide the cheese, tomatoes, and lettuce among the tortillas and serve immediately.

*Serving suggestion: Fresh Tomatillo Salsa (for recipe, see page 236).*

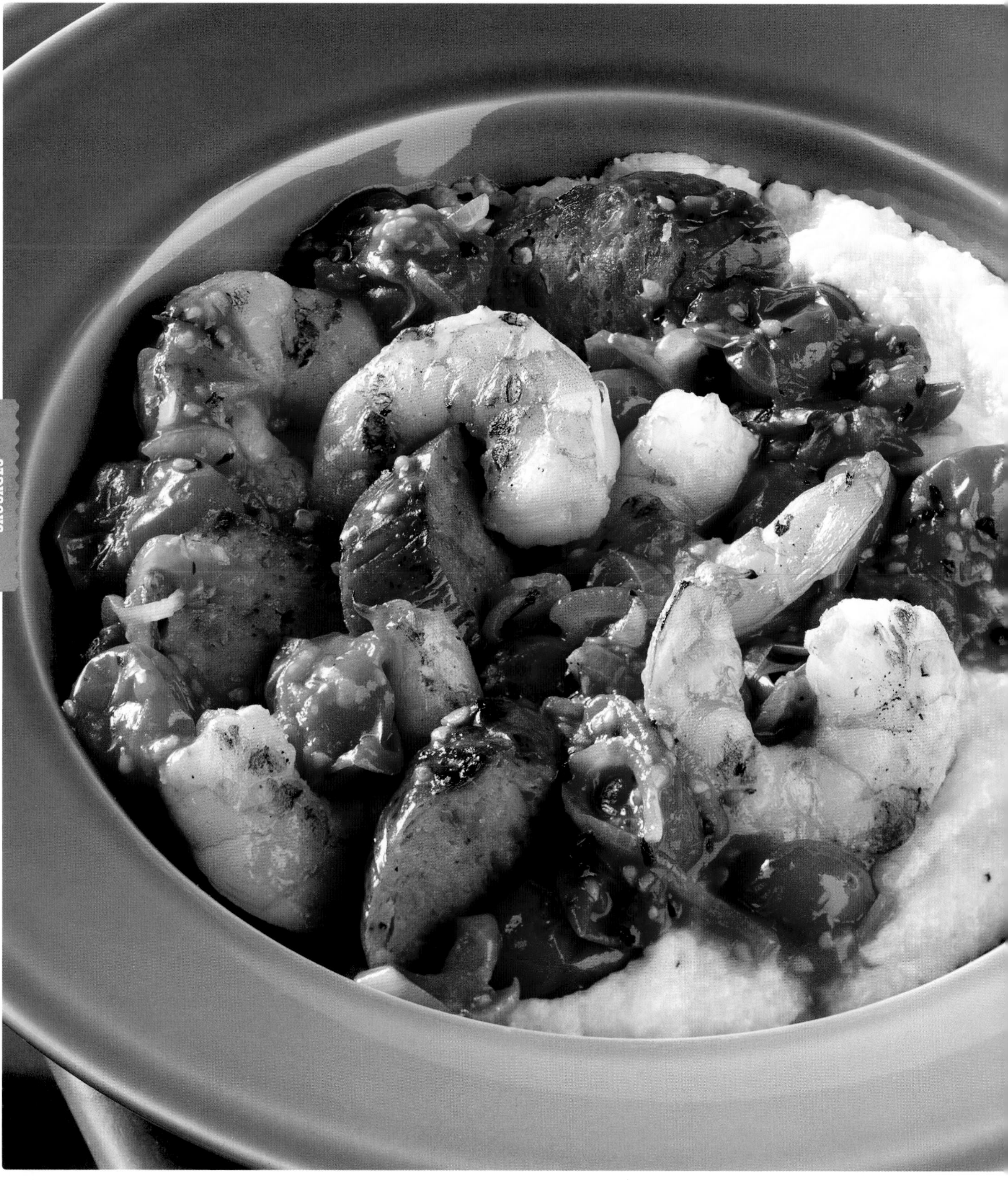

# SHRIMP, ANDOUILLE, AND TOMATO SAUCE
## OVER CHEDDAR GRITS

SERVES: **6** | PREP TIME: **30 MINUTES, PLUS ABOUT 25 MINUTES FOR THE SAUCE**
MARINATING TIME: **30 MINUTES** | GRILLING TIME: **8 TO 10 MINUTES**

24 large shrimp (21/30 count), peeled and deveined,
    tails removed
2 garlic cloves, minced or pushed through a press
    Extra-virgin olive oil

### SAUCE

1 medium yellow onion, cut in half and
    very thinly sliced
4 garlic cloves, minced or pushed through a press
1 teaspoon dried basil
¼ teaspoon crushed red pepper flakes
3 pints ripe grape tomatoes
1 tablespoon balsamic vinegar
1 teaspoon honey
½ teaspoon kosher salt
¼ teaspoon freshly ground black pepper

12 ounces fully cooked andouille sausage

### GRITS

3½ cups whole milk
3 tablespoons unsalted butter
¾ teaspoon kosher salt
1 cup quick-cooking grits (not instant grits)
1½ cups grated white cheddar cheese

1. Combine the shrimp, garlic, and 1 tablespoon oil and toss to coat. Cover and refrigerate the shrimp for 30 minutes.

2. Prepare the grill for direct cooking over medium-high heat (400° to 500°F).

3. In a large skillet over medium-high heat, warm 3 tablespoons oil. Add the onion, garlic, basil, and red pepper flakes and cook until the onion starts to soften, 2 to 3 minutes, stirring occasionally. Add the tomatoes and cook until they burst and are very tender, 18 to 20 minutes, stirring often. Stir in the vinegar and honey and cook for 1 minute. Remove from the heat and stir in the salt and pepper. Keep the sauce warm.

4. Grill the sausage over *direct medium-high heat*, with the lid closed, until nicely browned and heated through, 8 to 10 minutes, turning occasionally. During the last 2 to 4 minutes of grilling time, grill the shrimp over *direct medium-high heat* until firm to the touch and just becoming opaque in the center, turning once. Remove from the grill and cut the sausage on a diagonal into ½-inch slices. Cover the sausage and shrimp with foil to keep warm.

5. In a saucepan combine the milk, butter, and salt. Bring to a boil over medium-high heat, and then whisk in the grits in a slow, steady stream. Reduce the heat to medium and cook until the grits thicken, 4 to 5 minutes, stirring often. Add the cheese and stir until melted.

6. Divide the cheddar grits among bowls and top with equal amounts of tomato sauce, sausage, and shrimp. Serve warm.

> **FUN FACT**
>
> Southerners are serious about their grits. So much so that the small town of St. George, South Carolina, honors the coarsely ground corn with its annual Word Grits Festival—a three-day celebration with grits grinding, corn shelling, and a grits-eating contest, drawing crowds that exceed 45,000.

# ANDOUILLE PO'BOYS WITH CREOLE MUSTARD

SERVES: 4 | PREP TIME: **15 MINUTES** | GRILLING TIME: **4 TO 5 MINUTES**

**SLAW**

- ⅓ cup mayonnaise
- 2 tablespoons cider vinegar
- ½ small head green cabbage, coarsely shredded (4 cups)
- 1 cup thinly sliced red onion
- ½ cup bread-and-butter pickle chips, drained and finely chopped

<br>

- 4 fully cooked andouille sausages, each about 4 ounces and cut lengthwise in half
- 4 submarine sandwich buns, split
- ¼ cup Creole mustard
- ¼ cup mayonnaise
- 24 pickled jalapeño slices (from a jar)

1. Prepare the grill for direct cooking over medium heat (350° to 450°F).

2. Whisk the mayonnaise and vinegar, and then add the remaining slaw ingredients. Mix well.

3. Grill the sausages over *direct medium heat*, with the lid closed, until nicely browned and heated through, 4 to 5 minutes, turning occasionally.

4. Spread the bottom half of each bun with 1 tablespoon mustard. Spread the top half of each bun with 1 tablespoon mayonnaise. Top each bun with a sausage, slaw, and jalapeño slices. Serve immediately.

If you have trouble finding Creole mustard, substitute with country-style Dijon mustard and add a touch of hot pepper sauce.

SAUSAGES

# KIELBASA WITH PICKLED ONIONS, SPORT PEPPERS, AND CHEDDAR

SERVES: **4** | PREP TIME: **15 MINUTES** | PICKLING TIME: **AT LEAST 2 HOURS** | GRILLING TIME: **10 TO 12 MINUTES**

1 cup red wine vinegar
3 tablespoons granulated sugar
1 teaspoon kosher salt
⅛ teaspoon ground chipotle pepper
1½ cups thinly sliced red onions
2 tablespoons unsalted butter, softened
8 slices rye bread
1 package (14 ounces) Polska kielbasa
4 slices sharp cheddar cheese, each about 1 ounce
Yellow mustard
6–8 sport peppers, each cut crosswise

**1.** In a saucepan combine the vinegar, sugar, salt, and ground chipotle pepper. Bring to a boil over medium-high heat and then add the onions. Return to a boil over medium-high heat and cook for 1 minute. Remove from the heat and let stand at room temperature for at least 2 hours. Drain the onions before serving.

**2.** Prepare the grill for direct cooking over medium heat (350° to 450°F).

**3.** Butter one side of each bread slice. Cut the kielbasa crosswise into two pieces, and then cut each piece lengthwise in half. Grill the kielbasa over *direct medium heat*, with the lid closed, until nicely browned and heated through, 8 to 10 minutes, turning once. Cut each kielbasa quarter crosswise into two pieces (you should have eight pieces total).

**4.** Grill the bread, unbuttered side down first, over *direct medium heat* for 30 seconds to 1 minute. Turn the bread over, top four of the slices with a slice of cheese, and grill for 30 seconds to 1 minute more.

**5.** Arrange the bread slices on a work surface. Spread some mustard on the four bread slices without cheese, and then top each with two pieces of kielbasa, onions, sport peppers, and a cheese-topped piece of bread. Serve warm.

**FUN FACT**

We hope this tip cuts the mustard for you: what does that phrase mean anyway? Possibly originating in the early nineteenth century, it's a reference to the tall, fibrous, densely growing mustard plant. Cutting through the plants took skill, strength, and patience—so those who couldn't hack it simply didn't cut the mustard.

# MAPLE- AND CIDER-BRAISED BRATS
## WITH BACON AND FRIED SAUERKRAUT

SERVES: **6** | PREP TIME: **15 MINUTES** | GRILLING TIME: **16 TO 22 MINUTES** | SPECIAL EQUIPMENT: **LARGE DISPOSABLE FOIL PAN**

BRATS

 6  slices bacon
 1  medium yellow onion, cut in half and thinly sliced
 3  garlic cloves, minced or pushed through a press
1½  cups sauerkraut, drained well
 3  cups apple cider
 ¼  cup maple syrup
 6  fresh bratwurst
 6  submarine sandwich buns, split
    Whole-grain mustard

**1.** Prepare the grill for direct cooking over high heat (450° to 550°F).

**2.** In a large skillet over medium heat, fry the bacon until crisp, 10 to 12 minutes, turning occasionally. Transfer the bacon to paper towels to drain. Pour off all but 2 tablespoons of the bacon fat in the skillet. Return the skillet over medium heat, add the onion and garlic, and cook until slightly softened, 2 to 3 minutes, stirring often. Stir in the sauerkraut and cook until lightly browned, 4 to 5 minutes. Remove from the heat.

**3.** In a large disposable foil pan combine the cider and syrup. Add the bratwurst, place the pan over *direct high heat*, close the lid, and bring the liquid to a simmer. Continue simmering until the brats are evenly colored and have lost their raw look, 15 to 20 minutes, turning occasionally. Remove the brats from the pan and discard the liquid. Grill the brats over *direct high heat*, with the lid closed, until browned and fully cooked (160°F), 1 to 2 minutes, turning once or twice. During the last 30 seconds to 1 minute of grilling time, toast the buns, cut side down, over direct heat.

**4.** Warm the sauerkraut over medium heat. Spread mustard inside the buns and top each with a brat, one slice of bacon, and fried sauerkraut. Serve warm.

Sauerkraut is a fantastic topping and frying it in bacon fat takes it to a whole new level. The amount of saltiness in the sauerkraut varies by brand, so it is important to taste it before cooking to decide whether or not you should rinse it—just be sure to drain it well if you do. Most supermarkets carry canned sauerkraut near the canned vegetables, but the fresh sauerkraut sold in the refrigerated section is always much better.

# HOME OF THE BRAT

A haze hovers over the small city of 51,000 that sits on Lake Michigan, just an hour north of Milwaukee, Wisconsin. Open fires blaze in backyards across the land, and the local meat markets have been ransacked. Call it the bratwurst apocalypse, or simply call it summer in Sheboygan—these guys take their sausage seriously.

And for good reason. In 1860, 95 percent of the residents in Sheboygan County's Herman Township were German immigrants. To this day, German flags still proudly fly throughout the city of Sheboygan, and legendary homemade bratwurst line the butcher shop shelves. Residents run the annual Brat Trot (included in your entry fee is a post-race treat: a brat-on-a-stick) and attend the Brat Days festival, featuring such delicacies as the double brat, the brat egg roll, the brat taco, brat pizza, and brat jambalaya. Oh, and there was that formal legal battle with Bucyrus, Ohio, in 1970, which ultimately bestowed the coveted Bratwurst Capital of the World title upon the city of Sheboygan. The regional 'wurst pride in this Wisconsin town is real and it is relentless.

The textbook Sheboygan brat consists of coarsely ground pork that is seasoned with salt, pepper, and nutmeg (and sometimes mace, garlic, sage, or ginger) and stuffed into natural casings. And while pricking fresh brats with a fork and parboiling them in water, beer, or beer and onions before reduce the risk of exploding sausages) is a conventional practice across most of the United States, in Sheboygan, this standard of care is considered unorthodox and borderline silly.

True Sheboyganites skip the parboiling and pricking, classically cooking their brats low and slow over a charcoal fire, which keeps the juices inside and allows the pork to absorb the fire's smoky flavor. This method (read: fat and smoke) is what makes Sheboygan sausage far more flavorful than some of our other precooked, parboiled, smoked, or otherwise cured brat friends. For the most authentic of Sheboygan brats, once cooked through, they must then be served in a round, split hard roll called a semmel and dressed to perfection with brown mustard, dill pickle slices, and a heaping pile of grilled onions. Is your mouth watering yet?

Like Louisiana's crawfish boil, no social gathering in Sheboygan is complete without a brat fry. And by "brat fry," we mean an outdoor get-together that involves "frying" a massive amount of brats—without oil and without a deep fryer—but instead ... with a grill. According to the Sheboygan Convention and Visitor's Bureau, they do not grill their brats on a grill; they fry them—period. Sheboyganites unite in their brat terminology, even believing that their spelling is correct when writing: "I fryed brats this weekend." We'll let them have theirs, if we can keep ours. As they say, "It's just the Sheboygan way."

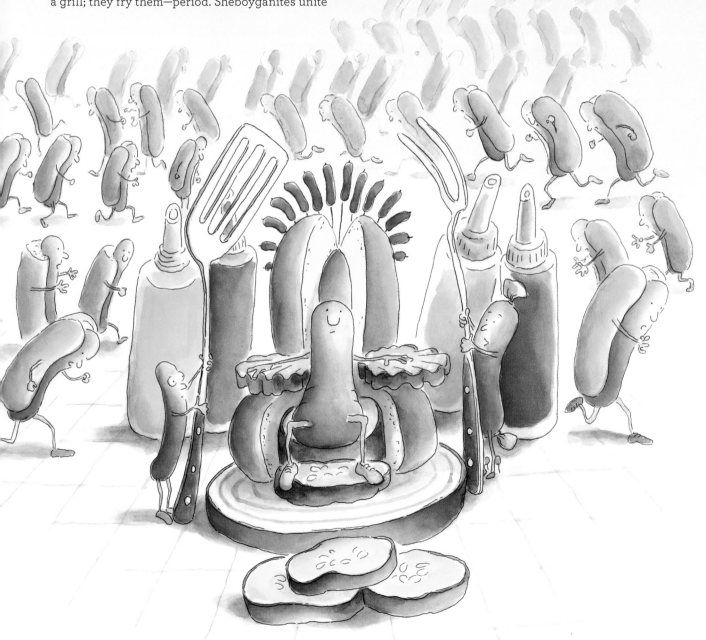

# GRILLED BRATS WITH SPICY TOMATO-CORN CHOWCHOW

SERVES: **6** | PREP TIME: **15 MINUTES** | GRILLING TIME: **15 TO 20 MINUTES**

### CHOWCHOW

- ¼ cup cider vinegar
- ¼ cup water
- 3 tablespoons packed brown sugar
- ½ teaspoon crushed red pepper flakes
- ½ teaspoon dried thyme
- 1 cup fresh corn kernels
- 2 plum tomatoes (slightly under ripe), seeded and cut into ½-inch dice
- ½ cup finely chopped green bell pepper
- ¼ cup finely chopped red onion
- 1 medium jalapeño chile pepper, seeded and minced

- 6 fresh bratwurst
- 6 hot dog buns, split
  Spicy brown mustard

Chowchow is a great relish to make when summer produce is at its peak. Try to purchase fresh corn as close to when you are going to use it as possible. Once it is picked, the sugars immediately begin to turn to starch, so the longer it sits, the less sweet and flavorful it will be.

**1.** Prepare the grill for direct cooking over medium-low heat (300° to 350°F).

**2.** In a medium saucepan combine the vinegar, water, brown sugar, red pepper flakes, and thyme. Bring to a boil over medium-high heat and cook for 1 minute. Add the corn, tomatoes, bell pepper, onion, and jalapeño, and return to a boil. Reduce the heat to medium and simmer for 10 minutes, stirring occasionally. Remove from the heat and let cool to room temperature.

**3.** Grill the bratwurst over *direct medium-low heat*, with the lid closed, until fully cooked (160°F), 15 to 20 minutes, turning occasionally. During the last 30 seconds to 1 minute of grilling time, toast the buns, cut side down, over direct heat.

**4.** Place each brat in a bun and top with mustard and tomato-corn chowchow. Serve warm.

# BEER BRATS WITH SAUERKRAUT, ONIONS, AND JALAPEÑOS

SERVES: **6**  |  PREP TIME: **15 MINUTES**  |  GRILLING TIME: **24 TO 26 MINUTES**  |  SPECIAL EQUIPMENT: **LARGE DISPOSABLE FOIL PAN**

1 bottle (12 ounces) lager
  Dijon or spicy brown mustard
2 tablespoons packed light
  brown sugar
½ teaspoon ground coriander
2 medium yellow onions, each
  cut in half and thinly sliced
6 fresh bratwurst
1 jar or bag (1 pound)
  sauerkraut, drained
2 jalapeño chile peppers,
  seeded and finely chopped
6 brat or torpedo rolls, split

BRATS

1. Prepare the grill for direct cooking over medium heat (350° to 450°F).

2. Whisk the lager, 2 tablespoons mustard, brown sugar, and coriander.

3. In a large disposable foil pan arrange the onions in an even layer. Add the bratwurst and pour the beer mixture over the top. Place the pan over *direct medium heat*, close the lid, and bring the mixture to a simmer. Simmer for about 20 minutes, turning the brats two or three times. Add the sauerkraut and jalapeños to the pan, and simmer for 2 to 3 minutes more.

4. Transfer the brats from the pan to the cooking grates and grill over *direct medium heat*, with the lid closed, until browned and fully cooked (160°F), 2 to 3 minutes, turning once. During the last 30 seconds to 1 minute of grilling time, toast the rolls, cut side down, over direct heat.

5. Place each brat in a roll and top with mustard and the sauerkraut mixture. Serve warm.

# SIDES &
# TOPPINGS

# JICAMA-APPLE SLAW
## WITH CREAMY YOGURT DRESSING

SERVES: **8 TO 10** | PREP TIME: **20 MINUTES** | STANDING TIME: **20 MINUTES**

# CLASSIC CREAMY SLAW

SERVES: **6 TO 8** | PREP TIME: **20 MINUTES**
CHILLING TIME: **2 HOURS TO 1 DAY**

### DRESSING

- ½ cup plain yogurt
- 3 tablespoons extra-virgin olive oil
- 2 tablespoons cider vinegar
- 1 tablespoon fresh lime juice
- 2 teaspoons granulated sugar
- 1½ teaspoons kosher salt
- 1 teaspoon ground cumin
- ½ teaspoon freshly ground black pepper

### SLAW

- 1 small jicama, about 1 pound, peeled, quartered, thinly sliced, and julienned
- ½ small head green cabbage, thinly sliced (4 cups)
- 2 large, ripe Granny Smith apples, quartered and thinly sliced
- ½ red onion cut in half and thinly sliced
- ½ cup roughly chopped fresh cilantro leaves

1. In a large bowl whisk the dressing ingredients. Add the slaw ingredients to the bowl and toss with the dressing.

2. Let the slaw stand at room temperature for 20 minutes, tossing occasionally, before serving.

If you have a mandoline or a food processor equipped with a slicing blade, use it to slice the jicama, cabbage, apples, and onion as thinly as possible.

### DRESSING

- ¾ cup mayonnaise
- 3 tablespoons white wine vinegar
- 2 tablespoons granulated sugar
- 1 teaspoon celery seed

  Kosher salt
  Freshly ground black pepper

### SLAW

- ½ small head green cabbage, thinly sliced (4 cups)
- 2 cups coarsely grated carrots
- 1 cup finely diced red bell pepper
- ½ cup roughly chopped fresh Italian parsley leaves

SIDES

# RED CABBAGE SLAW
## WITH CIDER-DILL VINAIGRETTE

SERVES: **8 TO 10** | PREP TIME: **20 MINUTES** | CHILLING TIME: **2 HOURS TO 1 DAY**

1. In a large bowl combine the dressing ingredients, including ¾ teaspoon salt and ½ teaspoon pepper, and whisk until the sugar and salt are dissolved. Add the slaw ingredients and mix well. Taste and add more salt and pepper, if desired. Cover and refrigerate until chilled, at least 2 hours or up to 1 day.

2. Before serving, drain the coleslaw in a colander and then transfer to a serving bowl.

### VINAIGRETTE
- ⅓ cup cider vinegar
- ⅓ cup canola oil
- ⅓ cup granulated sugar
- ¼ cup finely chopped fresh dill
- 1 tablespoon kosher salt
- ½ teaspoon freshly ground black pepper

### SLAW
- ½ medium head red cabbage, thinly sliced (6 cups)
- 1 English cucumber, about 14 ounces, thinly sliced
- 2 cups coarsely grated carrots
- 2 cups thinly sliced celery

1. In a large bowl combine the vinaigrette ingredients and whisk until the sugar and salt are dissolved. Add the slaw ingredients and mix well. Cover and refrigerate until chilled, at least 2 hours or up to 1 day.

2. Before serving, drain the slaw in a colander and then transfer to a serving bowl.

# MODERN MACARONI SALAD

SERVES: **8** | PREP TIME: **30 MINUTES** | GRILLING TIME: **10 TO 12 MINUTES**

## DRESSING

- ½ cup mayonnaise
- 1 teaspoon finely grated lemon zest
- 2 tablespoons fresh lemon juice
- 1 tablespoon Dijon mustard
- ¾ teaspoon kosher salt
- ¾ teaspoon freshly ground black pepper
- ½ teaspoon paprika
- ¼ teaspoon hot pepper sauce

- 8 ounces dried elbow macaroni
- 1 tablespoon extra-virgin olive oil
- 2 medium red bell peppers
- 1 cup thinly sliced celery
- 3 scallions (white and light green parts only), thinly sliced
- ½ cup thinly sliced kalamata olives
- ⅓ cup roughly chopped fresh Italian parsley leaves

1. In a nonreactive bowl whisk the dressing ingredients. Cover and refrigerate until ready to use.

2. Bring a large pot of salted water to a rolling boil. Add the macaroni and cook until al dente, 7 to 9 minutes. Drain and transfer to a large bowl. Toss with the oil. Cool to room temperature.

3. Prepare the grill for direct cooking over medium heat (350° to 450°F).

4. Grill the bell peppers over *direct medium heat*, with the lid closed, until blackened and blistered all over, 10 to 12 minutes, turning occasionally. Put the peppers in a bowl and cover with plastic wrap to trap the steam. Let stand for about 10 minutes. Carefully peel away and discard the charred skin. Remove and discard the stem, seeds, and ribs. Cut the peppers into medium dice.

5. To the bowl with the macaroni add the bell peppers, celery, scallions, olives, and parsley. Pour the dressing over the salad and toss to combine. Serve immediately, or cover and refrigerate until serving.

# CHEF'S MACARONI SALAD

SERVES: **6** | PREP TIME: **20 MINUTES**

### DRESSING

- ½ cup mayonnaise
- 3 tablespoons red wine vinegar
- 1¼ teaspoons kosher salt
- 1 teaspoon spicy brown mustard
- ½ teaspoon freshly ground black pepper
- ¼ teaspoon granulated sugar

- 8 ounces dried elbow macaroni
- ¼ medium red onion, finely chopped
- 2 ribs celery, finely diced
- ½ cup finely chopped fresh Italian parsley leaves

### TOPPINGS

- 2 ounces cooked ham, julienned
- 2 ounces cooked turkey breast, julienned
- 1 small heart of romaine, julienned
- 1 medium, ripe beefsteak tomato, cored, seeded, and finely diced
- ½ cup coarsely grated sharp cheddar cheese
- 2 hard-boiled eggs, finely chopped

Whenever you are cooking pasta, add plenty of salt to the boiling water—enough that the water tastes as salty as the ocean. Why? Because this is your one and only chance to season the pasta on the inside. After it's cooked, salt will only season the outside.

**1.** Combine the dressing ingredients.

**2.** Bring a large pot of salted water to a rolling boil. Add the macaroni and cook until al dente, 7 to 9 minutes. Drain and transfer to a wide serving bowl. Add the onion, celery, parsley, and dressing and toss to coat. Gently smooth the surface.

**3.** Arrange the toppings in stripes on top of the salad. Gently toss together before eating.

# ORZO SALAD WITH GRILLED FENNEL, TOMATOES, AND KALE

SERVES: 8 | PREP TIME: 40 MINUTES | GRILLING TIME: ABOUT 10 MINUTES

⅔ cup tightly packed fresh basil leaves

3 tablespoons white balsamic vinegar

Kosher salt

Freshly ground black pepper

Extra-virgin olive oil

1–2 fennel bulbs, about 1 pound total, trimmed, bulb(s) cut into quarters (leave core attached)

8 ounces dried orzo pasta

1 pound ripe red and yellow grape or cherry tomatoes, each cut in half

2–3 cups tightly packed whole baby kale leaves or roughly chopped regular kale leaves (3 ounces)

¾ cup coarsely grated (on the large holes of a box grater) Parmigiano-Reggiano® cheese (3 ounces)

1. In a food processor fitted with a metal blade, combine the basil, vinegar, ½ teaspoon salt, and ¼ teaspoon pepper, and pulse 10 times in one-second bursts. With the motor running, slowly add ½ cup oil through the feed tube. Continue to process until the vinaigrette is emulsified. Transfer to a very large bowl and set aside.

2. Prepare the grill for direct cooking over medium heat (350° to 450°F).

3. Brush the fennel with 1 tablespoon oil and season evenly with ¼ teaspoon salt and ⅛ teaspoon pepper.

4. Grill the fennel over *direct medium heat*, with the lid closed, until browned in spots and almost tender, about 10 minutes, turning three times. Remove from the grill and let rest while cooking the orzo.

5. Cook the orzo according to package directions. Drain and rinse briefly with cold water to cool slightly. Drain well. Transfer the orzo to the very large bowl with the vinaigrette. Toss to coat. Cut the fennel quarters crosswise into ¾-inch pieces (you may remove the core, if desired) and add to the bowl with the orzo. Add the tomatoes, kale, and cheese and mix gently. Season with salt and pepper. The salad can be served immediately or covered and refrigerated for up to 6 hours.

When you quarter fennel bulbs, leave some of the core attached to each piece. The core holds the leaves together on the grill.

SIDES

# EASY COLD NOODLE SALAD WITH PEANUT SAUCE AND CARROT

SERVES: **4** | PREP TIME: **20 MINUTES**

- 8 ounces dried fettuccine pasta
- 1 medium carrot, peeled and thinly sliced on a diagonal
- ½ cup smooth peanut butter
- ½ cup unsweetened coconut milk
- 2 tablespoons fresh lime juice
- 1 tablespoon packed light brown sugar
- 2 teaspoons Asian fish sauce
- 2 teaspoons peeled, grated fresh ginger
- 1 garlic clove, minced or pushed through a press
- ¼ teaspoon crushed red pepper flakes
- 1 English cucumber, about 12 ounces, halved lengthwise and thinly sliced into half-moons
- 3 scallions, ends trimmed and thinly sliced

1. Cook the fettuccine until al dente, according to package directions. During the last minute of cooking time, add the carrot. Drain, rinse under cold water, and drain again. Transfer to a large bowl.

2. In a blender combine the peanut butter, coconut milk, lime juice, brown sugar, fish sauce, ginger, garlic, and red pepper flakes and blend until smooth. Pour the mixture over the fettuccine, add the cucumber and scallions, and toss well. If the sauce seems too thick, stir in warm water a tablespoon at a time until the desired thickness is reached. Serve warm or at room temperature.

Called *nam pla* in Thailand and *nuoc mam* in Vietnam, fish sauce is an essential seasoning all over Southeast Asia. You need just a little bit of it to give savory dishes a pungent, salty accent.

SIDES

# DEVILED EGGS WITH HOT SAUCE

SERVES: 6 | PREP TIME: 10 MINUTES

6 large eggs
2 tablespoons mayonnaise
1 tablespoon finely chopped fresh dill
1 tablespoon whole milk
1 teaspoon Dijon mustard
Hot pepper sauce
¼ teaspoon kosher salt
¼ teaspoon freshly ground black pepper
12 very small sprigs fresh dill

1. Place the eggs in a single layer in a large saucepan and add enough water to cover them by at least 1 inch. Bring the water to a boil over high heat, uncovered. Then remove the saucepan from the heat, cover the saucepan, and let the eggs stand for 15 minutes. Drain the eggs and run cold water over them until cool to the touch.

2. Peel the eggs and cut each one lengthwise in half. Scoop out the yolks and put them in a bowl. Add the mayonnaise, chopped dill, milk, mustard, ¼ teaspoon hot pepper sauce (or to taste), salt, and pepper. Mix until well combined. Spoon the mixture into the egg whites. Garnish with dill sprigs and add another dash of hot pepper sauce, if desired.

To get the yolks to set in the middle of the egg whites, gently stir the eggs during the first couple minutes of cooking time.

# TOMATO AND AVOCADO SALAD WITH LEMON-CAPER VINAIGRETTE

SERVES: **4 TO 6** | PREP TIME: **15 MINUTES**

## VINAIGRETTE

- 2 tablespoons fresh lemon juice
- 1 tablespoon capers, drained and chopped
- 1 tablespoon finely chopped shallot
- 1 teaspoon Dijon mustard
- ½ teaspoon kosher salt
- ¼ teaspoon freshly ground black pepper
- ¼ cup extra-virgin olive oil

- 1 pint ripe yellow grape tomatoes, each cut in half
- ½ cup thinly sliced red onion
- 1 pound assorted ripe tomatoes, cored and each cut into 6 to 8 wedges
- 1–2 ripe Hass avocados, cut into slices

1. Whisk all the vinaigrette ingredients except for the oil. Add the oil in a steady stream, whisking constantly until the vinaigrette is emulsified.

2. In a bowl combine the grape tomatoes and onion with 1 tablespoon of the vinaigrette; toss well.

3. Spoon the grape tomatoes and onion onto the center of a large serving platter. Arrange the tomato wedges and avocado slices around the edge of the platter, and then drizzle with the remaining vinaigrette. The salad can be served immediately or covered and held at room temperature for up to 1 hour.

SIDES

# CHOPPED GREEK-STYLE SALAD

SERVES: **6 TO 8** | PREP TIME: **20 MINUTES**

## DRESSING

- 2 tablespoons fresh lemon juice
- 1 tablespoon red wine vinegar
- ½ teaspoon kosher salt
- ½ teaspoon freshly ground black pepper
- 1 small garlic clove, minced or pushed through a press
- ¼ cup extra-virgin olive oil

## SALAD

- 4–5 cups roughly chopped hearts of romaine
- 2 cups ½-inch-diced English cucumber
- 1 pint ripe grape or cherry tomatoes, each cut in half (quartered if large)
- 1 large red bell pepper, cut into ½-inch dice
- 1 cup canned chickpeas (garbanzo beans), rinsed and drained
- 4 ounces feta cheese, crumbled
- ½ cup finely chopped red onion
- ½ cup kalamata olives, each cut into quarters
- ¼ cup tightly packed fresh mint leaves, roughly chopped
- ¼ cup tightly packed fresh Italian parsley leaves, roughly chopped

1. Whisk all the vinaigrette ingredients except for the oil. Add the oil in a steady stream, whisking constantly until the dressing is emulsified.

2. In a serving bowl combine the salad ingredients. Add the dressing and toss well. Serve immediately.

# WARM BROCCOLI SALAD
## WITH CRISPY BACON, RED ONION, WALNUTS, AND RAISINS

SERVES: **4** | PREP TIME: **15 MINUTES** | GRILLING TIME: **12 TO 15 MINUTES** | SPECIAL EQUIPMENT: **CAST-IRON SKILLET**

### DRESSING
¼ cup whole-milk plain yogurt
¼ cup mayonnaise
1½ teaspoons red wine vinegar
½ teaspoon granulated sugar
½ teaspoon kosher salt
¼ teaspoon freshly ground black pepper
⅛ teaspoon ground cayenne pepper

½ cup walnut pieces
6 slices bacon
1 pound broccoli, cut into bite-sized florets
½ cup finely chopped red onion
½ cup raisins

1. Whisk the dressing ingredients.

2. Prepare the grill for direct cooking over medium heat (350° to 450°F) and preheat a cast-iron skillet.

3. Cook the walnuts in the skillet over *direct medium heat*, with the lid closed, until fragrant and golden, 2 to 3 minutes, stirring frequently. Remove the walnuts from the skillet.

4. Place the bacon in a single layer in the skillet. Fry over *direct medium heat*, with the lid closed, until the fat renders and the bacon is crisp, 10 to 12 minutes, turning occasionally. Transfer the bacon to paper towels to drain. Leave the bacon fat in the skillet. Add the broccoli and onion to the skillet and sauté over *direct medium heat*, with the lid closed, until crisp-tender, about 2 minutes. Transfer to a large bowl.

5. Coarsely chop the bacon. Add the bacon, walnuts, raisins, and the dressing to the large bowl and stir to combine. Serve warm, at room temperature, or cold.

**FUN FACT**

Broccoli, kale, cauliflower, kohlrabi, Brussels sprouts, cabbage: notice the similarity in taste, texture, aroma, and appearance? That's not surprising—they're cousins! All are members of the genus *Brassica*, and all likely originated in a humble wild cabbage species native to southern Italy.

# SCANDINAVIAN POTATO SALAD WITH FRESH HERBS

SERVES: **8 TO 10** | PREP TIME: **30 MINUTES** | CHILLING TIME: **1 TO 4 HOURS**

- 3 pounds small new potatoes, 1 to 1¼ inches in diameter
- 1 tablespoon plus 2 teaspoons kosher salt, divided
- ¼ cup extra-virgin olive oil
- 3 tablespoons white wine vinegar
- 1 garlic clove, minced or pushed through a press
- 2 teaspoons granulated sugar
- 2 teaspoons mustard powder
- 1 teaspoon freshly ground black pepper
- 3 scallions (white and light green parts only), thinly sliced
- ¼ cup finely chopped fresh Italian parsley leaves
- ¼ cup finely chopped fresh dill
- ¼ cup finely chopped fresh chives

1. Put the potatoes in a large saucepan and cover them with cold water by 2 inches. Add 1 tablespoon of the salt. Bring to a boil. Reduce the heat to medium and boil gently until the potatoes are tender but not mushy, 15 to 18 minutes. Drain and transfer to a large bowl.

2. Whisk the oil, vinegar, garlic, sugar, mustard powder, pepper, and the remaining 2 teaspoons salt. Pour over the warm potatoes, and then add the scallions. Toss to combine. Cover and refrigerate for 1 to 4 hours, tossing occasionally. Just before serving, stir in the parsley, dill, and chives.

# GRILLED POTATO SALAD WITH EGGS, CELERY, AND DIJON MAYO

SERVES: **6** | PREP TIME: **30 MINUTES** | GRILLING TIME: **20 TO 25 MINUTES** | CHILLING TIME: **AT LEAST 2 HOURS**

- 2 pounds yellow potatoes, about 1½ inches in diameter, each cut in half
- 1 tablespoon extra-virgin olive oil
- 2 teaspoons kosher salt, divided
- 2 teaspoons red wine vinegar
- ⅓ cup mayonnaise
- 1½ tablespoons Dijon mustard
- 1 teaspoon freshly ground black pepper
- 2 large hard-boiled eggs, chopped
- 1 cup finely chopped celery
- 1 cup finely chopped red onion, rinsed in a fine-mesh strainer under cold water
- ½ cup finely chopped fresh Italian parsley leaves

You can use any kind or any color of thin-skinned, low-starch (waxy) potatoes for this recipe. Just make sure to cut the potatoes into bite-sized pieces before grilling them. Avoid thick-skinned, starchy potatoes like russets—those are better suited for fries or mashed potatoes.

1. Prepare the grill for direct cooking over medium heat (350° to 450°F).

2. In a large bowl combine the potatoes, oil, and 1 teaspoon of the salt and turn to coat.

3. Grill the potatoes over *direct medium heat*, with the lid closed, until golden brown and tender, 20 to 25 minutes, turning occasionally. Return the potatoes to the large bowl. Sprinkle the vinegar over the potatoes and gently stir to combine. Cool to room temperature.

4. In a small bowl whisk the mayonnaise, mustard, pepper, and the remaining 1 teaspoon salt.

5. To the bowl with the potatoes add the mayonnaise mixture, the eggs, celery, onion, and parsley. Gently stir to combine. Cover and refrigerate for at least 2 hours. Serve chilled.

# NEW POTATO SALAD WITH BACON AND ONIONS

SERVES: **8** | PREP TIME: **20 MINUTES** | GRILLING TIME: **30 TO 37 MINUTES** | STANDING TIME: **1 HOUR (OPTIONAL)**

Extra-virgin olive oil
Kosher salt
Freshly ground black pepper
2½ pounds new potatoes, about 1½ inches
    in diameter, each cut in half
8 ounces thick-cut bacon, cut into ¼-inch dice
2 medium sweet onions, each cut crosswise
    into ½-inch slices
6 scallions (white part only), thinly sliced
3 tablespoons finely chopped fresh
    Italian parsley leaves
1 tablespoon finely chopped fresh thyme leaves
3 tablespoons sherry vinegar
3 tablespoons chicken broth *or* water

1. Prepare the grill for direct cooking over medium heat (350° to 450°F).

2. In a large bowl whisk 2 tablespoons oil, ½ teaspoon salt, and ½ teaspoon pepper. Add the potato halves and toss to coat.

3. Grill the potatoes over *direct medium heat*, with the lid closed, until golden brown and tender, 20 to 25 minutes, turning occasionally. When cool enough to handle, cut each potato half into two pieces and place in a large bowl. Cover and set aside at room temperature.

4. In a skillet over medium heat, fry the bacon until crisp, 10 to 12 minutes, turning occasionally. With a slotted spoon transfer the bacon to the bowl of potatoes; reserve the bacon fat.

5. Brush the onion slices on both sides with some of the reserved bacon fat and season with salt and pepper. Grill the onion slices over *direct medium heat*, with the lid closed, until lightly browned and tender, 10 to 12 minutes, turning and basting with the reserved bacon fat once. Cut each onion slice into quarters. Add to the potatoes along with the scallions, parsley, and thyme.

6. Combine the vinegar, broth, ¼ teaspoon salt, and ¼ teaspoon pepper. Slowly whisk in ⅓ cup oil. Pour the dressing over the potatoes and toss gently. Serve; or, to fully incorporate the flavors, cover and let stand at room temperature for about 1 hour before serving.

**SIDES**

**FUN FACT**

Contrary to what you may think, new potatoes are actually the same variety as many of the full-sized red, yellow, and white potatoes you see piled on your supermarket shelves. The difference is, the aptly named "new potato" is just a freshly harvested young potato with an edible paper-thin skin, a moist center, and a mildly sweet flavor.

# WATERMELON AND FETA SALAD WITH LIME AND MINT

SERVES: **6 TO 8** | PREP TIME: **20 MINUTES**

- 1 small, ripe seedless watermelon, 5 to 6 pounds
- ⅓ cup extra-virgin olive oil
- ½ cup finely chopped fresh fennel bulb
- 2 tablespoons fresh lime juice
- ½ teaspoon freshly ground black pepper
- ¼ teaspoon kosher salt
- 6 ounces feta cheese, crumbled
- ½ cup roughly chopped fresh mint leaves

1. Cut the watermelon into 1-inch slices. Cut away the rind and cut the flesh into 1-inch chunks. Put the watermelon chunks in a bowl and refrigerate until ready to serve.

2. Whisk the oil, fennel, lime juice, pepper, and salt to make a vinaigrette. Set aside.

3. When ready to serve, whisk the vinaigrette again and pour over the watermelon. Mix well. Add the cheese and mint. Mix again and serve immediately.

This salad is best eaten right away. Otherwise the watermelon juices will break down the nice, firm texture of the feta cheese.

# TROPICAL FRUIT SALAD WITH HONEY AND LIME

SERVES: 4 TO 6 | PREP TIME: 30 MINUTES

1 ripe papaya, about 1¼ pounds,
  peeled, seeded, and cut
  into ¾-inch pieces
1 ripe mango, about
  1 pound, peeled and cut
  into ¾-inch pieces
½ ripe, fresh pineapple, cored
  and cut into ¾-inch pieces
3 ripe kiwifruit, peeled and cut
  into ¼-inch-thick half-moons
  Finely grated zest and
  juice of 1 lime
1 serrano chile pepper, seeded
  and minced
1 tablespoon white wine vinegar
1 tablespoon honey
1 tablespoon minced fresh
  cilantro or mint leaves (optional)

1. In a large bowl combine
the ingredients. Gently toss.
Serve immediately.

Inside a mango is a
flat pit that runs from
top to bottom. To cut
around the pit, rotate
the mango so that the
pit runs parallel to the
blade of your knife.
Cut lengthwise along
each side of the pit.

# WHOLE-GRAIN RICE SALAD
## WITH HERBS, PINE NUTS, AND SOUR CHERRY VINAIGRETTE

SERVES: **8 TO 12** | PREP TIME: **40 MINUTES, PLUS ABOUT 45 MINUTES FOR THE RICE**

## RICE

- 5 cups water
- 2 tablespoons soy sauce
- 2 cups brown rice or brown rice blend

- 1 cup dried sour cherries
- 1 cup hot water
- ¼ cup red wine vinegar
- ¼ cup plus 1 tablespoon extra-virgin olive oil
- 3 tablespoons minced shallot
- 1½ teaspoons kosher salt
- ½ teaspoon ground black pepper
- ½ cup pine nuts, toasted
- 1 cup finely chopped celery
- 3 cups loosely packed fresh basil leaves, coarsely chopped
- 2 cups loosely packed fresh mint leaves, coarsely chopped
- 2 cups loosely packed fresh Italian parsley leaves, coarsely chopped

1. In a large saucepan with a tight-fitting lid, bring the water and soy sauce to a boil. Add the rice, cover, and simmer until tender and most of the water has been absorbed, about 45 minutes. Meanwhile, prepare the vinaigrette.

2. Combine the sour cherries and hot water. Set aside until the cherries are plumped, about 20 minutes. Drain, reserving both the soaking liquid and cherries (you should have about ¾ cup liquid). Put the liquid in a skillet and reduce over high heat to ⅓ cup, about 8 minutes (depending on the diameter of the skillet). Pour the reduction into a bowl and whisk with the vinegar, oil, shallot, salt, and pepper to make a vinaigrette.

3. Preheat a skillet over medium heat. Add the pine nuts and cook until golden brown, about 3 minutes, shaking the skillet occasionally and watching carefully to prevent burning.

4. In a serving bowl combine the rice with the vinaigrette, cherries, and celery. Stir in the fresh herbs. Cool to room temperature. Serve; or cover and refrigerate for up to 2 days. Add the pine nuts just before serving.

SIDES

# CORN AND BLACK BEAN SALAD

SERVES: **6 TO 8**  |  PREP TIME: **30 MINUTES**  |  GRILLING TIME: **10 TO 15 MINUTES**

## DRESSING

  3 tablespoons fresh lime juice
  1 teaspoon finely grated
    orange zest
  2 tablespoons fresh orange juice
1¼ teaspoons kosher salt
  ¼ teaspoon freshly ground
    black pepper

    Extra-virgin olive oil

## SALAD

  4 ears fresh corn, husked
  1 can (14 ounces) black beans,
    rinsed and drained
  1 red bell pepper, cut into
    ¼-inch dice
  1 English cucumber, cut into
    ¼-inch dice
  ½ cup finely chopped red onion
  ½ cup thinly sliced fresh
    basil leaves
  4 scallions (white and light green
    parts only), finely chopped
  3 ounces feta cheese, crumbled

1. Prepare the grill for direct cooking over medium heat (350° to 450°F).

2. Whisk the dressing ingredients, including 2 tablespoons oil.

3. Lightly brush the corn all over with oil, and then grill over *direct medium heat*, with the lid closed, until browned in spots and tender, 10 to 15 minutes, turning occasionally. Cut the kernels from the cobs over a serving bowl.

4. To the serving bowl add the remaining salad ingredients. Whisk the dressing again, and pour it over the salad. Toss gently to combine. Serve immediately.

**SIDES**

# FOOD EUPHORIA

We've all been there. The post-turkey slumber: propped up on the couch, football game on, sleepily lazy and oh-so-content after a huge holiday dinner. That sluggish, satisfied state is not just a result of stuffing yourself far beyond the socially acceptable lunch- or dinnertime dietary standards—it's a product of science. In fact, many foods create happiness, even euphoria, both physiologically (in our bodies) and psychologically (in our thoughts).

To understand the "how" of food happiness, we must first understand that our brain is our body's control center: It tells our hearts to beat, our eyes to blink, and our mouths to chew. Our brain also regulates our moods and can tell us when we're hungry, angry ... even "hangry" (the term used to describe a state of anger caused by lack of food—but that's another story in itself).

Happily, many foods help to produce mood-enhancing chemicals in the brain, such as serotonin and dopamine. Touted as the "happy hormone," serotonin calms our minds and regulates our moods and sleep cycles. Foods that aid in serotonin production include turkey, spinach, and bananas, among others. Thanksgiving Burger (page 98) or Chicken Popeye Slider (page 109), anyone?

Dopamine, then, is serotonin's euphoric counterpart that captains our brain's reward and pleasure centers. Like what you see? *Whoosh* ... dopamine production. Neuroimaging shows that these pleasure centers literally light up in the presence of "naughty" foods, such as those high in fat, sugar, or salt—very much like addicts' brain scans. *Zing! French fries!*

And while some foods physiologically affect our moods, others make us happy simply because they are delicious and familiar. We're talking the flame-broiled cheeseburgers, the savory casseroles, the hearty meat loaves, and the ooey-gooey mac-n-cheeses of the world—yep, comfort foods.

These types of foods provide happiness on a psychological level, and studies show that perhaps the comfort foods we crave are actually artifacts from our pasts. Comfort foods trigger happy memories and associations and provide a sense of well-being and security. Maybe it's Mom's homemade apple pie, or perhaps it's Dad's barbecued brats or Grandma's fried chicken. All of us have a certain food that "speaks" to us, some special dish that warms our hearts on an impenetrable level ... what's *yours*?

# CHILI-SPICED FRIES

SERVES: **4 TO 6** | PREP TIME: **25 MINUTES** | SOAKING TIME: **30 MINUTES** | COOLING TIME: **15 MINUTES**
FRYING TIME: **5 TO 6 MINUTES PER BATCH** | SPECIAL EQUIPMENT: **DEEP-FRY THERMOMETER**

## SPICES

1½ teaspoons kosher salt
 1 teaspoon ancho chile powder
½ teaspoon prepared chili powder
¼ teaspoon ground chipotle chile pepper
¼ teaspoon ground cumin

 4 russet potatoes, about 2½ pounds total
   Canola or vegetable oil

1. Combine the spices.

2. Fill a large bowl with cold water. Scrub the potatoes under cold water, and cut each lengthwise into ¼- to ⅓-inch slices. Then cut each slice lengthwise into ¼- to ⅓-inch strips. Transfer to the bowl of water. Let the potatoes soak for 30 minutes.

3. Drain the potatoes, and then pat dry with a towel. Lay them out in a single layer on several layers of paper towels.

4. Line a large sheet pan with several layers of paper towels. Pour enough oil into a large, deep pot to come 3 inches up the side. Attach a deep-fry thermometer to the side of the pot. Heat the oil on the stove top over medium heat until the temperature registers 325°F. Working in small batches to prevent the oil temperature from dropping too much, add some of the potatoes to the pot and cook until cooked through and beginning to brown slightly, about 4 minutes, maintaining the temperature between 300° and 325°F and moving them occasionally. Using a slotted spoon or tongs, transfer the potatoes to the prepared sheet pan. Repeat with the remaining potatoes, returning the oil temperature to 325°F between each batch. Allow all the potatoes to cool for 15 minutes before continuing.

5. Preheat the oven to 200°F.

6. Line another large sheet pan with several layers of paper towels. Increase the heat to medium-high and bring the oil temperature to 375°F. Divide the potatoes into three equal batches. Add one batch of potatoes to the oil and cook until crisp and deep golden brown, 1 to 2 minutes. Transfer the potatoes to the prepared sheet pan to drain, then transfer to a third sheet pan and hold in the oven. Return the oil temperature to 375°F, and repeat with the remaining two batches of potatoes, draining each batch on fresh paper towels.

7. Season the fries with the spices. Serve immediately.

Soak the cut potatoes in water for about 30 minutes to remove some starchiness, and then pat them dry with paper towels. The first round of frying is for cooking the fries to the center. The second round (at a higher temperature) is for making the surfaces brown and crispy.

# STEAK FRIES WITH ROSEMARY-LEMON AIOLI

SERVES: **4 TO 6** | PREP TIME: **15 MINUTES** | GRILLING TIME: **15 TO 17 MINUTES**

## AIOLI

- 1 cup mayonnaise
- ½ teaspoon finely grated lemon zest
- 1½ tablespoons fresh lemon juice
- 2 teaspoons minced garlic
- 2 teaspoons Dijon mustard
- 2 teaspoons minced fresh rosemary leaves

  Kosher salt
  Freshly ground black pepper
- 4 russet potatoes, about 3 pounds total
- 2 tablespoons extra-virgin olive oil

1. Prepare the grill for direct cooking over medium heat (350° to 450°F).

2. Whisk the aioli ingredients. Season with ¼ teaspoon salt and ¼ teaspoon pepper.

3. Scrub the potatoes under cold water and dry them with paper towels. Cut the potatoes lengthwise in half, and then cut each potato half lengthwise into ½-inch-thick slices. Place in a bowl and add the oil, 2 teaspoons salt, and 1 teaspoon pepper. Toss to coat.

4. Grill the potato slices over *direct medium heat,* with the lid closed, until tender and marked by the grill, 15 to 17 minutes, turning occasionally.

5. Serve the fries warm with rosemary-lemon aioli.

SIDES

# CURRY SWEET POTATO FRIES WITH SPICY YOGURT SAUCE

SERVES: 4 | PREP TIME: **15 MINUTES** | GRILLING TIME: **10 TO 15 MINUTES** | SPECIAL EQUIPMENT: **PERFORATED GRILL PAN**

## SAUCE

- ½ cup plain Greek yogurt
- 2 teaspoons fresh lime juice
- ½ teaspoon red curry paste
- ¼ teaspoon kosher salt
- 1 garlic clove, minced or pushed through a press

- 2 teaspoons curry powder
- 1 teaspoon kosher salt
- ½ teaspoon freshly ground black pepper
- 2 tablespoons extra-virgin olive oil
- 2 sweet potatoes, about 2 pounds total, peeled and ends trimmed

1. Prepare the grill for direct cooking over medium heat (350° to 450°F) and preheat a perforated grill pan.

2. Whisk the sauce ingredients.

3. In a large bowl combine the curry powder, salt, and pepper. Stir in the oil. Cut the potatoes into 4-by-½-by-½-inch sticks (discard any uneven pieces, as they would burn easily). Put the potatoes in the bowl with the oil and spices, and turn to coat evenly.

4. Spread the potatoes in a single layer on the grill pan and grill over *direct medium heat*, with the lid closed, until tender, 10 to 15 minutes, turning every few minutes to brown all sides.

5. Serve the fries warm with spicy yogurt sauce.

**FUN FACT**

Curry powder is actually a blend of up to 20 different spices, which can include turmeric (which gives it the characteristic golden color), coriander, cumin, fenugreek, paprika, pepper, cardamom, cinnamon, nutmeg, cloves, allspice, and more.

**SIDES**

# SMOKY BARBECUED BAKED BEANS

SERVES: 8 | PREP TIME: 15 MINUTES | GRILLING TIME: 1½ TO 2 HOURS
SPECIAL EQUIPMENT: 4 LARGE HANDFULS OAK, APPLE, OR CHERRY WOOD CHIPS; 12-INCH CAST-IRON SKILLET

- 3 slices thick-cut bacon, 4 to 5 ounces total, finely chopped
- 1 small yellow onion, finely chopped
- 1 medium jalapeño chile pepper, finely chopped (optional)
- 5 cans (each 15 ounces) navy beans or other small white beans, rinsed and drained
- 1¼ cups barbecue sauce
- 1 cup beef, chicken, or vegetable broth
- ⅓ cup molasses
- 2 tablespoons spicy brown mustard
- ½ teaspoon kosher salt
- ¼ teaspoon freshly ground black pepper

**SIDES**

If you're using a charcoal grill, replenish the charcoal as needed to maintain a steady temperature, adding about 8 unlit briquettes every 45 minutes to 1 hour. Leave the lid off the grill for about 5 minutes to help the new briquettes light.

1. Soak the wood chips in water for at least 30 minutes.

2. Prepare the grill for indirect cooking over medium-low heat (300° to 350°F).

3. In a 12-inch cast-iron skillet over medium-low heat, fry the bacon until barely browned, about 5 minutes, stirring often. Add the onion and jalapeño (if using), and cook until the onion is softened, about 3 minutes. Add the remaining ingredients and mix well.

4. Drain and add two handfuls of the wood chips to the charcoal or to the smoker box of a gas grill, following manufacturer's instructions, and close the lid. When the wood begins to smoke, cook the beans over *indirect medium-low heat*, with the lid closed, until the sauce has thickened and the beans are fully flavored with smoke, 1½ to 2 hours, stirring occasionally. Drain and add the remaining wood chips after 30 minutes of cooking time.

5. Serve the beans warm.

# SOUTHERN FRIED PICKLES WITH RÉMOULADE

SERVES: **6 TO 8** | PREP TIME: **20 MINUTES** | FRYING TIME: **ABOUT 1 MINUTE PER BATCH**
SPECIAL EQUIPMENT: **DEEP-FRY THERMOMETER**

## RÉMOULADE

- 1 cup mayonnaise
- 2 tablespoons coarse-grain Dijon mustard
- 2 tablespoons ketchup
- 1 tablespoon prepared horseradish
- 2 teaspoons capers, drained and chopped
- ½ teaspoon hot pepper sauce

- ⅔ cup all-purpose flour
- 1 tablespoon paprika
- 1 teaspoon garlic powder
- ½ teaspoon kosher salt
- ½ teaspoon freshly ground black pepper
- 1 large egg, beaten
- ⅔ cup well-shaken buttermilk
- 1 teaspoon hot pepper sauce
- 1½ cups panko bread crumbs
- 1 jar (16 ounces) dill pickle chips, drained and patted dry
  Canola or vegetable oil

1. Combine the rémoulade ingredients. Cover and refrigerate until ready to serve.

2. In a shallow bowl whisk the flour, paprika, garlic powder, salt, and pepper. In a separate, deeper bowl whisk the egg, buttermilk, and hot pepper sauce. Put the panko in a third bowl. Working with a few at a time, dip the pickles into the flour mixture, turning to coat, and then shake off the excess and dip them into the egg mixture. Shake off the excess egg mixture, and then dredge them through the panko. Place in a single layer on a sheet pan. Repeat with the remaining pickles.

3. Preheat the oven to 200°F. Line a sheet pan with paper towels, and have a second, unlined sheet pan at hand.

4. Pour enough oil into a large, deep pot to come 2 inches up the side. Attach a deep-fry thermometer to the side of the pot. Heat the oil on the stove top over medium-high heat until the temperature registers 350°F. Add one quarter of the pickles and cook until golden and crisp, about 1 minute, turning once, if necessary. Place the fried pickles on the lined sheet pan to blot the excess oil, and then transfer to the unlined sheet pan; keep warm in the oven. Repeat with the remaining pickles.

5. Serve the fried pickles warm with rémoulade.

# CLASSIC BUTTERMILK ONION RINGS

SERVES: **4 TO 6** | PREP TIME: **20 MINUTES** | STANDING TIME: **15 MINUTES**
FRYING TIME: **2 TO 4 MINUTES PER BATCH** | SPECIAL EQUIPMENT: **DEEP-FRY THERMOMETER**

2  cups well-shaken buttermilk
1  tablespoon paprika
1  teaspoon ground cumin
1  teaspoon freshly ground black pepper
2  yellow onions, 1¾ to 2 pounds total
2¼ cups all-purpose flour
1  tablespoon kosher salt
¾  teaspoon ground cayenne pepper
   Canola or vegetable oil
   Ranch dressing
   Ketchup
   Barbecue sauce

1. In a large bowl whisk the buttermilk, paprika, cumin, and pepper.

2. Cut the onions crosswise into ½-inch slices and separate them into rings. Add the onion rings to the buttermilk mixture and stir to coat. Let stand for 15 minutes, stirring occasionally.

3. Meanwhile, in a large, shallow bowl whisk the flour, salt, and cayenne pepper.

4. Preheat the oven to 200°F.

5. Line a sheet pan with parchment paper.

6. Pour enough oil into a large, deep pot to come 1 inch up the side. Attach a deep-fry thermometer to the side of the pot. Heat the oil on the stove top over medium-high heat until the temperature registers 350° to 375°F.

7. Working in batches, remove some of the onion rings from the buttermilk mixture and dredge them in the flour mixture. If desired, dip the onion rings back into the buttermilk and dredge them a second time in the flour mixture. Carefully add the onion rings to the hot oil and cook until they are golden, 2 to 4 minutes, turning once. Using tongs, transfer the onion rings to the prepared sheet pan and keep warm in the oven. Repeat with the remaining onion rings and flour mixture.

8. Serve the onion rings right away with your choice of condiment.

## A SALUTE TO KETCHUP

In praise of ketchup … or is it catsup? Either way, the tangy, tomato-loaded condiment seems to be the foundation upon which we've built a nation—or at least a culinary tradition. But like many American standbys, ketchup hails from far away. During their travels, eighteenth-century English explorers fell for a thin, fermented Asian fish sauce, which was brought back to Britain and adapted to eventually include tomatoes. The word "ketchup" is derived from its original, varied pronunciations.

But things got interesting here in the States when, in 1876, the H.J. Heinz Company began bottling its take on tomato ketchup, kicking off America's love affair with the condiment— which is now outsold only by mayonnaise and salsa. Beyond being tasty, ketchup is full of cancer-fighting lycopenes and is shelf stable due to its high acidity. It can even be used to polish brass (seriously)— but we much prefer it on our burgers.

# GRILLED AVOCADO AND JALAPEÑO GUACAMOLE

SERVES: **6 TO 8**  |  PREP TIME: **15 MINUTES**  |  GRILLING TIME: **6 TO 8 MINUTES**  |  CHILLING TIME: **30 MINUTES TO 1 HOUR**

3 ripe Hass avocados, about 2 pounds total, each cut in half and peeled

2 medium jalapeño chile peppers Extra-virgin olive oil

⅓ cup minced white onion, rinsed in a fine-mesh strainer under cold water

1 ripe plum tomato, cored, seeded, and finely chopped

¼ cup finely chopped fresh cilantro leaves

1 teaspoon kosher salt

2–3 tablespoons fresh lime juice Tortilla chips

1. Prepare the grill for direct cooking over medium heat (350° to 450°F).

2. Lightly brush the avocados and jalapeños with oil, and then grill over *direct medium heat*, with the lid closed, until the avocados are well marked and the jalapeños are blackened and blistered, 6 to 8 minutes, turning once.

3. Put the avocados in a bowl and coarsely mash with a fork. When the jalapeños are cool enough to handle, scrape away the blackened skin, remove the stem and seeds, and finely chop. To the bowl with the avocados, add the jalapeños, onion, tomato, cilantro, salt, and 2 tablespoons of the lime juice. Mix well. Add more lime juice, if desired. Place a piece of plastic wrap directly onto the surface of the guacamole to prevent it from browning. Refrigerate until cold, 30 minutes to 1 hour.

4. Serve the guacamole with tortilla chips.

SIDES

Make sure your avocados are perfectly ripe for maximum flavor and ease of mashing. Look for skins with a dark hue that are free of indentations, which could be an indicator of bruising. The avocado should yield to slight pressure when gently squeezed in the palm of your hand—avoid using your fingers or you'll likely bruise the fruit. (For a tip on ripening, see page 157.)

# CIDER-BRAISED SAUERKRAUT

SERVES: 8 | PREP TIME: 10 MINUTES, PLUS ABOUT 30 MINUTES COOKING TIME

- 2 tablespoons unsalted butter
- 1 medium yellow onion, cut in half and thinly sliced
- 2 garlic cloves, minced or pushed through a press
- 1 teaspoon caraway seed
- 1 teaspoon fennel seed
- 1 bay leaf
- ½ teaspoon kosher salt
- ¼ teaspoon ground black pepper
- 1 jar or bag (32 ounces) sauerkraut, drained and squeezed dry
- 2 cups apple cider or apple juice, preferably unfiltered

**FUN FACT**

A lot of people associate sauerkraut with Germany—after all, it is the German word for "sour cabbage." But fewer people know that the process of pickling cabbage actually originated in Asia or ancient Rome as an early form of preservation. No matter its source, it sure is a wonderful topping for hot dogs, brats, and sausages.

1. In a heavy saucepan over medium heat, melt the butter. Add the onion, garlic, caraway seed, fennel seed, bay leaf, salt, and pepper and sauté until the onion is softened, about 5 minutes. Add the sauerkraut and apple cider and bring the mixture to a boil. Lower the heat and allow the sauerkraut to simmer until all of the liquid has been absorbed, about 20 minutes. Remove the bay leaf.

2. Cool the sauerkraut to room temperature. Serve; or cover and refrigerate for up to 2 days. Bring to room temperature before serving.

# GRILLED SUMMER VEGETABLES WITH THREE DIPPING SAUCES

SERVES: **6** | PREP TIME: **45 MINUTES** | GRILLING TIME: **19 TO 23 MINUTES (TOTAL TIME, INCLUDING SAUCES)**

**SIDES**

6 zucchini, about 1¾ pounds total, each cut
   lengthwise in half (quartered if large)
1 globe eggplant, about 1 pound, ends trimmed,
   cut crosswise into ½-inch slices
1 pound asparagus, spears about ½ inch
   in diameter, tough ends trimmed
   Extra-virgin olive oil
1½ teaspoons kosher salt
1 teaspoon freshly ground black pepper
1 baguette
2 garlic cloves, each cut in half

1. Prepare the grill for direct cooking over medium heat
(350° to 450°F).

2. Brush the vegetables with oil and season evenly with
the salt and pepper.

3. Cut the baguette on a deep diagonal into long
¾-inch-thick slices. Lightly brush the baguette slices
on both sides with oil.

4. Grill the vegetables over *direct medium heat*, with
the lid closed, until tender and lightly charred on all
sides, 6 to 8 minutes for the asparagus and zucchini and
8 to 10 minutes for the eggplant, turning occasionally.
Transfer to a serving platter.

5. Toast the baguette slices over *direct medium heat*,
with the lid closed, for 1 minute, turning once. Rub both
sides of the baguette slices with the cut side of the garlic.
Transfer to the platter with the vegetables. Serve warm
with the dipping sauces.

## SPICY ROASTED RED PEPPER SAUCE

MAKES: **ABOUT 1¼ CUPS**

- 2 red bell peppers, each 7 to 8 ounces
- 1 large red jalapeño or Fresno chile pepper, seeded and coarsely chopped (about 2 tablespoons)
- 2 tablespoons extra-virgin olive oil
- 1 teaspoon ground cumin
- 1 teaspoon kosher salt
- 2 garlic cloves
- ½ teaspoon ground coriander
- ½ teaspoon freshly ground black pepper

1. Prepare the grill for direct cooking over medium heat (350° to 450°F).

2. Grill the bell peppers over *direct medium heat,* with the lid closed, until blackened and blistered all over, 10 to 12 minutes, turning occasionally. Transfer to a bowl and cover with plastic wrap to trap the steam. Let stand for about 10 minutes. Remove the bell peppers from the bowl and discard the charred skin, stems, and seeds and roughly chop. Transfer to a food processor. Add the remaining ingredients. Process until smooth. Serve; or cover and refrigerate for up to 1 day. Bring to room temperature before serving.

## HERBED BALSAMIC VINAIGRETTE

MAKES: ½ **CUP**

- 3 tablespoons balsamic vinegar
- 2 tablespoons chopped fresh basil leaves
- 1 tablespoon chopped fresh Italian parsley leaves
- 1 teaspoon minced garlic
- ½ teaspoon kosher salt
- ¼ teaspoon freshly ground black pepper
- ⅓ cup extra-virgin olive oil

1. In a small bowl whisk all the ingredients except for the oil. Add the oil in a steady stream, whisking constantly to emulsify. Serve; or let stand at room temperature for up to 2 hours. Whisk again just before serving.

## TZATZIKI SAUCE

MAKES: **ABOUT 1½ CUPS**

- ½ English cucumber, 6 to 7 ounces, coarsely grated on the large holes of a box grater
- 1 cup plain Greek yogurt
- 2 tablespoons finely chopped fresh mint leaves
- 1 tablespoon fresh lemon juice
- 2 teaspoons extra-virgin olive oil
- 1 medium garlic clove, minced or pushed through a press
- ½ teaspoon kosher salt
- ¼ teaspoon freshly ground black pepper

1. Place the grated cucumber in a strainer and press firmly to squeeze out the excess liquid. Discard the liquid. Transfer the cucumber to a small bowl. Add the remaining ingredients and stir to combine. Serve; or cover and refrigerate for up to 4 hours.

# CUCUMBER RELISH

MAKES: **ABOUT ¾ CUP**
PREP TIME: **10 MINUTES**
CHILLING TIME: **1 TO 3 HOURS**

  1 cucumber, about 12 ounces, peeled, seeded, and grated on the large holes of a box grater
  1 teaspoon kosher salt
  2 scallions (white and light green parts only), thinly sliced
  2 teaspoons minced fresh cilantro leaves
1½ teaspoons canola oil
  1 teaspoon rice vinegar
  1 teaspoon Asian fish sauce
  1 teaspoon packed brown sugar
  ½ teaspoon fresh lime juice
  ¼ teaspoon toasted sesame oil

1. In a colander toss the cucumber with the salt; let drain for 15 minutes.

2. When the cucumber has finished draining, squeeze out the excess moisture using a few paper towels. Whisk the remaining ingredients and fold in the cucumber. Cover and refridgerate for at least 1 hour or up to 3 hours.

# SOUR CREAM RAITA

MAKES: **ABOUT 1 CUP**
PREP TIME: **10 MINUTES**

  ½ English cucumber, about 10 ounces, halved lengthwise and thinly sliced
  ½ cup sour cream
  4 teaspoons fresh lemon juice
  1 tablespoon extra-virgin olive oil
  ¼ teaspoon curry powder
  ¼ teaspoon kosher salt
  1 small garlic clove, minced or pushed through a press

1. In a medium bowl combine all the ingredients.

# PICKLED OKRA

MAKES: **ABOUT 1¼ CUPS**
PREP TIME: **15 MINUTES**
BRINING TIME: **AT LEAST 1 HOUR**

  8 ounces fresh okra, rinsed and cut lengthwise in half
  5 tablespoons kosher salt, divided
1½ cups rice vinegar
  1 cup water
  ¼ cup finely chopped fresh dill
  1 teaspoon mustard seed
  1 bay leaf
  ½ teaspoon crushed red pepper flakes
  2 garlic cloves, smashed

1. In a colander toss the okra with 3 tablespoons of the salt and let drain for 10 minutes.

2. Meanwhile, in a saucepan combine the remaining ingredients, including the remaining 2 tablespoons salt. Bring to a simmer over medium-high heat and cook until the salt is dissolved, stirring occasionally. Rinse the okra thoroughly under cold water to remove the salt, and transfer to a nonreactive bowl or a quart-size glass jar. Pour the brine over the okra and cool to room temperature. Refrigerate for at least 1 hour before serving. The okra can be stored in the refrigerator in a covered container for up to 1 month.

TOPPINGS

# BABA GHANOUSH

MAKES: **ABOUT 1 CUP**
PREP TIME: **10 MINUTES**
GRILLING TIME: **ABOUT 20 MINUTES**

- 1 globe eggplant, about 1 pound
- ¼ cup tahini
- 3 tablespoons fresh lemon juice
- 1 tablespoon extra-virgin olive oil
- 2 large garlic cloves
- ½ teaspoon kosher salt
- ¼ teaspoon ground cumin
- ¼ teaspoon freshly ground black pepper

1. Prepare the grill for direct cooking over high heat (450° to 550°F).

2. Grill the eggplant over *direct high heat*, with the lid closed, until the flesh is so tender that you can slide a knife all the way through it without resistance, about 20 minutes. Remove from the grill and allow to cool.

3. Cut the eggplant lengthwise in half and scoop out the flesh. In a food processor fitted with a metal blade, combine the eggplant flesh with the remaining ingredients. Puree until smooth.

# JALAPEÑO SPREAD

MAKES: **ABOUT 1 CUP**
PREP TIME: **10 MINUTES**

- 1 ripe Hass avocado, roughly chopped
- 1 jalapeño chile pepper, seeded
- ⅓ cup sour cream
- ¼ cup mayonnaise
- 2 tablespoons fresh lime juice
- ½ teaspoon kosher salt

1. In a blender or food processor fitted with a metal blade, combine all the ingredients and process until smooth.

# SWEET AND SPICY TOMATO CHUTNEY

MAKES: **ABOUT 2 CUPS**
PREP TIME: **15 MINUTES, PLUS ABOUT 1 HOUR COOKING TIME**

- 1 tablespoon extra-virgin olive oil
- 1 cup finely chopped yellow onion
- 3 garlic cloves, minced or pushed through a press
- 2 teaspoons peeled, grated fresh ginger
- ¼ teaspoon crushed red pepper flakes, or to taste
- 2 pounds ripe plum tomatoes, cored, seeded, and finely chopped
- 1 medium green bell pepper, finely chopped
- ¾ cup cider vinegar
- ¼ cup honey
- ¾ teaspoon kosher salt
- ¼ teaspoon freshly ground black pepper
- ⅛ teaspoon ground cinnamon (optional)

1. In a nonreactive saucepan over medium heat, warm the oil. Add the onion, garlic, ginger, and red pepper flakes. Cook until the onion starts to soften, 2 to 3 minutes, stirring occasionally. Stir in the tomatoes and bell pepper, and cook until the tomatoes start to wilt, about 3 minutes. Add the remaining ingredients. Increase the heat to high, bring to a boil, and then reduce the heat to medium-low. Simmer, uncovered, until the mixture has thickened and reduced to about 2 cups, 45 to 55 minutes, stirring occasionally. Remove from the heat and cool completely before serving. The chutney can be stored in the refrigerator in a covered container for up to 1 week.

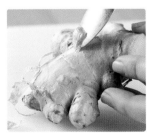

Before grating the ginger, scrape off the skin with the back of a spoon.

# RED BELL PEPPER HARISSA

MAKES: **ABOUT ¾ CUP**
PREP TIME: **10 MINUTES**
SPECIAL EQUIPMENT: **SPICE MILL OR MORTAR AND PESTLE**

1¾ teaspoons cumin seed
1 cup roasted red bell peppers (from a jar)
1 tablespoon fresh lemon juice
1 teaspoon ground coriander
½ teaspoon smoked paprika
½ teaspoon kosher salt
1 medium garlic clove
⅛ teaspoon ground cayenne pepper
⅛ teaspoon freshly ground black pepper
¼ cup plus 1 tablespoon extra-virgin olive oil

1. In a dry small skillet over medium heat, toast the cumin seed until fragrant and slightly darker in color, 2 to 3 minutes, stirring often. Remove from the heat and cool slightly. Transfer to a spice mill and finely grind.

2. In a food processor fitted with a metal blade, combine the toasted cumin with all the remaining ingredients except for the oil. Puree until almost smooth. With the motor running, gradually pour the oil through the feed tube and puree until the sauce is as smooth as possible. Transfer to a bowl and set aside at room temperature until ready to serve; or cover and refrigerate for up to 1 day. Bring to room temperature before serving.

# FRESH TOMATILLO SALSA

MAKES: **ABOUT 2 CUPS**
PREP TIME: **20 MINUTES**

8 ounces tomatillos, husked, rinsed, and roughly chopped
1 cup loosely packed fresh cilantro leaves
¼ cup roughly chopped white onion, rinsed in a fine-mesh strainer under cold water
1 medium jalapeño chile pepper, roughly chopped
1 garlic clove, roughly chopped
1 teaspoon fresh lime juice
½ teaspoon kosher salt

1. In a food processor fitted with a metal blade, combine all the ingredients. Pulse until finely chopped. Refrigerate until ready to serve.

# SUN-DRIED TOMATO PESTO

MAKES: **ABOUT ⅔ CUP**
PREP TIME: **10 MINUTES**

⅓ cup pine nuts
2 cups loosely packed fresh basil leaves
⅓ cup freshly grated Parmigiano-Reggiano® cheese
¼ cup oil-packed sun-dried tomatoes
2 garlic cloves
⅓ cup olive oil (not extra virgin)
Kosher salt

1. Preheat a skillet over medium heat. Add the pine nuts and cook until golden brown, about 3 minutes, shaking the skillet occasionally and watching carefully to prevent burning. Pour into a food processor fitted with a metal blade and let cool for a few minutes. Then add the basil, cheese, sun-dried tomatoes, and garlic. Pulse until the basil leaves are finely chopped. With the motor running, gradually pour the oil through the feed tube and process until the pesto is almost smooth. Season with salt.

TOPPINGS

# WEBER'S SECRET SAUCE

MAKES: **ABOUT ¾ CUP**
PREP TIME: **10 MINUTES**

- ¼ cup mayonnaise
- ⅓ cup sour cream
- 1–3 teaspoons hot pepper sauce
- 2 teaspoons fresh lemon juice
- 2 teaspoons finely chopped fresh chives
- ½ teaspoon dried parsley
- ½ teaspoon onion powder
- ½ teaspoon paprika
- ½ teaspoon dill weed
- ½ teaspoon mustard powder
- ¼ teaspoon granulated garlic
- ¼ teaspoon kosher salt
- ¼ teaspoon freshly ground black pepper

1. In a medium bowl whisk all the ingredients.

The secret to this sauce's success is the balanced blend of herbs and spices. First try it with just a little hot pepper sauce, and then add more to suit your taste. It is great on all kinds of burgers.

# CHERRY COLA BARBECUE SAUCE

MAKES: **ABOUT 4 CUPS**
PREP TIME: **10 MINUTES, PLUS ABOUT 1 HOUR COOKING TIME**

- 1 tablespoon unsalted butter
- 1 cup finely chopped yellow onion
- 3 garlic cloves, minced or pushed through a press
- 3 cups ketchup
- 2½ cups cherry cola (not diet)
- ½ cup packed light brown sugar
- ½ cup cherry preserves
- ¼ cup red wine vinegar
- 2 teaspoons prepared chili powder
- ¼ teaspoon ground cayenne pepper

1. In a saucepan over medium heat, melt the butter. Add the onion and garlic and cook until slightly softened, 5 to 6 minutes, stirring occasionally. Whisk in the remaining ingredients. Increase the heat to medium-high and bring to a boil, and then reduce the heat to medium-low and simmer, uncovered, until the mixture thickens and is reduced to 4 cups, 45 to 55 minutes, stirring occasionally. Serve warm; or cool completely and transfer to a covered container. The sauce can be refrigerated for up to 1 month. Reheat before serving.

TOPPINGS

# DRINKS

# TROPICAL RUM PUNCH

SERVES: 8 | PREP TIME: 5 MINUTES

10 ounces (1¼ cups) gold rum
3 cups cold fresh pineapple juice
2 cups cold mango nectar
1 cup cold guava nectar
¼ cup fresh lime juice
   Ice
   Ripe, fresh pineapple
   wedges (optional)
   Lime wedges (optional)

1. In a large pitcher combine the rum, pineapple juice, mango nectar, guava nectar, and lime juice; mix well.

2. Serve cold over ice. Garnish with pineapple wedges or lime wedges, if desired.

### COCKTAILS THAT COMPLEMENT BURGERS AND SAUSAGES

Rather than staunchly sticking with fussy pairings, we're advocates of the "drink what you like" style of sipping. However, we will admit: a carefully calculated food-drink match does wonders. Got robust flavors like bacon or sharp cheese? Consider something with a little tartness and fizz, such as our Cape Cod Berry Spritzers (page 246). Serving up spice? Tropical Rum Punch can tame the heat with sweet. Using poultry or seafood? The Spiked Coconut Shakes (page 246) counter the leanness with some heft. And when in doubt, margaritas (page 245) are perennial winners. Bottoms (and buns) up!

**VARIATION**

For a non-alcoholic version, substitute 1 cup of seltzer or club soda for the rum, and increase the fresh lime juice to ⅓ cup.

# POMITO

SERVES: 1 | PREP TIME: **5 MINUTES**

½ lime, cut into 3 wedges, divided
8 fresh mint leaves
1 teaspoon superfine sugar
Crushed ice
1 tablespoon fresh lime juice
1½ ounces light rum
1 ounce pomegranate liqueur
¼ cup pomegranate juice
(no sugar added)
3 tablespoons seltzer
1 fresh mint sprig

1. In the bottom of a collins glass, muddle two of the lime wedges with the mint leaves and sugar to extract the juice from the limes and the oils from the mint.

2. Fill the glass with crushed ice, and then add the lime juice, rum, pomegranate liqueur, and pomegranate juice. Top with the seltzer and stir. Garnish with the remaining lime wedge and mint sprig.

**VARIATION**

For a non-alcoholic version, muddle all 3 lime wedges. Replace the rum with an additional ¼ cup of pomegranate juice. Replace the pomegranate liqueur with an additional 2 tablespoons of seltzer.

# WATERMELON LEMONADE

SERVES: **8 TO 10** | PREP TIME: **15 MINUTES** | STANDING TIME: **15 MINUTES** | CHILLING TIME: **1 HOUR**

## SIMPLE SYRUP

- 2 cups water
- 1 cup granulated sugar
- ½ cup coarsely chopped fresh mint leaves

- 12 cups ripe, seedless watermelon cubes, about 4 pounds
- 1½ cups fresh lemon juice
  Ice
  Fresh mint leaves
  Watermelon wedges
- 1 lemon, cut crosswise into thin slices

1. In a saucepan over medium heat, combine the water and sugar and cook until the sugar dissolves, about 2 minutes, stirring occasionally. Remove from the heat, stir in the mint, and let stand for 15 minutes. Refrigerate for 1 hour. Strain, and discard the mint.

2. In a blender puree the watermelon and then pour through a fine-mesh strainer set over a bowl. Gently press on the solids to extract more of the juice. Discard any remaining solids. Transfer the watermelon juice to a pitcher.

3. To the pitcher add the lemon juice and 1½ cups of the chilled simple syrup; mix well (add more simple syrup, if desired). Serve over ice. Garnish with fresh mint, watermelon wedges, and lemon slices.

**VARIATION**

Substitute 12 cups of honeydew melon cubes for the watermelon, decrease the lemon juice to 1¼ cups, and omit the mint.

# PEACH, PLUM, AND BERRY ROSÉ SANGRIA

SERVES: **8** | PREP TIME: **20 MINUTES** | STANDING TIME: **15 MINUTES** | CHILLING TIME: **1 HOUR TO 1 DAY**

2 ripe, fresh peaches, cut into ½-inch chunks
2 ripe, fresh plums, cut into ½-inch chunks
1 cup ripe, fresh blackberries
1 cup ripe, fresh raspberries
1 cup ripe, fresh blueberries
3 tablespoons granulated sugar
2 cups cold peach nectar
1 bottle (750 ml) chilled rosé wine
2 ounces brandy (optional)
Ice

1. Combine the fresh fruit and sugar. Let stand at room temperature for 15 minutes, gently folding the fruit occasionally. Transfer to a large pitcher.

2. To the pitcher add the peach nectar, wine, and brandy (if using), stirring gently to mix. Chill for at least 1 hour or up to 1 day. Serve over ice.

## VARIATION

For a non-alcoholic version, substitute sparkling cider for the wine, leave out the brandy, and add ¼ cup fresh lemon juice.

# FROZEN STRAWBERRY-MANGO MARGARITAS
## WITH CHILI SALT RIMS

SERVES: **4** | PREP TIME: **20 MINUTES** | STANDING TIME: **15 MINUTES**

1 ripe mango, about 1 pound, peeled and
cut into cubes
1½ cups sliced ripe, fresh strawberries
⅓ cup granulated sugar
2 cups ice cubes
3 ounces good-quality tequila
2 ounces triple sec
⅓ cup fresh lime juice
2 teaspoons kosher salt
½ teaspoon prepared chili powder
1 lime wedge
4 slices lime (optional)
4 ripe, fresh strawberries (optional)

1. Combine the mango, strawberries, and sugar and let stand at room temperature for at least 15 minutes, stirring occasionally.

2. Transfer the strawberry-mango mixture to a blender and add the ice, tequila, triple sec, and lime juice. Puree the mixture on high.

3. On a small plate mix the salt and chili powder. Moisten the rims of four glasses with the lime wedge, and dip the rims into the salt mixture to coat. Divide the margaritas among the four glasses, and garnish with a lime slice and a strawberry, if desired.

# GINGER-LIME MARGARITA

SERVES: **1** | PREP TIME: **20 MINUTES** | STEEPING TIME: **1 HOUR**

**GINGER SYRUP** (MAKES 2 CUPS)
1 cup granulated sugar
1 cup water
2 cups peeled, sliced fresh ginger

1 tablespoon superfine sugar
½ teaspoon ground ginger
2 lime wedges, divided

**MARGARITA**
Crushed ice
Juice of 1 lime
1½ ounces good-quality tequila
3 tablespoons ginger syrup (from recipe above)

1. In a saucepan over medium heat, combine the granulated sugar and water and cook until the sugar dissolves, about 2 minutes, stirring occasionally. Remove from the heat, add the fresh ginger, cover, and allow to steep for 1 hour. Strain, and reserve the liquid.

2. On a small plate mix the superfine sugar and ground ginger. Moisten the rim of a rocks glass with one of the lime wedges, and dip the rim into the ginger sugar to coat. Fill a 12-ounce cocktail shaker with ice, lime juice, tequila, and ginger syrup. Shake, and pour into the glass. Garnish with the other lime wedge.

**VARIATION**

For a non-alcoholic version, fill a 12-ounce cocktail shaker with ice, the juice of 1 lime, and 3 tablespoons ginger syrup. Shake and pour into a rocks glass. Top with seltzer and stir. Garnish with a lime slice. For a more pronounced ginger flavor, replace the seltzer with ginger beer.

# CAPE COD BERRY SPRITZERS

SERVES: **6**  |  PREP TIME: **10 MINUTES**

- 1 cup ripe, fresh raspberries
- 1 cup chopped ripe, fresh strawberries
- 1 cup 100% cranberry juice, divided
- 1 bottle (750 ml) sparkling apple cider
  Ice
- 6 ripe, fresh strawberries
- 6 ripe, fresh raspberries

1. In a blender puree 1 cup raspberries, 1 cup strawberries, and ¼ cup of the cranberry juice. Pour the contents into a large pitcher and add the remaining ¾ cup cranberry juice. Slowly pour the sparkling cider down the inside wall of the pitcher to prevent excessive foaming. Add ice to the pitcher and gently stir.

2. Fill six glasses with ice, pour an equal amount of the spritzer into each glass, and garnish with a strawberry and a raspberry.

# SPIKED COCONUT SHAKES

SERVES: **2**  |  PREP TIME: **5 MINUTES**

- 1 pint coconut sorbet
- ⅔ cup cold unsweetened coconut milk
- 4 ice cubes
- 2 tablespoons agave nectar
- 2 ounces light rum
- 2 teaspoons fresh lime juice
- ¼ teaspoon coconut extract
  Toasted coconut flakes

1. In a blender combine all the ingredients, except for the toasted coconut flakes, and puree.

2. Divide the shake between two tall glasses. Garnish with the toasted coconut flakes.

**VARIATION**

For a non-alcoholic version, leave out the rum and increase the fresh lime juice to 1½ tablespoons.

DRINKS

# NEW YORK–STYLE EGG CREAM

SERVES: 1 | PREP TIME: 5 MINUTES

- 3 tablespoons chocolate or vanilla syrup
- ⅓ cup cold whole milk
- ¾ cup cold seltzer or club soda
  Whipped cream (optional)
  Chocolate sprinkles (optional)

1. In a tall glass combine the syrup and milk. Vigorously stir the syrup and milk while pouring in the seltzer in a steady stream. The constant stirring will help to give the egg cream its traditional creamy head of froth.

2. Garnish the egg cream with whipped cream and chocolate sprinkles, if desired.

Egg creams typically contain neither eggs nor cream. So … why the name? One story says that this late nineteenth-century New York invention snagged its namesake for the white foam top layer, which resembles beaten egg whites.

# PEACH AND STRAWBERRY SMOOTHIES

SERVES: 4 TO 6 | PREP TIME: 5 MINUTES

- 3 ripe, fresh peaches, about 1 pound total, peeled and roughly chopped
- 1 pound frozen whole strawberries
- 1 cup lemonade
- ½ cup plain yogurt
- 2 tablespoons honey *or* agave nectar, or to taste

1. In a large blender puree the peaches, frozen strawberries, lemonade, and yogurt. Add the honey. Blend once more. Divide the smoothie among four to six glasses. Serve cold.

# GRILLING GUIDE

| TYPE | THICKNESS/ WEIGHT | APPROXIMATE GRILLING TIME | INTERNAL TEMP |
|---|---|---|---|
| Beef, ground | ½ inch thick | **6 to 8 minutes** direct medium-high heat (400° to 500°F) to medium doneness | 160°F |
| | ¾ inch thick | **8 to 10 minutes** direct medium-high heat (400° to 500°F) to medium doneness | 160°F |
| | 1 inch thick | **9 to 11 minutes** direct medium-high heat (400° to 500°F) to medium doneness | 160°F |
| Grass-fed beef, ground | ¾ inch thick | **7 to 9 minutes** direct medium heat (350° to 450°F) to medium doneness | 160°F |
| | 1 inch thick | **8 to 10 minutes** direct medium heat (350° to 450°F) to medium doneness | 160°F |
| Bison, ground | ¾ inch thick | **7 to 9 minutes** direct medium heat (350° to 450°F) to medium doneness | 160°F |
| | 1 inch thick | **8 to 10 minutes** direct medium heat (350° to 450°F) to medium doneness | 160°F |
| Lamb, ground | ¾ inch thick | **8 to 10 minutes** direct medium-high heat (400° to 500°F) to medium doneness | 160°F |
| | 1 inch thick | **9 to 11 minutes** direct medium-high heat (400° to 500°F) to medium doneness | 160°F |
| Pork, ground | ¾ inch thick | **8 to 10 minutes** direct medium-high heat (400° to 500°F) to medium doneness | 160°F |
| | 1 inch thick | **10 to 12 minutes** direct medium heat (350° to 450°F) to medium doneness | 160°F |
| Poultry, ground | ½ inch thick | **7 to 9 minutes** direct medium-high heat (400° to 500°F) to medium doneness | 165°F |
| | ¾ inch thick | **8 to 10 minutes** direct medium-high heat (400° to 500°F) to medium doneness | 165°F |
| | 1 inch thick | **11 to 13 minutes** direct medium heat (350° to 450°F) to medium doneness | 165°F |
| Seafood, chopped | ¾ inch thick | **6 to 8 minutes** direct medium heat (350° to 450°F) | 145°F |
| Hot dog | 3-ounce link | **4 to 5 minutes** direct medium heat (350° to 450°F) | |
| Sausage, raw | 3-ounce link | **20 to 25 minutes** direct medium heat (350° to 450°F) until fully cooked | 160°F |
| Sausage, precooked | 3-ounce link | **8 to 10 minutes** direct medium heat (350° to 450°F) until hot | |